Machine Learning Algorithms and Applications

Scrivener Publishing
100 Cummings Center, Suite 541J
Beverly, MA 01915-6106

Sustainable Computing and Optimization

The objective of the series is to bring together the global research scholars, experts, and scientists in the research areas of sustainable computing and optimization from all over the world to share their knowledge and experiences on current research achievements in these fields. The series aims to provide a golden opportunity for the global research community to share their novel research results, findings, and innovations to a wide range of readers. Data is everywhere and continuing to grow massively, which has created a huge demand for qualified experts who can uncover valuable insights from the data. The series will promote sustainable computing and optimization methodologies in order to solve real life problems mainly from engineering and management systems domains. The series will mainly focus on the real-life problems, which can suitably be handled through these paradigms.

Submission to the series:

Dr. Prasenjit Chatterjee
Department of Mechanical Engineering,
MCKV Institute of Engineering, Howrah - 711204, West Bengal, India
E-mail: dr.prasenjitchatterjee6@gmail.com

Dr. Morteza Yazdani
Department of Management, Universidad Loyola Andalucia, Seville, Spain
E-mail: morteza_yazdani21@yahoo.com

Dr. Dilbagh Panchal
Department of Industrial and Production Engineering,
Dr. B. R. Ambedkar National Institute of Technology (NIT) Jalandhar, Punjab, India
E-mail: panchald@nitj.ac.in

Publishers at Scrivener
Martin Scrivener (martin@scrivenerpublishing.com)
Phillip Carmical (pcarmical@scrivenerpublishing.com)

Machine Learning Algorithms and Applications

Edited by

Mettu Srinivas,
National Institute of Technology, Warangal, India

G. Sucharitha
Institute of Aeronautical Engineering,
Hyderabad, India

and

Anjanna Matta
Faculty of Science and Technology, IFHE,
Hyderabad, India

Wiley Global Headquarters
111 River Street, Hoboken, NJ 07030, USA

For details of our global editorial offices, customer services, and more information about Wiley products visit us at www.wiley.com.

Limit of Liability/Disclaimer of Warranty
While the publisher and authors have used their best efforts in preparing this work, they make no representations or warranties with respect to the accuracy or completeness of the contents of this work and specifically disclaim all warranties, including without limitation any implied warranties of merchantability or fitness for a particular purpose. No warranty may be created or extended by sales representatives, written sales materials, or promotional statements for this work. The fact that an organization, website, or product is referred to in this work as a citation and/or potential source of further information does not mean that the publisher and authors endorse the information or services the organization, website, or product may provide or recommendations it may make. This work is sold with the understanding that the publisher is not engaged in rendering professional services. The advice and strategies contained herein may not be suitable for your situation. You should consult with a specialist where appropriate. Neither the publisher nor authors shall be liable for any loss of profit or any other commercial damages, including but not limited to special, incidental, consequential, or other damages. Further, readers should be aware that websites listed in this work may have changed or disappeared between when this work was written and when it is read.

Library of Congress Cataloging-in-Publication Data

ISBN 978-1-119-76885-2

Cover image: Pixabay.Com
Cover design by Russell Richardson

Set in size of 11pt and Minion Pro by Manila Typesetting Company, Makati, Philippines

10 9 8 7 6 5 4 3 2 1

Contents

Part 3: Machine Learning for Security Systems 175

Ritesh Vyas, Tirupathiraju Kanumuri, Gyanendra Sheoran and Pawan Dubey

Umita Deepak Joshi, Vanshika, Ajay Pratap Singh, Tushar Rajesh Pahuja, Smita Naval and Gaurav Singal

Part 4: Machine Learning for Classification and Information Retrieval Systems   247

Acknowledgments

This book is based on research conducted at various leading technical institutions on different topics regarding the machine and deep learning platforms used throughout India. We are grateful to the many authors and co-authors who contributed their research work for use in the successful completion of this book. We are also grateful to our colleagues for their encouragement to start the process of working on the book, persevere throughout it, and finally publish it.

We gratefully acknowledge NIT Warangal and the Faculty of Science & Technology, ICFAI Foundation for Higher Education, Hyderabad, for providing the use of their facilities to carry out the work on this book. Finally, we would like to acknowledge with gratitude, the support and love from our parents, life partners and children.

Preface

Nowadays, machine learning has become an essential part of many commercial and industrial applications and research developments. It has expanded its roots in areas ranging from automatic medical diagnosis in healthcare to product recommendations in social networks. Many people think that machine learning can only be applied by large companies with extensive research teams. In this book, we try to show you how you yourself can easily adopt machine learning to build solutions for small applications and the best way to go about it. With the knowledge presented herein, you can build your own system to find the faults in a company's manufactured products and the fake profiles in social networks. This book clearly explains the various applications of machine and deep learning for use in the medical field, animal classification, gene selection from microarray gene expression data, sentiment analysis, fake profile detection in social media, farming sectors, etc.

For the ambitious machine learning specialists of today who are looking to implement solutions to real-world machine learning problems, this book thoroughly discusses the various applications of machine and deep learning techniques. Each chapter deals with the novel approach of machine learning architecture for a specific application and its results, including comparisons with previous algorithms. In order to present a unified treatment of machine learning problems and solutions, many methods based in different fields are discussed, including statistics, pattern recognition, neural networks, artificial intelligence, sentiment analysis, control, and data mining. Furthermore, all learning algorithms are explained in a way that makes it easy for students to move from the equations in the book to a computer program.

The Editors
June 2020

Part 1

MACHINE LEARNING FOR INDUSTRIAL APPLICATIONS

A Learning-Based Visualization Application for Air Quality Evaluation During COVID-19 Pandemic in Open Data Centric Services

Priyank Jain* and Gagandeep Kaur†

*Dept. of CSE & IT, Jaypee Institute of Information Technology,
Noida, Uttar Pradesh, India*

Abstract

Air pollution has become a major concern in many developing countries. There are various factors that affect the quality of air. Some of them are Nitrogen Dioxide (NO_2), Ozone (O_3), Particulate Matter 10 (PM_{10}), Particulate Matter 2.5 ($PM_{2.5}$), Sulfur Dioxide (SO_2), and Carbon Monoxide (CO). The Government of India under the Open Data Initiative provides data related to air pollution. Interpretation of this data requires analysis, visualization, and prediction. This study proposes machine learning and visualization techniques for air pollution. Both supervised and unsupervised learning techniques have been used for prediction and analysis of air quality at major places in India. The data used in this research contains the presence of six major air pollutants in a given area. The work has been extended to study the impact of lockdown on air pollution in Indian cities as well.

Keywords: Open Data, JSON API, OpenAQ, clustering, SVM, LSTM, prediction, Heat Map visualizations

**Corresponding author*: priyankjn62@gmail.com
†*Corresponding author*: gagandeep.kaur@jiit.ac.in

Mettu Srinivas, G. Sucharitha and Anjanna Matta (eds.) Machine Learning Algorithms and Applications, (3–22) © 2021 Scrivener Publishing LLC

1.1   Introduction

1.1.1   Open Government Data Initiative

These days, Open Government Data (OGD) is gaining momentum in providing sharing of knowledge by making public data and information of governmental bodies freely available to private citizens in system processable formats so as to reuse it for mutual benefits. OGD is a global movement and has its roots in the initiative started in 2009 by the US President as a Memorandum on Transparency and Open Government providing transparency in government projects and collaborations through sharing of data by public administration and industry to private citizens. Indian Government also has joined this initiative and provides free access to the data for development of applications, etc., so as to be able to reuse the information for mutual growth of industry and government. Open Data is the raw data made available by governments, industry, as well as NGOs, scientific institutions, and educational organizations and as such is not an individual's property.

The growth in the field of Open Data surely asks for new tools and techniques that can support it. Digital transformation needs companies to look out for new tools and techniques so as to be able to support the increasing need for faster delivery of services at large numbers of delivery points. Technologies like SaaS, mobile, and Internet of Things are gaining grounds in providing increase in endpoints and thus enabling the success of Open Data Initiative.

1.1.2   Air Quality

A report, State of Global Air 2017, by Institute for Health Metrics published recently [1] stated that, in the year 2015, there have been 1,090,400 deaths in India only due to an increase in $PM_{2.5}$. High concentration of $PM_{2.5}$ in the air is majorly caused by burning of petroleum fuels, household fuels, wooden fuels, agricultural fires, and industry related pollutants and contaminants. In 2015, India and Bangladesh came next to North African and Middle East countries in terms of places with high concentration of $PM_{2.5}$ in air.

The report compares the ambient concentrations to the air quality guidelines established by the WHO in 2005. Based on the report by WHO, in the year 2015, 92% of the world's population and 86% of Indian population lived in unsafe areas exceeding safe limits. It is therefore need of the hour to develop tools that can provide better forecasting and easy understanding of the surrounding environment to naive users with lowest cost possible. Air Quality Index (AQI) is a commonly used index by agencies to provide information about quality of air in the vicinity to its residents.

The irony of today's Internet world is that even when we are inundated with large quantities of data or information, we as humans still struggle with its rightful interpretation. Extracting meaningful information from plain textual data in old tabular formats is an extraneous task. It is under these circumstances that data visualizations play a vital role.

The objective of this work was to build a machine learning–based visualization app for air quality evaluation and air pollution assessment by assessing various parameters by which air is getting polluted. Existing approaches did not account for variations in values of parameters at different locations. That is why we have trained different models for different locations to capture the trends better.

1.1.3   Impact of Lockdown on Air Quality

COVID-19 is a highly infectious disease caused by a newly discovered Coronavirus which was firstly identified in Wuhan, Central China. It has taken more than 460,000 lives as on 20th June, 2020, around the world. Due to this pandemic, a nationwide lockdown was imposed in India from 24th March, 2020, which extended up to several weeks. It is observed that lockdown could help in reducing pollution levels to a certain extent. This study tries to capture the variations in air pollution levels with and without lockdown.

1.2   Literature Survey

Air pollution occurs when particulates ($pm_{2.5}$ and pm_{10}), biological molecules, and other harmful substances are introduced into Earth's atmosphere. Natural processes and human activities can both generate air pollution. Air pollution can be further classified into two sections: visible air pollution and invisible air pollution.

Proactive monitoring and control of our natural and built environments is important in various application scenarios. Semantic Sensor Web technologies have been well researched and used for environmental monitoring applications to expose sensor data for analysis in order to provide responsive actions in situations of interest [2]. A sliding window approach that employs the Multilayer Perceptron model to predict short-term PM 2.5 pollution situations is integrated into the proactive monitoring and control framework [2]. Time series data in practical applications always contain missing values due to sensor malfunction, network failure, outliers, etc. [3]. A spatiotemporal prediction framework based on missing value processing algorithms and deep recurrent neural network (DRNN) has been proposed [3]. A generic methodology for weather forecasting is proposed by the help of incremental K-means clustering algorithm in [4]. Air pollution data are available to the public as numeric values on the concentration of pollutants in the air on a web page [5, 6]. The numeric information is not conducive to determining the air pollution level intuitively [6]. To address this problem, the study developed and implemented a program for visualizing the air pollution level for six pollutants by obtaining real-time air pollution data using API and generating a keyhole markup language (KML) file defined to visualize the data on Google Earth intuitively [6]. Visualization method is intuitive and reliable through data quality checking and information sharing with multi-perspective air pollution graphs [7]. This method allows the data to be easily understood by the public and inspire or aid further studies in other fields [7]. As the tools are invented using spatial-temporal visualization and visual analytics for general visualization purposes of geo-referenced time series data of air quality and environmental data, they can be applied to other environmental monitoring data (temperature, precipitation, etc.) through some configurations [8].

According to a survey mentioned in [9], pollution levels in many cities across the country reduced down drastically only after a few days of imposing lockdown. Also, as discussed in the study [10], lockdown could be the effective alternative measure to be implemented for controlling air pollution.

The results above show us that all these machine learning techniques can be used for prediction and evaluating air pollution thereafter. Implementation details are described in the next section.

1.3 Implementation Details

There are several paradigms that can be implemented to classify the quality of air. The novelty of the application is to predict the future air quality of different places in detail with estimated values of various parameters along with its air quality and AQI. The application is able to visualize data in an efficient and descriptive way which is hard to analyze numerically in its raw form.

1.3.1   Proposed Methodology

Our proposed methodology steps have been discussed as follows:

1. Fetch real-time air quality data through an API of Open Data.
2. Clustering of air quality data based on AQI and assigning classes of air quality from good to severe.
3. Train a Support Vector Machine (SVM) model on the previously clustered data.
4. Train different time series Long Short-Term Memory (LSTM), a Recurrent Neural Network (RNN) model for different places to predict the future air quality of that place based on the previous trend.
5. Assign air quality and AQI to the observed/predicted values of the parameters. AQI is assigned based on the worst 24-hour average of all the parameters.
6. Different visualizations of the past data and future predictions using Heat Maps, Graphs, etc.
7. Compare variations in different parameters contributing toward air pollution at different places.
8. Provide a user-friendly web app to predict and analyze air quality.

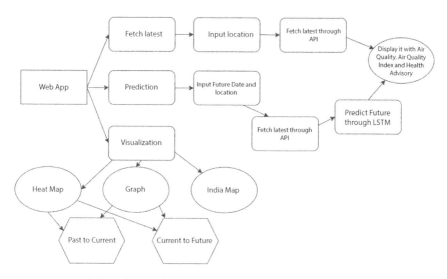

Figure 1.1 Workflow of the application.

Figure 1.1 shows the detailed description of the working of the application. The latest data for specific location/place is fetched using Restful API in JSON format from the Open Data Repository. Prediction is also done for the future air quality using the past values. The predicted data is displayed with an adequate message through the web app to the user. Visualization involved displaying the results in human understandable format. For that, Heat Maps were generated and appropriate messages were displayed based on the WHO guidelines. The results were also displayed through graphs to show connectivity between different values. Finally, the outputs were also displayed on the Indian map.

1.3.2   System Specifications

Main hardware requirements are high computational power CPU such as an i5/i7 Intel processor or equivalent. The system must be able to fulfill both primary and secondary high memory requirements approximately around 50-GB HDD and 4–8 GB of RAM. Main software requirements consist of any open source operating system, Python language with dependencies like scikit-learn, and other packages and libraries like pandas, numpy, matplotlib, bokeh, flask, tensorflow, and theano.

1.3.3   Algorithms

1. *K-Means Clustering*: The K-means algorithm takes a set of input values and, based on parameter k, clusters the values into k clusters. The division of values into k clusters is based on a similarity index in which data values having close similarity index are grouped into one cluster and another set of values is grouped into another cluster [11]. Distance measures like Euclidean, Manhattan, and Minkowski are some of the similarity indices that are used for clustering. We have used clustering because our dataset values were to be divided into classes. We choose six classes, *viz.*, Good, Satisfactory, Moderately Polluted, Poor, Very Poor, and Severe.

2. *Support Vector Machine Algorithm (SVMA) for Prediction*: SVMAs are an age old excellent algorithms in use for solving classification and regression problems. SVM provides a supervised learning model and is used to analyze the patterns in the data. In SVM, a linear model is applied to convert

non-linear class boundaries to linear classes. This is done by reducing the high-dimensional feature vector space. Kernel selection is an integral part of SVMs. Different kernels exist and we have used linear and Radial Basis Function (RBF) for our experiments. The outputs have been discussed under results. Two major kinds of SVM considered are therefore linear-based modeling and non-linear based modeling.

3. *Recurrent Neural Network LSTM Algorithm (LSTM-RNN)*: Contemporary Neural Networks such as Feed Forward Neural Networks (FFNNs) are different from Recurrent Neural Networks (RNNs) because they are trained on labeled data and forward feed is used till prediction error gets minimized.

RNNs are different from FFNNs because the output or result received at stage $t - 1$ impacts the output or result received at stage t. In RNN, there are two input values: first one being the present input value and second one being the recent past value. Both inputs are used to compute the new output.

Figure 1.2 shows the simple form of RNN. For a hidden state (h_t) which is non-linear transformation in itself, it can be computed using a combination of linear input value (I_t) and recent hidden past value $(h_t - 1)$. From the figure, it can be observed that the output result is computable using the present dependent hidden state h_t. The output O_t holds dependence on probability p_t which was computed using a function called softmax. Softmax was only computed in the last layer of RNN-based classification before the final result was received.

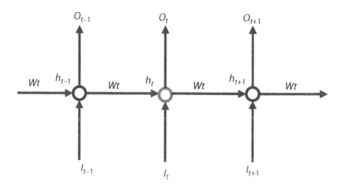

Figure 1.2 Basic steps of recurrent neural network.

Since RNN in itself suffers from two gradient problems of vanishing gradients and exploding gradients, therefore there have been two modifications to the basic RNN. Gates have been provided to control the impact of the multiplying factor that is majorly responsible for increase (explosion) in gradient (multiplying factor if larger than one) or decrease (vanishing) in gradient (multiplying factor if less than one). We now have LSTM and Gated Recurrent Unit (GRU). LSTM has been used in our work [12].

Because we were trying to predict future values based on present and past pollution data values that were in time series and had lags, therefore LSTM suited our use case. LSTM learns from the historical data to not only classify but also to process the results and predict the future scores without getting affected by gradient incumbencies.

1.3.4   Control Flow

In terms of control flow, the working of our model can be explained with respect to training model and testing model:

1. *Training Model*: As the first step of the training model, the data is fetched from the OpenAQ Open Data Community and is pre-processed to remove any kind of noise from the data. The cleaned world data is passed for K-means clustering. Before setting the number of clusters required to classify the data we measured Silhouette coefficient to determine the optimal number of clusters required. On the second hand, the cleaned single place data is passed to the LSTM for different places. The output of the world data clustering and LSTM training of single place data is passed to measure the performance using MAE and RMSE values. Also, the world data after clustering is assigned labels using the AQI table. The labeled data is then split into testing data and training data. SVM training is done with values of parameters as input and air quality as output. At the end, 10-fold cross-validations were done and performances were measured using confusion matrix, precision and recall parameters.

2. *Testing Model*: Under testing, new data was fetched using API. It was passed to the respective places LSTM. Future values of all parameters were predicted by the LSTM. This was passed as input to the SVM and the final result was prediction of air quality and assignment of AQI was done.

1.4   Results and Discussions

The open data is being provided by *OpenAQ* organization [13]. Their aim is to help people fight air pollution by providing open data and open-source tools. The data is obtained from government bodies as well as research groups and aggregated by OpenAQ. OpenAQ API was used to fetch the latest data in data frame and saved in .csv format for computations. Figure 1.3 shows the screenshot of data fetched on 6th June, 2020 for Visakhapatnam, India.

1. *K-Means Clustering Outcomes*: As explained in the methodology section, we applied K-means clustering to determine the classes via clusters for our unsupervised data. In order to find out the optimal number of clusters required, Silhouette coefficient was calculated. The Silhouette coefficient is calculated using the mean intra-cluster distance (a) and the mean nearest-cluster distance (b) for each sample where b is the distance between a sample and the nearest cluster that the sample is not a part of. The value of Silhouette coefficient for a sample is $(b - a)/max\ (a, b)$. For our experiments, we kept it equal to 7 using the Elbow method. After clustering, the clustered data were assigned labels for air quality using the AQI table. The required range for different air control parameters is shown in Table 1.1.

   We worked on six parameters, namely, NO_2, O_3, PM_{10}, $PM_{2.5}$, SO_2, and CO. To build the LSTM model, we trained our model for 14 different places in India, namely, Visakhapatnam (GVMC Ram Nagar), Ajmer (Civil Lines), Alwar, Vasundhara (Ghaziabad), Gurgaon (Vikas Sadan), Bandra (Maharashtra), Bhiwadi Industrial Area, Bengaluru (BWSSB Kadabesanaha), Amritsar (Golden Temple), Anand

Visakhapatnam

Date & Time	NO2	O3	PM10	PM2.5	SO2	CO
2020-06-06 06:00:00	22.10	41.00	93.00	14.00	11.30	400.00

Figure 1.3 Screenshot of fetched data.

Table 1.1 Range of AQI categories.

AQI category (range)	PM₁₀ (24hr)	PM₂.₅ (24hr)	NO₂ (24hr)	O₃ (8hr)	CO (8hr)	SO₂ (24hr)	NH₃ (24hr)	Pb (24hr)
Good (0–50)	0–50	0–30	0–40	0–50	0–1.0	0–40	0–200	0–0.5
Satisfactory (51–100)	51–100	31–60	41–80	51–100	1.1–2.0	41–80	201–400	0.5–1.0
Moderately polluted (101–200)	101–250	61–90	81–180	101–168	2.1–10	81–380	401–800	1.1–2.0
Poor (201–300)	251–350	91–120	181–280	169–208	10–17	381–800	801–1200	2.1–3.0
Very poor (301–400)	351–430	121–250	281–400	209–748	17–34	801–1,600	1,200–1,800	3.1–3.5
Severe (401–500)	430+	250+	400+	748+	34+	1600+	1800+	3.5+

Vihar, R K Puram, Punjabi Bagh, NSIT (Dwarka), and Sector 62 Noida. First of all, K-means clustering was applied.

2. *SVM outcomes*: The data values (1,870) were divided into training and testing sets. We took 80% for the training set and 20% for the testing set. The clustered data was trained on SVM against air quality so that air quality could be determined based on the values of all parameters. Sklearn library was used for it [14]. SVM was cross-validated using GridSearchCV (k = 10) technique. Results on 374 test samples could be seen in Table 1.2. Best parameter set found was {c: 0.1, gamma: 0.001, kernel: linear}.

3. *LSTM outcomes*: To build the LSTM model, we trained our model for 14 different places in India, namely, Visakhapatnam (GVMC Ram Nagar), Ajmer (Civil Lines), Alwar, Vasundhara (Ghaziabad), Gurgaon (Vikas Sadan), Bandra (Maharashtra), Bhiwadi Industrial Area, Bengaluru (BWSSB Kadabesanaha), Amritsar (Golden Temple), Anand Vihar, R K Puram, Punjabi Bagh, NSIT (Dwarka), and Sector 62 Noida. Five thousand samples were used for training and 500 samples for testing of each model.

Each model had different values for different parameters like kernel initializer, batch size, and epochs during hyper parameter tuning. We used Keras library in Python [15]. The performance was evaluated with two metrics: Mean

Table 1.2 Precision, recall, and F1-score.

Classes	Precision	Recall	F1-Score
Moderate	1.0	0.99	0.99
Poor	1.0	0.95	0.97
Satisfactory	0.98	1.0	0.99
Severe	1.0	1.0	1.0
Very Poor	1.0	1.0	1.0
Avg/total	0.99	0.99	0.99
Final Accuracy: 0.9893			

Absolute Error (MAE), Root Mean Square Error (RMSE). Table 1.3 shows the MAE and RMSE values received. MAE is calculated by $(\sum|y - x|)/n$, and RMSE is calculated by $\sqrt{(\sum y - x)^2/n}$ where y is predicted value and x is actual value.

Figure 1.4 shows the prediction values for Bengaluru City at present hour as well as for 2 days 3 hours after 13th

Table 1.3 MAE and RMSE scores for different epochs.

Test MAE for 1	8.864
Test RMSE for 1	12.122
Test MAE for 2	17.996
Test RMSE for 2	35.390
Test MAE for 3	23.820
Test RMSE for 3	35.938
Test MAE for 4	6.021
Test RMSE for 4	9.269

Prediction at Bengaluru (BWSSB Kadabesanaha) at present hour

Date & Time	NO2	PM2.5	SO2	CO
13 19:00:00	21.68	15.82	3.29	392.25

Air Quality Index: 21.68
Air Quality: Good
Health Advisory: None
Health Impacts: Minimal Impact.

Prediction at Bengaluru (BWSSB Kadabesanaha) after 2 days and 3 hours

Date & Time	NO2	PM2.5	SO2	CO
15 22:00:00	21.68	15.82	3.29	392.25

Air Quality Index: 21.68
Air Quality: Good
Health Advisory: None
Health Impacts: Minimal Impact.

Figure 1.4 Predicted values in Bengaluru in December, 2017.

December, 2017. Figure 1.5 shows the prediction values for 2 days 3 hours after 6th June, 2020. We observed that on an average Bengaluru is a cleaner city as compared to other cities even during November and December. It was realized that it could have been due to rainy weather. Bengaluru gets rain almost every day and due to which the majority of air pollutants get washed down thus resulting into reduced air pollution.

Figure 1.6 shows the predicted values at present hour and for future one day 3 hours for Anand Vihar, New Delhi, after 13th December, 2017. New Delhi suffers from heavy pollution and therefore the quality of observed air was very poor. $PM_{2.5}$ level remains high, making the air not only toxic but also prone to causing breathing problems. We have also generated advisory for the users of the app. Figure 1.7 shows the predicted values for 1 day and 3 hours for Anand Vihar, New Delhi, after 6th June, 2020. It could clearly be seen that pollution levels have drastically reduced and air quality has also become better due to imposed lockdown as there is less traffic and industrial waste emissions.

The experiments were performed for batch sizes of 10, 24, 15, 8, and 6 with epochs of 10 and 100. The MAE Scores

Prediction at Bengaluru (BWSSB Kadabesanaha) at present hour

Date & Time	NO2	PM2.5	SO2	CO
6 16:00:00	14.64	0.79	1.31	116.84

Air Quality Index: 13.76
Air Quality: Good
Health Advisory: None
Health Impacts: Minimal Impact.

Prediction at Bengaluru (BWSSB Kadabesanaha) after 2 days and 3 hours

Date & Time	NO2	PM2.5	SO2	CO
8 19:00:00	14.12	0.89	0.09	111.47

Air Quality Index: 14.12
Air Quality: Good
Health Advisory: None
Health Impacts: Minimal Impact.

Figure 1.5 Predicted values in Bengaluru in June, 2020.

Prediction at Anand Vihar at present hour

Date & Time	NO2	O3	PM10	PM2.5	SO2
13 19:00:00	92.27	55.40	24.88	457.75	14.18

Air Quality Index: 456.94
Air Quality: Very Poor
Health Advisory: … State of Emergency …. Everyone should avoid all physical activity outdoors.
Health Impacts: May cause respiratory illness to the people on prolonged exposure.
Effect may be more pronouced in people with lung and heart diseases.

Prediction at Anand Vihar after 1 day and 3 hours

Date & Time	NO2	O3	PM10	PM2.5	SO2
14 22:00:00	92.17	55.38	24.60	459.60	14.16

Air Quality Index: 458.83
Air Quality: Very Poor

Figure 1.6 Predicted values in New Delhi in December, 2017.

Prediction at Anand Vihar at present hour

Date & Time	NO2	O3	PM10	PM2.5	SO2
6 16:00:00	35.94	56.07	39.09	127.31	6.11

Air Quality Index: 115.53
Air Quality: Satisfactory
Health Advisory: Sensitive groups should reduce prolonged or heavy exertion.
Health Impacts: May cause minor breathing discomfort to sensitive people.

Prediction at Anand Vihar after 1 day and 3 hours

Date & Time	NO2	O3	PM10	PM2.5	SO2
7 19:00:00	37.05	43.51	41.39	141.06	6.44

Air Quality Index: 138.64
Air Quality: Moderate

Figure 1.7 Predicted values in New Delhi in June, 2020.

for LSTM Hyper Parameters for NO_2, O_3, PM_{10}, $PM_{2.5}$, and SO_2 are shown in (Table 1.4), and after careful analysis of the LSTM Hyper Parameter scores, we zeroed in on the batch size with minimum bias.

Table 1.4 MAE scores for LSTM hyper parameters.

Batch size	Epochs	NO_2	O_3	PM_{10}	$PM_{2.5}$	SO_2
10	10	22	52	142	64	14
24	100	17	22	142	52	13
15	100	13	19	139	51	13
8	10	16.8	25.4	124	44.8	13
6	10	13	25	119.7	44	13

4. *Data Visualization*: One of the main objectives of the project was to provide better visualizations to the normal people who are not able to interpret the relations between different values of the air pollutants. We therefore generated the Heat Maps of different parameters. Individual Heat Maps for the parameters as well as combined Heat Maps for the parameters have been provided.

   Figure 1.8 shows the Heat Map for Ozone gas O_3 for 12th and 13th December, 2017. From the map, we could observe that O_3 suffers maximum fluctuations between day and night intervals. O_3 levels reduce at midnight and are very high on 13th December evening time. This could be due to heavy vehicular traffic during evening hours. Figure 1.9 shows Heat Map for O_3 for 6th to 8th June, 2020 which clearly shows reduction in O_3 levels during less vehicular traffic and reduced industrial emissions.

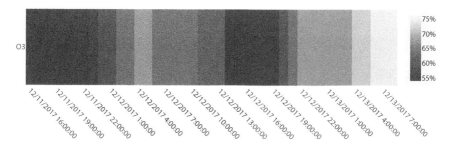

Figure 1.8 Heat map for ozone O_3 for day and night in December, 2017.

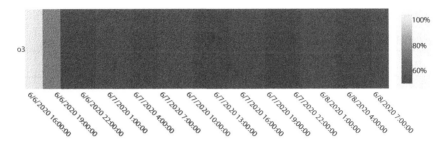

Figure 1.9 Heat map for ozone O_3 for day and night in June, 2020.

Figure 1.10 shows the Heat Map for all the parameters for the days 11th, 12th, and 13th December, 2017, at Sector 62, Noida. From the Heat Maps it could be observed that $PM_{2.5}$ is the main pollution causing parameter in the Air. It could also be observed that it remains at dangerous levels on all days and during Days as well as Nights. Figure 1.11 shows the Heat Map for all the parameters for the days 6th, 7th and 8th June, 2020 at Sector 62, Noida. The reduced levels of all pollutants could clearly be seen from the Heat Map as

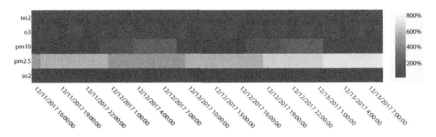

Figure 1.10 Heat map for all parameters for 3 days and nights in December, 2017.

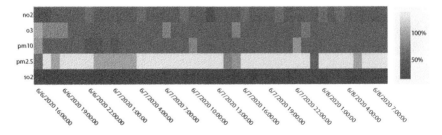

Figure 1.11 Heat map for all parameters for 3 days and nights in June, 2020.

a result of imposed lockdown. However, $PM_{2.5}$ still remains the top contributing factor toward pollution in the area.

Figure 1.12 shows the predicted values of O_3 for Anand Vihar, New Delhi in December, 2017, and decline in O_3 levels can be observed. Figure 1.13 shows the predicted values

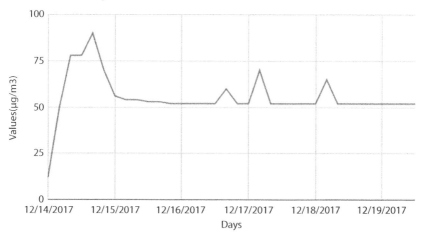

Current to Future Analysis of O3 at Anand Vihar

Figure 1.12 Predicted values for O_3 for Anand Vihar, New Delhi.

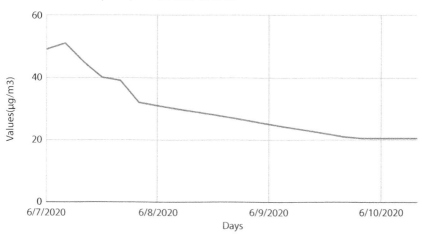

Current to Future Analysis of pm10 at Sector-62 Noida

Figure 1.13 Predicted values for PM_{10} for Sector 62, Noida.

of PM_{10} for Sector 62, Noida in June, 2020, and decline in levels could be observed.

The quality of air as shown in Figure 1.14 could also be observed/predicted for the major cities of India. This helped the user to study the quality of air throughout the country. The figure shows the quality of air as severe (magenta), very poor (yellow), poor (cyan), moderate (red), satisfactory (green), and good as blue dot on the map. It was realized that smaller cities, towns, and villages in India have good air quality. It is only the Metropolitan cities and the areas surrounding these cities that suffer from worst air quality.

From our project, we had some major findings. It was found that the values of different parameters of air depend

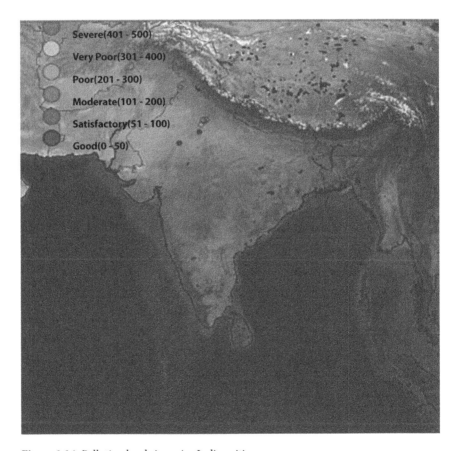

Figure 1.14 Pollution levels in major Indian cities.

on the latest past records (few days to a month) and not on many previous months. While retrieving real-time values through API for different parameters, sometimes, null or zero values occur. This might be due to malfunctioning of the sensors or inappropriate weather conditions. Zero or very less values might also occur at night because of the fact that certain parameters like O_3 mix with other chemical compounds to form other compounds and consequently their value reduces. No_2 and SO_2 are also sometimes interacting and hence their abrupt values. The raw data is much easier to understand through visualizations for a common man. Also, lockdown is expected to be the effective alternative measure to be implemented for controlling air pollution.

1.5 Conclusion

After applying K-means clustering using Silhouette coefficient, the data is divided into seven clusters. The SVM is successfully able to classify the data into its respective air quality class with accuracy of 99%. The LSTM models for different places have been tuned accordingly to minimize MAE and RMSE. The proposed model could be used for various purposes like predicting future trends of air quality, assessing past trends of air quality, visualizing data in an effective way, issuing health advisory, and providing health effects (if any) based on the current air quality. Various parameters can be compared and it could be determined which pollutant is affecting more in a particular area and accordingly actions could be taken beforehand. Anyone could get inference from the data easily which is tough to analyze numerically and could take certain actions to control air pollution in any area.

References

1. IHME and HEI State of Global Air/2017, A special report on global exposure to air pollution and its disease burden. State of Global Air, vol. 1, 1–17, 2017.
2. Li, H., Fan, H., Mao, F., A visualization approach to air pollution data exploration—a case study of air quality index (PM2. 5) in Beijing, China. *Atmosphere*, 7, 3, 35, 2016.
3. Lu, W., Ai, T., Zhang, X., He, Y., An interactive web mapping visualization of urban air quality monitoring data of China. *Atmosphere*, 8, 8, 148, 2017.

4. Kumar, A., Sinha, R., Bhattacherjee, V., Verma, D. S., & Singh, S., Modeling using K-means clustering algorithm. *1st International Conference on Recent Advances in Information Technology (RAIT)*, vol. 1, 554–558, IEEE, 2012.

5. Fan, J., Li, Q., Hou, J., Feng, X., Karimian, H., Lin, S., A spatiotemporal prediction framework for air pollution based on deep RNN. *ISPRS Annals of the Photogrammetry, Remote Sensing and Spatial Information Sciences*, vol. 4, p. 15, 2017.

6. Pereira, R.L., Sousa, P.C., Barata, R., Oliveira, A., Monsieur, G., CitySDK Tourism API-building value around open data. *J. Internet Serv. Appl.*, 6, 1, 1–13, 2015.

7. Adeleke, J.A., Moodley, D., Rens, G., Adewumi, A.O., Integrating statistical machine learning in a semantic sensor web for proactive monitoring and control. *Sensors*, 17, 4, 807, 2017.

8. Kim, S.H., Choi, J.W., Han, G.T., Air pollution data visualization method based on google earth and KML for Seoul air quality monitoring in real-time. *Int. J. Software Eng. Its Appl.*, 10, 10, 117–128, 2016.

9. Sharma, S., Zhang, M., Gao, J., Zhang, H., Kota, S.H., Effect of restricted emissions during COVID-19 on air quality in India. *Sci. Total Environ.*, 728, 138878, 2020.

10. Mahato, S., Pal, S., Ghosh, K.G., Effect of lockdown amid COVID-19 pandemic on air quality of the megacity Delhi, India. *Sci. Total Environ.*, 730, 139086, 2020.

11. Lloyd, S., Least squares quantization in PCM. *IEEE Trans. Inf. Theory*, 28, 2, 129–137, 1982.

12. Hochreiter, S. and Schmidhuber, J., Long short-term memory. *Neural Comput.*, 9, 8, 1735–1780, 1997.

13. Hasenkopf, C. A., Flasher, J. C., Veerman, O., & DeWitt, H. L., OpenAQ: A Platform to Aggregate and Freely Share Global Air Quality Data. *AGU Fall Meeting Abstracts*, 2015, A31D-0097, 2015.

14. Pedregosa, F., Varoquaux, G., Gramfort, A., Michel, V., Thirion, B., Grisel, O., Vanderplas, J., Scikit-learn: Machine learning in Python. *J. Mach. Learn. Res.*, 12, 2825–2830, 2011.

15. Manaswi, N. K., Understanding and working with Keras, *Deep Learning with Applications Using Python,* vol. 1, pp. 31–43, Springer, 2018.

Automatic Counting and Classification of Silkworm Eggs Using Deep Learning

Shreedhar Rangappa[1*], Ajay A.[1] and G. S. Rajanna[2]

[1]Intelligent Vision Technology, Bengaluru, India
[2]Maharani Cluster University, Sheshadri Road, Bengaluru, India

Abstract

The method of using convolutional neural networks to identify and quantify the silkworm eggs that are laid on a sheet of paper by female silk moth. The method is also capable of segmenting individual egg and classifying them into hatched egg class and unhatched egg class, thus outperforming image processing techniques used earlier. Fewer limitations of the techniques employed earlier are described and attempt to increase accuracy using uniform illumination of a digital scanner is illustrated. The use of a standard key marker that helps to transform any silkworm egg sheet into a standard image, which can be used as input to a trained convolution neural network model to get predictions, is discussed briefly. The deep learning model is trained on silkworm datasets of over 100K images for each category. The experimental results on test image sets show that our approach yields an accuracy of above 97% coupled with high repeatability.

Keywords: Deep learning, convolution neural network, datasets, accuracy, silkworms, fecundity, hatching percentage

2.1 Introduction

In the last decade, machine learning has gained the popularity that no sequential programming approach has reached in a century in various fields of engineering. Deep learning/convolution neural network (CNN) is a part of a machine learning approach that solves a given problem without

*Corresponding author: 44shree@gmail.com

Mettu Srinivas, G. Sucharitha and Anjanna Matta (eds.) Machine Learning Algorithms and Applications, (23–40) © 2021 Scrivener Publishing LLC

explicitly providing the features to be considered to generate useful results. These advanced techniques are predominantly deployed in the engineering field. However, disciplines such as medical imaging [1], microbiology [2], and finance [3] are vastly adopting machine learning to achieve superior results.

Further, some areas of science still use the conventional approach of solving the problem, and sericulture is one among them. The sericulture industry involves the art and science of host plant cultivation as well as silkworm rearing to produce natural silk products. Silk is the queen of textiles and globally India is the second-largest producer of four different types of silk. Thus, sericulture serves as the base for economic, social, scientific, political, and intellectual advancements [4]. The fecundity (number of eggs laid by fertilized female silk moth), hatching percentage (silkworm birth rate), survival percentage (disease and environment tolerant), and silk productivity are a few economic traits (parameters) on which entire silk industry thrives. Manual counting of eggs is in vogue to quantify fecundity and hatching percentage parameters. Many automatic methods (image processing and new hardware design) have been attempted with lower accuracy [5]. A new approach of automatic counting and classifying eggs is described in this paper to quantify fecundity and hatching percentage accurately which provides required rearing information to harvest successful silk cocoon crops.

The chapter describes a few conventional approaches and their drawbacks and, further, introduce the CNN approach adopted in this paper and to explain the specifications of each model trained to surpass the results provided by other image processing techniques.

2.2   Conventional Silkworm Egg Detection Approaches

Manual counting of silkworm egg is in practice in countries like India, China, Thailand, and other Asian countries [6]. The silkworm eggs are small-sized [5], approximately 2 to 3 mm in diameter, densely populated in small clusters. Hence, the manual counting process will be tediously associated with prolonged time and is susceptible to human error. The inconsistency in determining the fecundity and hatching percentage impacts the overall cocoon crop performance and Silk productivity.

Many techniques have been implemented to measure the quantity of egg laid, such as designing hardware [6, 7], and using image processing techniques. The primary focus in previously published papers was to segment the silkworm egg from the background using different image processing techniques such as low contrast image setting [8], contrast enhancement followed by image morphological operations [7], image patch centroid analysis [6], image channel conversion from RGB to HSV to identify the region of interest (ROI) [9], using Gaussian mixture model [10], and using Hough transforms (blob analysis) [11, 12]. The accuracy achieved in these techniques completely depends on the consistency of the experimental conditions such as the color of the sheet on which the silkworm eggs were laid, the size of the eggs, and uniform illumination while capturing a digital image of eggs. By altering any one of these parameters, the results vary drastically, and hence designing an image processing algorithm for every possible scenario becomes laborious. Also, the method used in these techniques to capture digital data of the eggs was to use digital cameras, operated manually without any preset illumination parameter and hence resulting in poor accuracy.

2.3   Proposed Method

Two of the main parameters that vary during capturing digital data for image processing are the size of the silkworm egg and uniform illumination spread across the image. Firstly, since the image processing (including blob analysis) algorithms are designed to identify a particular egg size or range of egg sizes, exceeding this limit causes error in the final result. Since no constant distance is set between the egg sheet and camera, in any of the earlier papers, the pixel size of captured eggs varies which causes the problem to the image processing algorithm. Also, the irregular distribution of illumination over ROI causes the digital cameras to record the data slightly in a different way, which may over saturate or under saturate the ROI. The image processing algorithms such as contrast stretch and histogram equalization perform well on the limited scenario and do not provide complete confidence to enhance low-quality data.

To overcome these issues, a constant illumination light source with a fixed distance between camera and egg sheets of a paper scanner is used to capture the digital data of the silkworm egg sheets. Since the distance between the camera array of the paper scanner is fixed, the egg size can be approximated to stay within a specific range, i.e., around 28 to 36 pixels in diameter in our experiment. However, not all manufacturers of paper scanner follow strict dimensions while designing, hence the silkworm eggs scanned with different scanner results are found to be different. For example, the eggs scanned with Canon® scanner have a diameter of 28 to 32 pixels under, while 36 to 40 pixels with Hewlett-Packard® (HP) scanners for the same resolution and dots per inch (dpi).

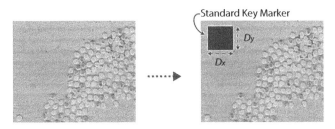

Figure 2.1 Adding a key marker on the silkworm egg sheet.

Also, by changing the scanner parameters such as resolution and dpi, the resulting egg diameter is of different pixels size for the same scanner. Hence, a key marker is printed on the egg sheet before it is scanned to capture the details in a digital format. The dimension of the key marker is 100×100 pixels (10×10 mm) which are considered as a standard dimension in our experiment. Let $R(hxw)$ be the standard resolution required by the image processing algorithm, while $R'(h'xw')$ be the resolution at which the egg sheet is scanned and R'' is the resulting resolution of the image. Also, let (D_x, D_y) be the standard dimensions of the key marker, while (D'_x, D'_y) is the key marker dimension calculated from the new scan. Figure 2.1 shows a part of the silkworm egg sheet before and after the key marker was stamped. Figure 2.1 (left) represents the original egg sheet while Figure 2.1 (right) represents the egg sheet with key marker stamped. Equations (2.1) to (2.3) represent the method of converting images with any dpi into the standard dpi by comparing the dimensions (D_x, D_y) *with* (D'_x, D'_y), where R'' values are used in image processing platforms such as MATLAB to resize the image sheet to match the standard required dimensions.

$$d_x = (D_x - D'_x) \tag{2.1}$$

$$d_y = (D_y - D'_y) \tag{2.2}$$

$$R'' - h' - d_x \times w' - d_y \tag{2.3}$$

2.3.1 Model Architecture

To overcome the problem with conventional image processing algorithms as stated in Section 2.2, machine learning (ML) techniques were employed to segment the eggs from the background (egg sheet). The features to be considered for segmentation such as color (grayscale pixel values), the diameter of eggs was collected manually using image processing and feature engineering, later fed into various ML algorithms (KNN, decision trees, and SVM). ML algorithms provide accuracy over 90% but fail when the input data is of a different class (breed in terms of sericulture field) when compared to the class for which the algorithm was trained since the color of eggs is not the same for different breeds of the silkworm. To overcome this issue, a supervised CNN technique is used which requires the true label while the features are selected automatically. The primary aim of our approach was to accurately count several silkworm eggs present in a given digital image and further classify them into respective classes such as hatched and unhatched. Figure 2.2 represents a sample digital image of the egg sheet with a different class of eggs being marked with specific colors manually. The eggs marked with green color represent the *hatched class* (HC), while eggs marked with red color represent the *unhatched class* (UHC).

To identify the core features of the eggs, for segmenting them from the background sheet and to classify them into respective categories, a simple deep learning technique was used with four hidden layers to provide results that are much more accurate compared to conventional methods. Deep learning models are trained using TensorFlow framework to provide three different results such as foreground-background segmentation, detecting eggs, and classifying detected egg.

The core deep learning model used in our experiments is shown in Figure 2.3. The model consists of convolution layers, max-pooling layers, and fully connected layers. These layers are trained to identify the features of egg, while the last layer is modified to provide categorical or continuous data. The core CNN model is trained using a stride of (2×2) and kernel of (5×5) for convolution, with (2×2) max pooling and a fully connected

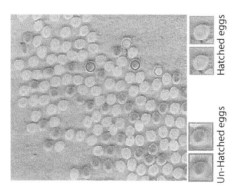

Figure 2.2 Silkworm egg classes: hatched eggs and unhatched eggs.

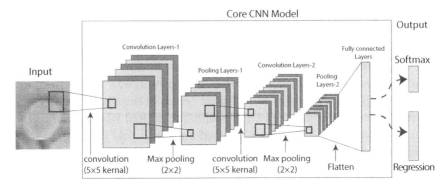

Figure 2.3 Core CNN model.

layer consisting of 3200 neurons. The input to the CNN model is a 32×32 dimension image with three color channels, RGB.

2.3.2 Foreground-Background Segmentation

The basic requirement for accurate counting of silkworm egg is to perform foreground-background (FB) segmentation. In the previous attempts, the background was segmented based on the intensity value of the eggs [8]. The region that has no pixel values corresponding to the eggs is considered as background and discarded before the image processing stage. However, this is not ideal in all situations, since the silkworm eggs laid on the sheet may also contain urine from the silkworms that discolor the background. The urinated background dries into a white layer that resembles an egg pixel intensity value close to 230 for an 8-bit grayscale image.

The resolution of the digital data that is fed into the CNN model is another reason to perform segment the background before the class of eggs is determined. The eggs are of the size around 32×32 pixels after scanning, while the entire sheet of silkworm eggs is of the size 5008×6984 pixels (in our experiment). If the entire sheet was fed to the CNN model with an input image size of 32×32 pixels with a sliding window method, then the model must classify 35M images that would be computationally expensive for a system without GPU support.

To overcome this issue, the FB CNN model was trained with an input data of 128×128 pixels, three-channel RGB image that was fed to the core CNN model, as shown in Figure 2.3, to provide categorical output using the softmax activation function. Some of the corresponding specifications of the FB CNN model are provided in Table 2.1 along with accuracy scores. Using a 128×128 pixel input to the FB CNN model, the entire

Table 2.1 Specifications of foreground-background (FB) segmentation CNN model.

Input image	Activation/ output	Training samples	Test samples	Validation samples	Test loss	Accuracy on the test set	Accuracy on the validation set
128×128	SoftMax 2 class-(0/1)	142×10^3	64.3×10^3	9.6×10^3	0.1242	96.1554%	96.6422%

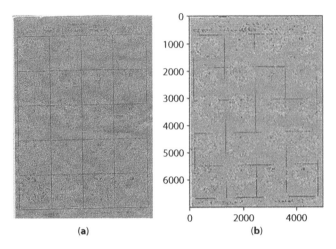

Figure 2.4 Foreground-background segmentation of entire silkworm egg sheet (a) (input) and (b) (output).

silkworm egg sheet is divided into square grids of 128 × 128 with a stride of 128, resulting in an image set of 2K images that must be processed for categorical results as foreground or background class. Figure 2.4 represents the segmentation of the entire silkworm egg sheet, where the foreground (presence of egg) and background (absence of egg) are represented by a green color (pixels) and red color, respectively. Further processing is only carried out for pixels represented in green color that minimizes computational time and increase final accuracy as background pixels are dropped out of the data processing cycle.

2.3.3   Egg Location Predictor

After segmentation of egg pixels from background pixels, the next step is to determine the location of the eggs. Many CNN models have been introduced such as Fast-RCNN [13] and YOLO [14] to predict the location of the object using the Intersect over Union method. There are two main reasons for not considering well-known techniques to locate the eggs. Firstly, in these methods the object/ROI dimensions are over 100 × 100, irregular in size, and the method has been trained for different bounding box dimensions. These techniques become unacceptable to determine the location of the egg, as the eggs have an average size of 28 × 28 pixels to 36 × 36 pixels. Moreover, the shape of the egg remains similar with minor deformation that can be neglected; hence, training for different dimension bounding box will not yield any good result. Secondly, these methods have the limitation of how many similar class objects can be recognized within a single bounding box, which are two objects for YOLO [14]. Since the eggs are small, many eggs will be present within a 100 × 100 grid image that may belong to the same class and hence may not be detected.

The specification of the egg location predictor CNN model is represented in Table 2.2, where the input to the core CNN model has been changed to 32 × 32 pixels, three-channel RGB image. Here, the output is a regression that provides the location of the egg center (x, y) rather than a bounding box (four corner points). The training dataset consists of both the class images, i.e., hatched eggs and unhatched eggs. The positive samples consist of images where an individual egg is visible completely, while the negative samples consist of eggs that are partially visible and have multiple egg entries. Figure 2.5 represents the classifier model that is trained to determine positive and negative samples, and the positive samples are later trained to predict the egg center location in terms of pixel values. Further, during the practical application, the center location of the egg predicted is used to crop a single egg data to be fed into a classifier that determines the class of the selected egg into HC or UHC. Figure 2.6 represents an overall result of locating egg centers using egg location predictor CNN model for one of the test data sheets where all egg centers are marked with a blue dot. A sliding window of (32 × 32) with a stride of (4, 4) was used to achieve the results.

2.3.4   Predicting Egg Class

The sliding window method is used to generate input images, and a single egg may be represented by many image windows each of size 32 × 32. Euclidean distance equation, $\sqrt{(x1-x2)^2+(y1-y2)^2}$, was used to select the egg center by combining all the egg location predictions that fall within a certain user-defined distance limit. $(x1, y1)$ and $(x2, y2)$ are the reference pixel and pixel under consideration. Since the egg diameter is well within the range of 28 to 32 pixels, a distance limit is set that is equal to the radius of the egg, i.e., 16 pixels. Any center locations that fall within this limit are considered to be representing same egg and hence combined to generate single egg location that can be then cropped by using Equations (2.4) to (2.7), where (x_a, y_a) are the resulting egg location after averaging all predicted egg locations that fall within distance limits. (x, y) pixel is the original location while w, h represents the width and height of the image to be cropped that is equal to 32 pixels. The resulting

Table 2.2 Specifications of egg location CNN model.

Input image	Activation/ output	Training samples	Test samples	Validation samples	Test loss	Validation loss
32×32	Regression Center of the egg (x, y)	439×10^3	51.6×10^3	25.8×10^3	0.5488	0.5450

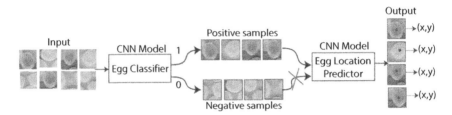

Figure 2.5 CNN training model to predict egg location in terms of pixel values.

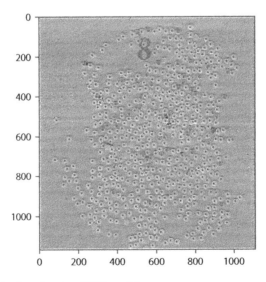

Figure 2.6 Result of egg location CNN model.

Table 2.3 Specification of egg class predicator CNN model.

Input image	Activation/output	Training samples	Test samples	Validation samples	Test loss	Accuracy on the test set	Accuracy on the validation set
32 × 32	SoftMax 2 class-(0/1)	2.4×10^6	80.2×10^3	30×10^3	0.0077	99.8115%	99.7981%

images are fed into the egg class predictor CNN model, which provides categorical data to distinguish the input image into class HC or UHC. The specification of the egg class predictor CNN model is represented in Table 2.3.

$$x = x_a - 16 \tag{2.4}$$

$$y = y_a - 16 \tag{2.5}$$

$$w = x_a + 16 \tag{2.6}$$

$$h = y_a + 16 \tag{2.7}$$

The overall result of egg classification and counting yields an accuracy greater than 97%, and Figure 2.7 represents the result generated using the proposed method where green dots represent the hatched eggs while red dots represent unhatched eggs. Some of the areas of the images are zoomed and shown separately in Figure 2.7 since the input image is too big to fit in the page and eggs are minuscule to see any features.

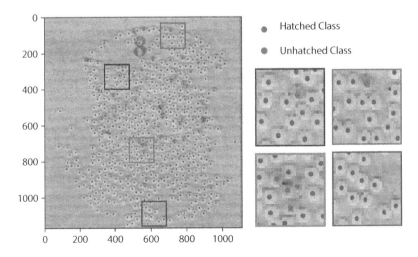

Figure 2.7 Result of egg classification generated by the proposed method.

2.4   Dataset Generation

In comparison with the conventional method of extracting egg count information using digital images that hardly require any training data, the proposed method that employs the CNN technique required large datasets to learn the features automatically to provide the required results. The CNN method uses plenty of training data along with test and validation datasets as the number of hidden layers increases.

There are many datasets available for free that can be downloaded to train our own CNN models to classify handwritten digits, identify objects, and many more. But there is no single public dataset available corresponding with the sericulture field especially silkworm egg counting or classification. So, in our work, training datasets were generated by cropping class images from the silkworm egg sheet and providing class labels and other features that are necessary for CNN training such as egg center location. Over 400K image set was generated for egg location and FB class and over 100K image set for individual classes (HC and UHC). Also, data augmentation is implemented to increase the datasets.

2.5   Results

The trained CNN models were tested with new silkworm egg sheets that were scanned using a Canon® paper scanner at 600 dpi, to classify and count the number of eggs. These digital datasets were completely isolated from the training step; thereby, the trained CNN models had to predict the results than providing learned results. Table 2.4 represents the performance of the overall CNN model trained using our datasets. The performance of a few datasets is shown due to space restriction. It can be observed that CNN models trained with two hidden layers perform superior to the conventional techniques by providing accuracy of over 97%. The accuracy shown in Table 2.4 is the accuracy of the number of eggs counted and accuracy in classifying the eggs. The model consistently outperforms the conventional computer vision/image processing technique of silkworm counting and classification with accuracy over 97% for newer data of the same breed. The inference time shown in Table 2.4 was performed on an Nvidia GPU (GTX 1060).

The model performance drops to newer egg data that are completely different in color and texture, which were not available in the training dataset. This happens due to the nature of different breed eggs that are spatially

Table 2.4 Performance of the CNN model results on test datasets.

Test sample	True count	Count prediction	Time (sec)	Class scores			Accuracy (%)
				HC	UHC		
MSR1_001.jpg	588	586	11.83	437	149		99.65
MSR1_002.jpg	534	526	8.99	473	53		98.68
MSR1_003.jpg	554	556	10.42	491	65		99.28
MSR1_004.jpg	539	528	9.81	501	27		97.95
MSR1_005.jpg	597	588	11.14	562	26		98.32

different from the trained model. Collecting and training a deep learning model to a different breed of silkworm eggs will resolve these issues, which is under action.

2.6   Conclusion

In this paper, CNN-based silkworm egg counting and classification model that overcomes many issues found with conventional image processing techniques is explained. The main contribution of this paper is in four-folds. First, a method to generalize the method of capturing silkworm egg sheet data in a digital format using normal paper scanners rather than designing extra hardware, which eliminates the need for additional light sources to provide uniform illumination while recording data and maintain high repeatability.

Second, the scanned digital data can be transformed into standard size by using key markers stamped onto the egg sheets before scanning. This allows the user to resize the dimension of digital data and later use it in an image processing algorithm or CNN without introducing dimensionality error.

A dataset has been put together containing over 400K images representing different features of silkworm eggs. The CNN and other models that need a lot of training, testing and validation data can easily use this dataset to skip the data generation phase which is the third contribution.

Fourth, a CNN model has been trained using the dataset that is designed to predict the egg class and count the number of eggs per egg sheet. With over 97% accuracy the model outperforms many conventional approaches with only 4 hidden layers and a fully connected layer.

The model performs accurately in quantifying (counting) different breed silkworm eggs, but new datasets become necessary to predict the class labels for new silkworm breed for which the model is not trained. This is because HC class eggs have high pixel intensity throughout the egg surface while UHC has dark pixels at the center surrounded with high-value pixels for the egg breed used on our experiment. This color feature may not be the same as other breed silkworm eggs, and hence, additional data becomes important that can be fed into already trained CNN using transfer learning. Also, the egg location model performs well with new breed data, the training dataset to determining the class of eggs can be easily generated with minimal human effort.

Acknowledgment

The authors would like to thank Smt. R. Latha S-B and Mr. P. B. Vijayakumar S-C of KSSRDI, KA, IN for providing silkworm egg sheets for this study.

References

1. Xue, Y. and Ray, N., Cell Detection in Microscopy Images with Deep Convolutional Neural Network and Compressed Sensing, *CoRR*, abs/1708.03307, *arXiv preprint arXiv:1708.03307*, 2017.

2. Zieliński, B., Plichta, A., Misztal, K., Spurek, P., Brzychczy-Włoch, M., Ochońska, D., Deep learning approach to bacterial colony classification. *PLoS One*, 12, 9, e0184554, 2017.

3. Abe, M. and Nakayama, H., Deep learning for forecasting stock returns in the cross-section, in: *Lecture Notes in Computer Science (including subseries Lecture Notes in Artificial Intelligence and Lecture Notes in Bioinformatics)*, vol. 10937 LNAI, pp. 273–284, 2018.

4. Kumar, D.A., Silkworm Growth Monitoring Smart Sericulture System based on Internet of Things (IOT) and Image Processing. *Int. J. Comput. Appl.*, 180, 18, 975–8887, 2018.

5. S.P., Rajanna, G.S., Chethan, D., Application of Image Analysis methods for Quantification of Fecundity in Silkworm Bombyx mori L, in: *International Sericulture Commission*, Research Papers, 2015 (http://www.inserco.org/en/previous_issue).

6. Kiratiratanapruk, K., Watcharapinchai, N., Methasate, I., Sinthupinyo, W., Silkworm eggs detection and classification using image analysis, in: *2014 International Computer Science and Engineering Conference, ICSEC 2014*, pp. 340–345, 2014.

7. Pandit, A., Rangole, J., Shastri, R., Deosarkar, S., Vision system for automatic counting of silkworm eggs, *2014 International Conference on Information Communication and Embedded Systems, ICICES 2014*, no. 978, pp. 1–5, 2015.

8. Kiratiratanapruk, K. and Sinthupinyo, W., Worm egg segmentation based centroid detection in low contrast image, in: *2012 International Symposium on Communications and Information Technologies, ISCIT 2012*, pp. 1139–1143, 2012.

9. Pathan, S., Harale, A., Student, P.G., A Method of Automatic Silkworm Eggs Counting System. *Int. J. Innovative Res. Comput. Commun. Eng.*, 4, 12, 25, 2016.

10. K.P.R., Sanjeev Poojary, L., M.G.V., S.N.K., An Image Processing Algorithm for Silkworm Egg Counting. *Perspect. Commun. Embedded-Syst. Signal-Process. (PiCES)*, 1, 4, 2566–932, 2017.

11. Matas, J., Galambos, C., Kittler, J., Robust Detection of Lines Using the Progressive Probabilistic Hough Transform. *Comput. Vision Image Understanding*, 78, 1, 119–137, Apr. 2000.

12. Nikitha, R.N., Srinidhi, R.G., Harshith, R., Amar, T., Raghavendra, C.G., Reckoning the hatch rate of multivoltine silkworm eggs by differentiating yellow grains from white shells using blob analysis technique, in: *Advances in Intelligent Systems and Computing*, vol. 709, pp. 497–506, 2018.

13. F. und T. des L. N.-W. Ministerium für Innovation and Wissenschaft, Faster R-CNN: Towards Real-Time Object Detection with Region Proposal Networks. *Advances in neural information processing systems*, 2015.

14. Özdener, A.E. and Rivkin, A., You Only Look Once: Unified, Real-Time Object Detection Joseph. *Drug Des. Devel. Ther.*, abs/1506.02640, 11, 2827–2840, 2015.

3

A Wind Speed Prediction System Using Deep Neural Networks

Jaseena K. U.[1,2]* and Binsu C. Kovoor[1]

[1]Division of Information Technology, School of Engineering, Cochin University of Science and Technology, Kochi, Kerala, India
[2]Department of Computer Applications, MES College Marampally, Aluva, Kochi, Kerala, India

Abstract

The demand for renewable energy sources has improved significantly due to the depletion of fossil fuels at a tremendous rate. The usage of conventional energy sources is making the environment more polluted. So, wind and other renewable energy sources have got more significance and demand. Low cost and availability are the key factors that make wind one of the most dominant renewable sources of energy. Wind speed prediction has applications in various domains such as wind power stations, agriculture, navy, and airport operations. Wind speed can be predicted depending on various environmental factors such as dew point, humidity, temperature, and pressure. Deep Neural Networks (DNNs) are particular types of neural networks that can process and analyze massive datasets by applying a series of trained algorithms and are capable of making predictions based on past data. This chapter suggests a DNN model to forecast daily average wind speed using massive datasets. The metrics used to estimate the accuracy of the prediction system are mean absolute error, root mean squared error, and R^2. Performance comparison of the proposed model with Artificial Neural Network, Support Vector Machine, and Random Forests are analyzed, and the experimental outcomes demonstrate that the proposed model is more efficient and effective.

Keywords: Wind speed prediction, Artificial Neural Networks, deep learning, Deep Neural Networks

*Corresponding author: jaseena.mes@gmail.com

Mettu Srinivas, G. Sucharitha and Anjanna Matta (eds.) Machine Learning Algorithms and Applications, (41–60) © 2021 Scrivener Publishing LLC

3.1   Introduction

Energy sources are an inevitable part of every developing country for their industrial and agricultural activities. Wind energy is observed to be the most promising and environment-friendly source of renewable energy that can be used for power generation. Wind speed prediction is an essential activity as the wind has many applications in various domains such as agriculture, industry, marine applications, military, and airport applications. In wind power generators, effective and precise wind speed prediction is a necessity for generating electricity. The cultivation of certain crops also depends on wind speed. It also plays a significant role during the rocket launching process. Wind speed forecasting can be accomplished with the help of historical wind speed data. Wind speed is weather dependent, and the recurrent behavior of wind speed makes the accurate prediction a challenging task [1]. Hence, the development of accurate wind speed forecasting models has got more significance, and several systems are being implemented for enhancing accuracy. In this big data era, traditional computational intelligence models could take a considerable amount of time to extract relevant information from big datasets. However, the incredible potential of deep learning helps to process and analyze extensive datasets for better feature learning and pattern analysis.

Current prediction systems can be grouped into four categories, namely, physical, statistical, Artificial Intelligence (AI), and hybrid systems, depending on the methods employed for forecasting [2]. Physical systems utilize mathematical models to forecast future states. Statistical models are linear models and are suited for short-term wind speed forecasting. The most commonly employed statistical models for wind speed forecasting are Autoregressive Integrated Moving Average (ARIMA), multiple regression, and Vector Autoregression (VAR). The development of AI has inspired the development of intelligent prediction models. These models have proven to be robust and effective when compared to statistical models. AI models can efficiently manage non-linear datasets and demonstrate better predictive performance. AI systems are further divided into machine learning predictors and deep learning predictors. Artificial Neural Networks (ANNs), Extreme Learning Machine (ELM), and Support Vector Machine (SVM) are the popular machine learning models used for forecasting wind speed. Machine learning techniques are prevalent for predictive systems, in which ANNs are frequently employed as they can learn nonlinear functions. Deep learning uses neural networks with deep architectures that cover many layers of non-linear processing stages. Subsequently, Deep Neural Networks (DNNs) are successfully implemented to predict wind speed due to their high prediction accuracy. Hybrid models are made by combining two or more linear or nonlinear models. These are the latest models that offer the best performance. Yet, another classification found in the literature based on the prediction period is the short, medium, and long term.

He and Xu [3] built a model to forecast wind speed using SVM with two types of kernel functions, namely, polynomial and wavelet kernel functions. The results proved the effectiveness of employing combined learning functions over a single function. Yang *et al.* [4] recommended a forecasting model to predict wind power using the representative unit method, where the Least Square SVM (LSSVM) approach is employed to forecast wind power. Finamore *et al.* [5] suggested a feed forward neural network model for predicting wind power and compared its performance with the persistence model. Yu *et al.* [6] built a hybrid model to forecast wind speed based on WPD (wavelet packet decomposition) and Elman neural network. The ANN model developed by Filik and Filik [7] utilized weather parameters such as temperature, wind speed, and pressure, and the effect of these variables is also investigated. Tarade and Katti [8] carried out an in-depth survey on the existing wind speed forecasting models based on ARIMA, ANN, and Polynomial Curve Fitting. Liu *et al.* [9] suggested a hybrid model employing wavelet, wavelet packet, time series, and ANN. Wavelet Packet ANN model outperformed all other models. Ramasamy *et al.* [10] detailed a wind speed prediction system using ANN to predict wind speed at eleven locations in Himachal Pradesh. Ghorbani *et al.* [11] suggested an hourly wind speed prediction model based on ANN and Genetic Expression Programming (GEP) using 8 years of data from Colorado, USA, from 2005 to 2012 and compared the results with multiple linear regression model and persistence model. Mi *et al.* [2] defined a new hybrid method employing wavelet, ELM, and outlier correction algorithm. Distortions in the dataset are reduced by applying the wavelet domain.

Khandelwal *et al.* [12] recommended a wind speed forecasting system using Discrete Wavelet Transform (DWT), ARIMA, and ANN, where the original signal is partitioned into low and high-frequency components using DWT. Low-frequency components are then trained using ARIMA and high-frequency components using ANN. Yousefi *et al.* [13] devised a wind speed forecasting system using Wavelet Transform (WT) and ANN. The results showed that the prediction accuracy was significantly improved and thus the effectiveness of the proposed model was tested. Shao *et al.* [14] demonstrated a wind speed prediction system based on the AdaBoost neural network, which initially denoise the wind speed data using WT to improve accuracy. Cui *et al.* [15] suggested a model using a neural network for wind speed prediction, where enhanced empirical mode decomposition is adopted to decompose the input data. The model parameters are optimized using bat algorithm, and the simulation results revealed the superiority of the suggested model. Senthil [16] developed three different wind speed forecasting models based on machine learning. The authors employed backpropagation neural networks, Radial Basis Function (RBF), and nonlinear autoregressive network with exogenous inputs (NARX) model to predict wind speed. The results proved that the NARX model surpassed the other two models in the wind speed prediction. The application of the mutual information feature selection method increased the prediction accuracy of the NARX model. Hui et al. [17] proposed a two-stage wind power prediction model that employs fuzzy clustering and RBF networks to predict wind power.

In most of the models presented in the literature, single hidden layer architectures are used. For training a neural network with more hidden layers, deep learning architecture has to be employed. Deep learning utilizes both developments in computing power and unique types of neural networks that can automatically extract essential features from massive datasets. Bali et al. [18] conducted a detailed and comprehensive survey of various deep learning–based wind speed forecasting systems. The proposed survey provided better and efficient methods to assess the effectiveness of the approaches employed for wind speed forecasting. Coa et al. [19] performed a complete review of the accuracy of wind speed prediction models by combining recurrent neural network (RNN) with multivariate and univariate ARIMA models. The authors suggested that the nonlinear RNN model achieved better performance compared to ARIMA models. Khodayar and Teshnehlab [20] recommended a stacked autoencoder DNN model for extremely short-term forecasts of wind speed in Colorado, USA. Sergio and Ludermir [21] and Liu et al. [22] described deep learning–based models for forecasting wind speed. The transfer learning–based model implemented by Hu et al. [23] used a DNN architecture with shared hidden layer that is suitable for datasets with deficit data.

The analysis of the literature reveals that the forecasting performance of the models can be enhanced by employing neural networks with more hidden layers. Moreover, with more hidden layers, the system will be able to learn the features more accurately. Hence, in this chapter, an optimal DNN-based system for predicting daily average wind speed of a meteorological station in Stanford, California, is proposed. Initially, experiments are done to determine reliable and optimal configuration for the

DNN model. The effectiveness of this model is analyzed with other popular machine learning models. The main highlights of the chapter are presented below.

(1) A study was conducted to find the optimal configuration for DNNs.
(2) Investigation of the efficiency of the proposed system using quantitative error indicators and coverage percentage value.
(3) Assessment of the recommended model with other popular machine learning models.
(4) Simulation results reveal the dominance of the proposed system over other systems.

The chapter is organized as follows. The proposed methodology is explained in Section 3.2. The results achieved by the system are described in Section 3.3, followed by conclusions in Section 3.4.

3.2 Methodology

The proposed framework is presented in this section with an introduction to DNNs. The primary objective is to predict daily average wind speed using an optimal DNN architecture. In order to find out the optimum configuration for the DNN architecture, initially, a parametric study of various network parameters is conducted. The parameters considered for the study are the count of hidden layers, count of neurons in each hidden layer, and the learning rate. Accuracy of the proposed optimal model is then compared with popular and widely used machine learning models like ANNs, Random Forests (RF), Decision Trees (DT), SVM, and Linear Regression (LR).

3.2.1 Deep Neural Networks

Deep learning, a subset of machine learning, comprises of many layers of neural networks capable of learning from massive datasets. Deep learning has a hierarchical structure of neural networks by which data can be processed with a nonlinear approach [24]. The main advantage of deep learning is that its performance increases as the volume of data increases. The architecture of a DNN with four hidden layers is shown in Figure 3.1. The neurons in the input layer receive features as input, which are then transferred to the next hidden layer. Each neuron applies a nonlinear

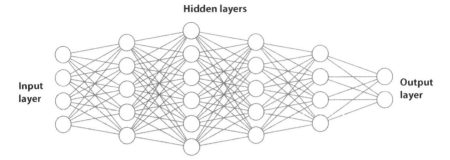

Figure 3.1 Deep Neural Network architecture.

transformation on its input to produce outputs with the help of activation functions. The output layer performs classification and regression tasks. The association between input X and output Y of a neural network at layer i can be represented as in Equation (3.1).

$$Y_i = g\left(\sum_{j=1}^{n} W_{ij}X_j + b_i\right) \qquad (3.1)$$

where W_{ij} represents the weight of the connection between neurons, b_i represents the bias of the neuron i, and g is the activation function.

Each neuron in the hidden and output layers aggregates its input values and then applies an activation function to it. The Rectified Linear Unit (ReLU) is a nonlinear activation function used in the majority of the DNN models. It is used with the hidden layers of a neural network. The equation of ReLU activation function is given by Equation (3.2).

$$f(z) = \begin{cases} 0 \; for \; z < 0 \\ z \; for \; z \geq 0 \end{cases} \qquad (3.2)$$

During the learning process, the network learns by adjusting the weights of the connections using an optimization algorithm to achieve the desired output. The selection of activation functions and optimization algorithms are crucial in assessing the quality and learning capability of a DNN. Adagrad, a gradient-based optimization algorithm, is used for optimizing the objective function in neural networks [25]. In this algorithm, the parameter $\emptyset$, where $\emptyset$ is a vector of W and b (i.e., [W,b]), is updated by using Equations (3.3) and (3.4) to optimize an objective function f(∅).

$$\emptyset_{t+1} = \emptyset_t + \nabla \emptyset_t \tag{3.3}$$

$$\nabla \emptyset_t - - \frac{l}{\sqrt{\sum_{T=1}^{t} gT^2}} \cdot g_t \tag{3.4}$$

where W represents weights, b represents biases, $\nabla\emptyset_t$ is the change in parameter $\emptyset_t$, l is the learning rate which controls the step size in the direction of the negative gradient, and g_t represents the gradient of the parameter at t^{th} iteration. L2 norm of all previous gradients is computed by the denominator of Equation (3.4). The learning rate is not constant throughout the entire learning process. The new learning rate is computed each time by dividing each current gradient by an L2 norm of past observed gradients for that component [25]. This characteristic is mainly valuable for training DNNs.

3.2.2   The Proposed Method

The different phases in the proposed framework are presented in Figure 3.2. The phases include data acquisition, data pre-processing, model selection and training, performance evaluation, and visualization.

3.2.2.1   Data Acquisition

The acquisition of data is an essential step because the quality and quantity of data collected will directly determine the quality of our predictive model. Meteorological data observations from the Stanford (Palo Alto of Santa Clara County) Meteorological station of California from January 1996 to March 2018 were selected for this research work. Stanford, CA, USA is located at 37.42°N, and 122.17°W, and an elevation of 7 ft above sea level. The datasets for the experiments are downloaded from www.wunderground.com. Environmental factors like wind speed, temperature, sea level pressure, dew point, humidity, and visibility are collected daily. Table 3.1 provides statistical information about the data collected from the Stanford weather station. The distribution of the average wind speed data from January 1996 to March 2018 is depicted in Figure 3.3 using both distribution charts and histograms.

The feature names are represented using abbreviations in Table 3.1. The abbreviations T, DP, H, SP, V, and WS, represent temperature, dew point,

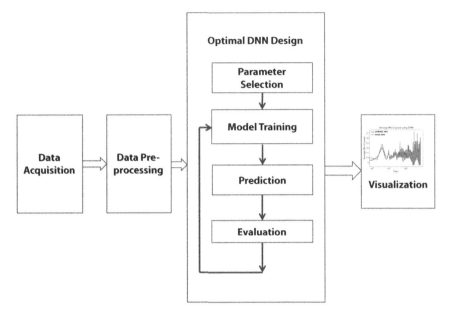

Figure 3.2 Framework of the proposed methodology.

humidity, sea level pressure, visibility, and wind speed, respectively. The variables low, avg, and high are synonyms for minimum, average, and maximum, respectively.

3.2.2.2   Data Pre-Processing

Real-world data often has missing values for a variety of reasons, such as unrecorded values and data corruption. Missing values may affect the quality of results. Therefore, it is necessary to impute missing values before processing the data. In this study, missing values are imputed using mean values. MinMax normalization technique is applied to the datasets to standardize data after missing values are imputed. MinMax normalization technique normalizes data between 0 and 1 using the equation given in Equation (3.5).

$$v' = \frac{v - min}{max - min} \tag{3.5}$$

where v is the original value and v' is the value obtained after normalization. The variables *min* and *max* are minimum and maximum values of the samples, respectively.

Table 3.1 Statistical information of data collected from Stanford Station.

Feature	Units	Parameter type	Mean	Std	Min	Max
T_high	Degree Celsius	Input	20.53	5.09	0	42
T_avg	Degree Celsius	Input	15.42	4.26	0	31
T_low	Degree Celsius	Input	10.68	4.34	−4	24
DP_high	Degree Celsius	Input	11.93	4.05	−6	26
DP_avg	Degree Celsius	Input	9.78	4.27	−11	21
DP_low	Degree Celsius	Input	7.19	4.85	−43	19
H_high	Percentage	Input	87.50	9.46	18	100
H_avg	Percentage	Input	67.30	11.62	17	100
H_low	Percentage	Input	50.13	14.31	4	100
SP_high	Hectopascals	Input	1018.31	4.99	993	1055
SP_avg	Hectopascals	Input	1016.66	4.81	989	1035
SP_low	Hectopascals	Input	1015.03	5.00	970	1034
V_high	Kilometer	Input	26.19	7.17	1	32
V_avg	Kilometer	Input	20.88	6.84	0	32
V_low	Kilometer	Input	15.66	8.24	0	32
WS_high	Kilometer/Hr	Input	25.13	12.14	0	230
WS_avg	Kilometer/Hr	Output	11.98	4.74	0	35

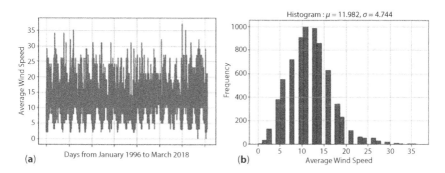

Figure 3.3 Distribution of average wind speed: (a) distribution chart and (b) histogram.

3.2.2.3 Model Selection and Training

Models that are suitable for big data processing are selected to forecast wind speed. The proposed model employs a four-hidden layer DNN with 0.01 as the learning rate and ReLU as the activation function. Four hidden layers with 25, 20, 10, and 5 neurons in the first, second, third, and fourth hidden layers, respectively, are chosen as the optimal configuration using trial and error method. The procedure adopted in this study to find optimal configuration is described in Section 3.3.1. The neuron count in the input layer corresponds to the number of features in the input dataset. The output layer has one neuron corresponding to predicted wind speed. The configuration of the DNN architecture is demonstrated in Figure 3.4. In the figure, the features, namely, temperature, humidity, dew point, pressure, visibility, and high wind speed, are given as input to the DNN architecture. Each hidden layer extracts the abstract features from the input and passes it to the next hidden layer. Finally, the output layer transfers the predicted average wind speed as the output.

The model is trained using data from 1996 to 2013, and the prediction accuracy of the model is then assessed using data from 2014 to 2018. Since the collected data is time-series data, a six-fold time-series cross-validation is applied for evaluating the model accuracy. The dataset is divided into different folds sequentially, and they are trained and evaluated separately. The forecasting accuracy of the model is then compared with various machine learning models. The ANN model employed for comparison is developed with two hidden layers, with 20 neurons each and 0.001 as a learning rate.

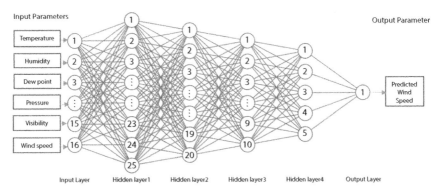

Figure 3.4 The architecture of the proposed DNN model.

3.2.2.4   Performance Evaluation

Assessment plays a vital role in any prediction model. Therefore, the performance assessment of the proposed DNN system is done to evaluate its effectiveness. The prediction accuracy of the model is computed using error indices root mean squared error (RMSE), mean absolute error (MAE), and R^2. RMSE is demarcated as the square root of the average of squared differences between predicted data $(\hat{y})$ and the actual data (y), which is given in Equation (3.6).

$$RMSE = \sqrt{\frac{1}{n}\sum_{j=1}^{n}(y_j - \hat{y}_j)^2} \qquad (3.6)$$

MAE is the absolute variation among the predicted (y^) and actual data (y) as shown in Equation (3.7).

$$MAE = \frac{1}{n}\sum_{j=1}^{n}|y_j - \hat{y}_j| \qquad (3.7)$$

R^2, the coefficient of determination, is a metric that illustrates the closeness of the data to the regression line. It is computed using equation (3.8), which measures the effectiveness of the model. It ranges from 0% and 100%. Higher R^2 values represent smaller differences between the observed and predicted values.

$$R^2 = \frac{Variance\ Explained\ by\ the\ model}{Total\ Variance} \qquad (3.8)$$

3.2.2.5   Visualization

Visualization is yet another essential step in any predictive system. In this study, scatter plots and semi-log plots are employed to visualize the results. Scatter plots are utilized to analyze graphically, the difference between actual and predicted values, and these plots are further employed to assess the efficiency of the system. The variation of predicted values from actual values can be visualized more precisely using semi-log plots.

3.3　Results and Discussions

3.3.1　Selection of Parameters

The construction of the optimal DNN model is based on the selection of learning rate, number of inputs, outputs, count of hidden layers, and the count of neurons in each hidden layer. A DNN architecture with four hidden layers is selected initially, and then, experiments are conducted by altering the learning rate and the count of neurons in each hidden layer. Four combinations are randomly selected for number of hidden neurons, such as (20,20,20,10), (25,20,15,10), (25,20,10,5), and (25,25,10,5). The different learning rates considered for the study are 0.01, 0.02, 0.001, and 0.002. Table 3.2 illustrates the effect of various parameters investigated during the

Table 3.2 Effect of various parameters.

Number of neurons in hidden layers	Learning rate	RMSE	MAE	R^2
(20, 20, 20, 10)	0.01	2.8684	2.1118	64.90
(20, 20, 20, 10)	0.02	2.8777	2.1111	64.67
(20, 20, 20, 10)	0.001	2.8775	2.1134	64.64
(20, 20, 20, 10)	0.002	2.8602	2.1049	65.01
(25, 20, 15, 10)	0.01	3.0012	2.1808	61.57
(25, 20, 15, 10)	0.02	2.9748	2.2055	62.25
(25, 20, 15, 10)	0.001	4.0504	2.9430	30.01
(25, 20, 15, 10)	0.002	3.7289	2.6933	40.68
(25, 20, 10, 5)	**0.01**	**2.8207**	**2.0781**	**66.56**
(25, 20, 10, 5)	0.02	2.8425	2.0894	65.53
(25, 20, 10, 5)	0.001	2.8355	2.0810	65.70
(25, 20, 10, 5)	0.002	2.9370	2.1642	63.20
(25, 25, 10, 5)	0.01	2.9315	2.1890	63.34
(25, 25, 10, 5)	0.02	2.8898	2.1307	64.37
(25, 25, 10, 5)	0.001	3.6713	2.6243	42.50
(25, 25, 10, 5)	0.002	2.8411	2.1003	65.56

Table 3.3 Optimum configuration.

Parameter	Value
Count of input layer neurons	16
Count of hidden layers	4
Count of hidden layer neurons	(25, 20, 10, 5)
Learning rate	0.01
Count of output layer neurons	1

experiments. It can be observed that the architecture with the number of hidden neurons (25, 20, 10, and 5) in the corresponding hidden layers with learning rate 0.01 achieves low RMSE and MAE values and high R^2 value. The architecture with hidden neurons (25, 20, 10, and 5) in the hidden layers attains the RMSE value of 2.8207, MAE value of 2.0781, and an R^2 value of 66.56. Hence, this configuration has been chosen as optimal configuration. The DNN system with optimal architecture is represented in Table 3.3.

3.3.2   Comparison of Models

The proposed DNN system to forecast average wind speed is compared with other machine learning models to evaluate its effectiveness. The predicted values and actual values are compared to assess the quality of the developed DNN model using quantitative error indicators RMSE, MAE, and R^2. Table 3.4 presents the attained performance assessment results of the developed models. Smaller values of RMSE and MAE denote higher accuracy of the forecasts, while larger values of R^2 show a higher linear relationship between the predicted and actual values. It can be perceived from the table that the suggested DNN model achieves minimum error values in terms of RMSE and MAE and maximum R^2 value compared to other models. The results presented in the table illustrate that the implemented DNN system is efficient for predicting average wind speed with a minimal RMSE of 2.8207 and MAE of 2.0781. The higher R^2 value also substantiates the effectiveness of the developed DNN model. The prediction accuracy of the various models in terms of RMSE, MAE, and R^2 is represented in Figure 3.5. The figure illustrates that the developed DNN system performs well with lowest MAE and RMSE values and highest R^2 value.

The prediction capability of the developed DNN, ANN, RF, and SVM models is analyzed graphically by plotting the predicted data against

Table 3.4 Comparison of models.

Algorithm	Average wind speed		
	RMSE	MAE	R^2 (%)
DT	3.0062	2.2845	60
RF	2.8892	2.2182	63
SVM	2.8612	2.1102	64
ANN	3.0626	2.2943	62
LR	3.3207	2.4431	51
DNN	**2.8207**	**2.0781**	**67**

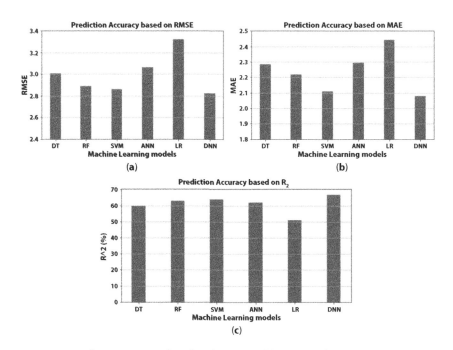

Figure 3.5 Prediction accuracy based on (a) RMSE, (b) MAE, and (c) R_2.

the recorded (actual) data using scatter plots. DNN, ANN, RF, and SVM models are considered for visualization because they produced comparable results. The scatter plots of predicted daily data against the recorded data to predict wind speed using various models are illustrated in Figure 3.6.

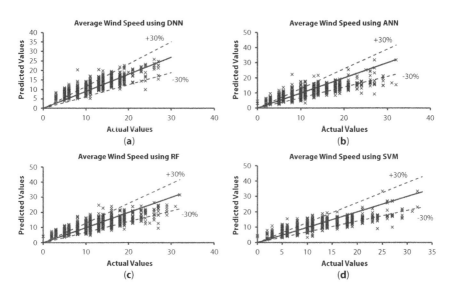

Figure 3.6 Comparison of predicted against the actual values (a) Average wind speed using DNN (b) Average wind speed using ANN (c) Average wind speed using RF (d) Average wind speed using SVM.

The effectiveness of the models can be further evaluated by drawing two lines closer to the regression line starting from the origin with slopes 1.3 and 0.7, respectively. The goodness of the model can be calculated by counting the data points lying inside the ±30% boundary lines. Thus, the percentage coverage of the data points lying inside the ±30% boundary lines can be determined using the equation given in (3.9). The percentage coverage values of various wind speed prediction models are presented in Table 3.5. The observations show that 83.95% of the points lie within the ± 30% boundary of the regression line in the case of the DNN model. However, with ANN, RF, and SVM models, only 78.42%, 76.31%, and

Table 3.5 Coverage of points within the boundary of the regression line.

Algorithm	No. of points within ±30% boundary (out of 1427)	Coverage %
ANN	1119	78.42
RF	1089	76.31
SVM	1158	81.15
DNN	**1198**	**83.95**

81.15% of the points lie within the ± 30% boundary of the regression line, respectively. It can therefore be concluded that the proposed DNN system exhibits better predictive accuracy when compared other models.

$$Coverage \% = \frac{No.\ of\ points\ within\ the\ boundary}{Total\ Number\ of\ points} \tag{3.9}$$

Semi-log plots are used to visualize the variation in observed and recorded values more precisely. Semi-log plots of predicted average wind speed data against the recorded data of DNN, ANN, RF, and SVM models are illustrated in Figure 3.7. It is observed that there is a slight deviation in the predicted values from the actual values of the proposed DNN model compared to other machine learning models. The variation of predicted values from the actual values seems to be higher for SVM, ANN, and RF models. Because the prediction accuracy is high compared to SVM, ANN,

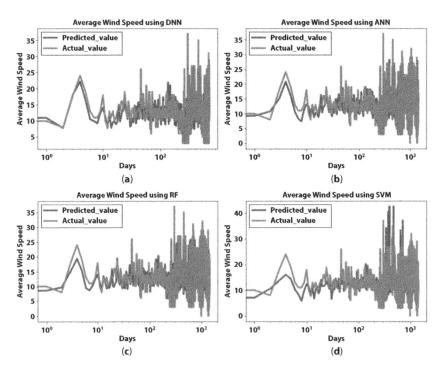

Figure 3.7 Comparison of prediction accuracy of DNN and other models (a)Average wind speed using DNN (b) Average wind speed using ANN (c) Average wind speed using RF (d) Average wind speed using SVM.

and RF models, the study concludes that DNNs can be employed effectively to forecast daily average wind speed.

3.4   Conclusion

The proposed framework investigates the effects of various model parameters and selects an architecture with low RMSE and MAE value as the most appropriate architecture for predicting average wind speed. The data collected from Stanford weather station has been utilized for the experiments. The optimal DNN architecture with hidden neurons (25, 20, 10, and 5) in the hidden layers from 1 to 4 is employed for the study. Performance comparison of the proposed DNN model is performed with the benchmark models, such as SVM, ANN, and RF models. The developed DNN model outperforms the other prediction models with a minimum RMSE value of 2.8207, MAE of 2.0781, and a maximum R^2 value of 67%. Analysis of the experimental outcomes illustrates the effectiveness of the proposed DNN system for predicting wind speed. Optimization algorithms to enhance further the performance of the predictive model will be deliberated in future works. Other deep learning–based wind speed forecasting models using RNNs will also be considered as future directions.

References

1. Wang, X., Guo, P., Huang, X., A review of wind power forecasting models. *Energy Proc.*, 12, 770–778, 2011, https://doi.org/10.1016/j.egypro.2011.10.103.
2. Mi, X.W., Liu, H., Li, Y.F., Wind speed forecasting method using wavelet, extreme learning machine and outlier correction algorithm. *Energy Convers. Manage.*, 151, 709–722, 2017, https://doi.org/10.1016/j.enconman.2017.09.034.
3. He, J. and Xu, J., Ultra-short-term wind speed forecasting based on support vector machine with combined kernel function and similar data. *EURASIP J. Wirel. Commun. Netw.*, 2019, 1, 248, 2019, https://doi.org/10.1186/s13638-019-1559-1.
4. Yang, M., Liu, L., Cui, Y., Su, X., Ultra-Short-Term Multistep Prediction of Wind Power Based on Representative Unit Method. *Math. Probl. Eng.*, 2018, 1936565, 11, 2018, https://doi.org/10.1155/2018/1936565.
5. Finamore, A.R., Galdi, V., Calderaro, V., Piccolo, A., Conio, G., Grasso, S., Artificial neural network application in wind forecasting: An one-hour-ahead wind speed prediction, *5th IET International Conference on Renewable Power Generation (RPG) 2016*, 1–6, 2016, https://doi.org/10.1049/cp.2016.0545.

6. Yu, C., Li, Y., Xiang, H., Zhang, M., Data mining-assisted short-term wind speed forecasting by wavelet packet decomposition and Elman neural network. *J. Wind Eng. Ind. Aerodyn.*, 175, 136–143, 2018, https://doi.org/10.1016/j.jweia.2018.01.020.

7. Filik, Ü. B. and Filik, T., Wind speed prediction using artificial neural networks based on multiple local measurements in Eskisehir. *Energy Proc.*, 107, 264–269, 2017, https://doi.org/10.1016/j.egypro.2016.12.147.

8. Tarade, R.S. and Katti, P.K., A comparative analysis for wind speed prediction, in: *2011 International Conference on Energy, Automation and Signal*, 2011, December, IEEE, pp. 1–6, https://doi.org/10.1109/iceas.2011.6147167.

9. Liu, H., Tian, H.Q., Pan, D.F., Li, Y.F., Forecasting models for wind speed using wavelet, wavelet packet, time series and Artificial Neural Networks. *Appl. Energy*, 107, 191–208, 2013, https://doi.org/10.1016/j.apenergy.2013.02.002.

10. Ramasamy, P., Chandel, S.S., Yadav, A.K., Wind speed prediction in the mountainous region of India using an artificial neural network model. *Renewable Energy*, 80, 338–347, 2015, https://doi.org/10.1016/j.renene.2015.02.034.

11. Ghorbani, M.A., Khatibi, R., FazeliFard, M.H., Naghipour, L., Makarynskyy, O., Short-term wind speed predictions with machine learning techniques. *Meteorol. Atmos. Phys.*, 128, 1, 57–72, 2016, https://doi.org/10.1007/s00703-015-0398-9.

12. Khandelwal, I., Adhikari, R., Verma, G., Time series forecasting using hybrid ARIMA and ANN models based on DWT decomposition. *Proc. Comput. Sci.*, 48, 1, 173–179, 2015, https://doi.org/10.1016/j.procs.2015.04.167.

13. Yousefi, M., Hooshyar, D., Yousefi, M., Khaksar, W., Sahari, K.S.M., Alnaimi, F.B., II, An artificial neural network hybrid with wavelet transform for short-term wind speed forecasting: A preliminary case study, in: *2015 International Conference on Science in Information Technology (ICSITech)*, 2015, October, IEEE, pp. 95–99, https://doi.org/10.1109/icsitech.2015.7407784.

14. Shao, H., Wei, H., Deng, X., Xing, S., Short-term wind speed forecasting using wavelet transformation and AdaBoosting neural networks in Yunnan wind farm. *IET Renewable Power Gener.*, 11, 4, 374–381, 2016, https://doi.org/10.1049/iet-rpg.2016.0118.

15. Cui, Y., Huang, C., Cui, Y., A novel compound wind speed forecasting model based on the back propagation neural network optimized by bat algorithm. *Environ. Sci. Pollut. Res.*, 27, 7, 7353–7365, 2020, https://doi.org/10.1007/s11356-019-07402-1.

16. Senthil, K.P., Improved prediction of wind speed using machine learning. *EAI Endorsed Trans. Energy Web*, 6, 23, 1–7, 2019, https://doi.org/10.4108/eai.13-7-2018.157033.

17. Hui, H., Rong, J., Songkai, W., Ultra-Short-Term Prediction of Wind Power Based on Fuzzy Clustering and RBF Neural Network. *Adv. Fuzzy Syst.*, 2018, 9805748, 7, 2018, https://doi.org/10.1155/2018/9805748.

18. Bali, V., Kumar, A., Gangwar, S., Deep learning based wind speed forecasting-A review, in: *2019 9th International Conference on Cloud Computing,*

Data Science & Engineering (Confluence), 2019, January, IEEE, pp. 426–431, https://doi.org/10.1109/confluence.2019.8776923.

19. Cao, Q., Ewing, B.T., Thompson, M.A., Forecasting wind speed with recurrent neural networks. *Eur. J. Oper. Res.*, 221, 1, 148–154, 2012, https://doi.org/10.1016/j.ejor.2012.02.042.

20. Khodayar, M. and Teshnehlab, M., Robust deep neural network for wind speed prediction, in: *2015 4th Iranian Joint Congress on Fuzzy and Intelligent Systems (CFIS)*, 2015, September, IEEE, pp. 1–5, https://doi.org/10.1109/cfis.2015.7391664.

21. Sergio, A.T. and Ludermir, T.B., Deep learning for wind speed forecasting in northeastern region of Brazil, in: *2015 Brazilian Conference on Intelligent Systems (BRACIS)*, 2015, November, IEEE, pp. 322–327, https://doi.org/10.1109/bracis.2015.40.

22. Liu, H., Mi, X., Li, Y., Smart deep learning based wind speed prediction model using wavelet packet decomposition, convolutional neural network and convolutional long short term memory network. *Energy Convers. Manage.*, 166, 120–131, 2018, https://doi.org/10.1016/j.enconman.2018.04.021.

23. Hu, Q., Zhang, R., Zhou, Y., Transfer learning for short-term wind speed prediction with deep neural networks. *Renewable Energy*, 85, 83–95, 2016, https://doi.org/10.1016/j.renene.2015.06.034.

24. Nielsen, M.A., *Neural networks and deep learning*, vol. 2018, Determination press, San Francisco, CA, 2015.

25. Zeiler, M.D., Adadelta: an adaptive learning rate method. arXiv:1212.5701. https://arxiv.org/abs/1212.5701, 2012.

4

Res-SE-Net: Boosting Performance of ResNets by Enhancing Bridge Connections

Varshaneya V.*, S. Balasubramanian† and Darshan Gera‡

Department of Mathematics and Computer Science, Sri Sathya Sai Institute of Higher Learning, Prasanthi Nilayam, Anantapur District, India

Abstract

One of the ways to train deep neural networks effectively is to use residual connections. Residual connections can be classified as being either identity connections or bridge connections with a reshaping convolution. Empirical observations on CIFAR-10 and CIFAR-100 datasets using a baseline ResNet model, with bridge connections removed, have shown a significant reduction in accuracy. This reduction is due to lack of contribution, in the form of feature maps, by the bridge connections. Hence, bridge connections are vital for ResNet. However, all feature maps in the bridge connections are equally important. In this work, an upgraded architecture "Res-SE-Net" is proposed to further strengthen the contribution from the bridge connections by quantifying the importance of each feature map and weighting them accordingly using Squeeze-and-Excitation (SE) block. It is demonstrated that Res-SE-Net generalizes much better than ResNet and SE-ResNet on the benchmark CIFAR-10 and CIFAR-100 datasets.

Keywords: Deep residual learning, weighting activations, bridge connections, ResNet, Squeeze-and-Excitation Net

4.1 Introduction

Deep neural networks are increasingly being used in a number of computer vision tasks. One great disadvantage of training a very deep network

---

*Corresponding author: varshaneya.v@gmail.com
†*Corresponding author*: sbalasubramanian@sssihl.edu.in
‡*Corresponding author*: darshangera@sssihl.edu.in

Mettu Srinivas, G. Sucharitha and Anjanna Matta (eds.) Machine Learning Algorithms and Applications, (61–76) © 2021 Scrivener Publishing LLC

is the vanishing gradient problem which delays the convergence. This is alleviated to some extent by initialization techniques mentioned in [1] and [2] and batch normalization [8]. It is observed in [3] that accuracy stagnates and degrades subsequently as the network becomes deeper. They argue that this degradation is not caused by over-fitting and that adding more layers to an already "deep" model results in an increase in train and test errors. Therefore, in order to make training of deep networks possible, they introduce "ResNets". ResNet [3] attends to this problem by emphasizing on learning residual mapping rather than directly fit input to output. This is achieved by introducing skip connections which ensure a larger gradient is flown back during the backpropagation.

After ResNet a plethora of variants like ResNeXt [14], DenseNet [7], ResNet with stochastic depth [6], and preactivated ResNet [4] have been proposed that makes training very deep networks possible. All these variants have either focused on pre-activation or split-transform-merge paradigm or dense skip connections or dropping layers at random. But none have investigated the bridge connections in ResNet that connect two blocks with a varying number of feature maps. In this work, the effect of bridge connections in ResNet is investigated, and subsequently, a novel network architecture called **Res-SE-Net** is proposed that outperforms the baseline ResNet and SE-ResNet.

4.2 Related Work

Training deep networks had been a concern until ResNets [3] were introduced. ResNet emphasizes on learning residual mappings rather than directly fit input to output. After ResNet, a lot of its variants have been proposed. Fully preactivated ResNet [4] performs activation before addition of identity to the residue to facilitate unhindered gradient flow through the shortcut connections to earlier layers. This makes training of a 1001 layered deep network possible. ResNeXt [14] follows a model which is like Inception net [13], by splitting the input to ResNet block into multiple transformation paths and subsequently merging them before identity addition. The number of paths is a new hyperparameter that characterizes model capacity. With higher capacity, the authors have demonstrated improved performance without going much wider or deeper. DenseNet [7] further exploits the effect of skip-connections by densely connecting through skip-connections the output of every earlier layer to every other following layer. The connections are made using depth concatenation and not addition. The authors argue that such connections would help in feature reuse and thereby an unhindered information flow. In Ref. [6], the weight layers in the ResNet block are randomly dropped thereby only keeping skip-connections active in these layers. This gives rise to an ensemble of ResNets similar to dropout [12]. Dropping weight layers depend on "survival probability". This idea outperforms the baseline ResNet. Another important architecture that won the 2017 ILSVRC[1] competition is SE-ResNet [5]. This winning architecture has in its base a ResNet with an SE block introduced between the layers of ResNet. This block quantifies the importance of feature maps instead of considering all of them equally likely. This has resulted in a significant level of improvement in performance of the ResNet.

Though ResNet has been studied in detail, to the best of our knowledge there has not been any work focusing on bridge connections in ResNet. In this work, the effectiveness of bridge connections is investigated and a novel architecture namely "Res-SE-Net" is proposed. This architecture consists of an SE block in the bridge connection to weigh the importance of feature maps. The proposed architecture demonstrates a superior performance on CIFAR-10 and CIFAR-100 benchmark datasets over baseline ResNet and SE-ResNet.

4.3   Preliminaries

4.3.1   ResNet

The idea behind ResNets [3] is to make a shallow architecture deeper by adding identity mapping from a previous layer to the current layer and then applying a suitable non-linear activation. Addition of skip-connections facilitates larger gradient flow to earlier layers thereby addressing the degradation problem as mentioned in [3]. The building block of a ResNet is depicted in Figure 4.1. Here, x is identity and F(x) is called the residual mapping.

ResNet comprises of a stack of these blocks. A part of the 34-layer ResNet is shown in Figure 4.2. The skip-connections that carry activations within a block are referred to as identity skip-connections and those that carry from block to another are called as bridge connections.

---

[1] http://image-net.org/challenges/LSVRC/.

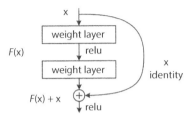

Figure 4.1 ResNet module (adapted from [3]).

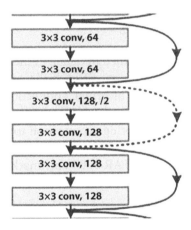

Figure 4.2 Bridge connection in ResNet (adapted from [3]).

The dotted connection is an example of a bridge connection. It involves a 1×1 convolution to increase the number of feature maps from 64 to 128 and a down sampling operation to reduce their spatial dimension. In its absence, F(x) and x will have incompatible dimensions to be added.

4.3.2   Squeeze-and-Excitation Block

Filters in a convolutional layer capture local spatial relationships in the form of feature maps. These feature maps are further used as they are, without any importance being attached to them. In other words, each feature map is treated independently and equal. This may allow insignificant features that are not globally relevant to propagate through the network, thereby affecting the accuracy. Hence, to model the relationship between the feature maps, SE block is introduced in [5]. This enhances the quality of representations produced by a convolutional neural network. SE block performs a recalibration of features so that the global information is used to weight features from the feature map that are more "informative" than the rest.

The SE block has two operations, *viz.*, squeeze and excitation. Features are first passed to the "squeeze" operation to produce a descriptor for each of the feature maps by aggregating along each of their spatial dimensions [5]. The descriptor produces an embedding of a global distribution of channel-wise feature responses. This allows information from the global receptive field of the network to be used by all its layers. The squeeze operation is followed by an "excitation" operation, wherein the embedding produced is used to get a collection of modulation weights for every feature map. These weights are applied to the feature maps to generate weighted feature maps as shown in Figure 4.3. In Figure 4.3, the input $X \in R^{H \times W \times C}$ is fed to global pooling function which outputs a vector of dimension $1 \times 1 \times C$. Its dimension is further reduced by r using a fully connected layer, which is followed by ReLU activation [10]. This constitutes a squeeze operation. The output of squeeze operation is then upsampled to dimension $1 \times 1 \times C$ using another fully connected layer followed by sigmoid activation which gives weights for each of the channels. This constitutes an excitation operation. The input X is thus rescaled using the output of

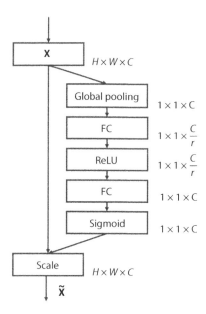

Figure 4.3 Squeeze-and-Excitation block (adapted from [5]).

excitation to get the weighted feature map which is $\tilde{X} \in R^{H \times W \times C}$ as shown in Figure 4.3.

SE blocks add negligible extra computation and can be included in any part of the network [5]. SE-ResNet module is a ResNet module with each residual mapping passing through a SE block which is added with identity connection. SE-ResNet is a stack of SE-ResNet modules.

4.4   Proposed Model

The motivation for the proposed model is presented prior to its elucidation. As shown in Figure 4.2, bridge connections (represented as dotted lines) connect two blocks of ResNet that have a different number of feature maps and different spatial dimensions. The following subsection discusses the effect of bridge connections in ResNet.

4.4.1   Effect of Bridge Connections in ResNet

Tables 4.1 and 4.2 compare the performance of various ResNet architectures with and without bridge connections, respectively. The performance without bridge connections drastically drops, particularly in ResNet-56 and ResNet-110. This comparison stresses the importance of bridge connections. However, in the original ResNet [3], all feature maps in the bridge connections are weighted equally. It is to be noted that SE-ResNet [5] weights the feature maps along the non-skip connections, based on their importance. The importance is learnt using a simple feed forward network that adds negligible computations. This idea motivated us to quantify the importance of feature maps that arise in bridge connections.

Table 4.1 Performance of baseline ResNets.

Architecture	CIFAR-10 Top-1	(Acc %) Top-5	CIFAR-100 Top-1	(Acc %) Top-5
Res-20	91.4	99.74	67.37	91.06
Res-32	92.32	99.73	69.8	91.25
Res-44	93.57	99.81	73.15	92.9
Res-56	93.16	99.82	73.8	92.99
Res-110	93.66	99.77	73.33	92.7

Table 4.2 Performance of baseline ResNets without bridge connections.

Architecture	CIFAR-10 (Acc %)		CIFAR-100 (Acc %)	
	Top-1	Top-5	Top-1	Top-5
Res-20	90.48	99.71	67.37	91.06
Res-32	90.38	99.62	69.8	91.25
Res-44	87.62	99.51	73.15	92.9
Res-56	77.46	98.55	48.65	76.67
Res-110	92.42	99.83	1.00	5.00

4.4.2   Res-SE-Net: Proposed Architecture

The novel architecture incorporates an SE block in each of the bridge connection of a ResNet. Figure 4.4 shows an illustration of a modified bridge connection. The proposed model Res-SE-Net has a similar architecture as mentioned in [3]. Specifically, our architecture is as follows.

The input image is of the size 32×32. The first layer is a 3×3 convolutional layer, which is followed by batch normalization [8] and ReLU [10]. This is followed by a stack of ResNet modules. A group of ResNet modules within the stack which have the same number of feature maps constitute a block. Average-pooling follows the stack of ResNet modules. The final layer is a fully connected layer followed by softmax activation, which predicts the probability of an input belonging to a class. The sub-sampling of feature-maps is done in the first convolutional layer of every block, by performing the convolution with a stride of 2. There is a reduction in the size of feature maps and an increase in their number from one block to another. Hence, to take activations from one block to another, the bridge connection downsamples the feature map size and increases their number by using 1×1 convolution with stride 2.

An SE block [5] is added on to the bridge connection just after downsampling. This ensures that when the feature maps are taken from one block to another, they are weighted according to the content that they carry. Hence, those features that are more relevant are given higher importance. The downsampled feature maps are sent from the previous block to the next one, so the weighting process must be done after downsampling in order to give more importance to the downsampled feature maps. Doing this before downsampling would reduce the significance of the weighted features. This is the primary reason for adding SE layer after downsampling and not before.

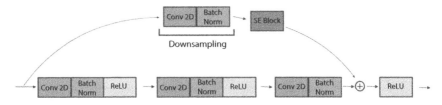

Figure 4.4 Modified bridge connection.[2]

It is also found empirically that adding SE layer before the downsampling process gives less accuracy compared to adding it after downsampling.

4.5   Experiments

4.5.1   Datasets

All experiments are conducted on CIFAR-10 [9] and CIFAR-100 [9] datasets. The CIFAR-10 dataset consists of 50,000 training images and 10,000 test images in 10 classes, with 5,000 training images and 1,000 test images per class. The CIFAR-100 dataset consists of 50,000 training images and 10,000 test images in 100 classes, with 500 training images and 100 test images per class. There are 20 main classes which contain these classes. The size of images in both the datasets is 32×32 and all of them are RGB images.

4.5.2   Experimental Setup

The experiments on ResNets considered ResNets of varying depths such as 20, 32, 44, 56, and 110 layers. The implementations are coded in Pytorch [11]. The code for baseline ResNet[3] and SE-ResNet[4] have been adapted from existing implementations and modified. The following data augmentation techniques are used:

- Padding with 4 pixels on each side.
- Random cropping to a size of 32×32 from the padded image.
- Random horizontal flip.
- Standard normalization.

---

[2] Image from Andrew Ng's Deep Learning course and modified with an SE block.
[3] Adapted from https://github.com/bearpaw/pytorch-classification.
[4] Adapted from https://github.com/moskomule/senet.pytorch.

Table 4.3 Hyperparameters.

Hyperparameter	Value
Initial learning rate	0.1
Weight decay	0.0001
Momentum	0.9
Batch size	128

The images are only normalized at the test time. The input to the network is of size 32×32. The architecture of the network used, for both CIFAR-10 and CIFAR-100 datasets, is mentioned in Section 4.4. The training starts with an initial learning rate of 0.1, and subsequently, it is divided by 10 at 32,000 and 48,000 iterations. The training is done for a maximum of 64,000 iterations. Stochastic Gradient Descent (SGD) is used for updating the weights. The weights in the model are initialized by the method described in [2], and further, batch normalization [8] is adopted. The hyperparameters used are enlisted in Table 4.3.

4.6   Results

Tables 4.1, 4.4, and 4.5 report the accuracies obtained by baseline ResNets, baseline SEResNets, and Res-SE-Nets, respectively. As evident from Table 4.1, the best performing ResNet is ResNet-110 with Top-1 accuracies of 93.66% and 73.33% on CIFAR-10 and CIFAR-100, respectively. Similarly,

Table 4.4 Performance of baseline SE-ResNets.

Architecture	CIFAR-10 (Acc %)		CIFAR-100 (Acc %)	
	Top-1	Top-5	Top-1	Top-5
SE-ResNet-20	92.1	99.7	68.31	90.69
SE-ResNet-32	93.08	99.83	70.09	92.12
SE-ResNet-44	93.71	99.77	71.2	91.78
SE-ResNet-56	93.64	99.76	71.42	91.28
SE-ResNet-110	93.79	99.74	72.99	92.71

Table 4.5 Performance of proposed model.

Architecture	CIFAR-10 (Acc%)		CIFAR-100 (Acc%)	
	Top-1	Top-5	Top-1	Top-5
Res-SE-Net-20	91.9	99.75	67.99	91.03
Res-SE-Net-32	92.79	99.82	69.93	91.95
Res-SE-Net-44	94.08	99.83	73.83	93.54
Res-SE-Net-56	93.64	99.87	74.29	93.45
Res-SE-Net-110	94.53	99.87	74.93	93.48

from Table 4.4, the best performing SE-ResNet is SE-ResNet-110 with Top-1 accuracies of 93.79% and 72.99% on CIFAR-10 and CIFAR100, respectively. It is clear from Table 4.5 that, our model, Res-SE-Net-110 reporting Top-1 accuracies of 94.53% and 74.93% on CIFAR-10 and CIFAR-100 datasets respectively, significantly overwhelms the baseline ResNets and SE-ResNets. It can further be observed from Table 4.5, that Res-SE-Net-44 performs exceedingly well compared to baseline ResNets and SE-ResNets. In fact, Res-SE-Net-44 can outperform ResNet-110 and SE-ResNet-110 by a significant margin of 0.42% and 0.29% on CIFAR-10 dataset, respectively. On CIFAR-100 dataset, Res-SE-Net-44 dominates over ResNet-110 and SE-ResNet-110 by a margin of 0.5% and 0.84%. It is to be noted that Res-SE-Net-44 has 61.75% and 62.06% lesser number of parameters compared to ResNet-110 and SE-ResNet-110, respectively. Res-SE-Net-56 too exhibits outstanding performance on CIFAR-100 dataset compared to baseline ResNets and SE-ResNets, and near on-par performance on CIFAR-10 dataset with baseline ResNets and SE-ResNets. This strongly emphasizes the gravity of the proposed idea to activate the feature maps in bridge connections by their importance. The proposed idea enables a reasonably deep network with lesser number of parameters to outperform very deep networks.

The improvement in accuracies of Res-SE-Nets, for both the datasets in comparison to baseline ResNets [3] and SE-ResNets [5] are tabulated in Tables 4.6 and 4.7, respectively. Res-SE-Net outperforms baseline ResNet by 0.566%, i.e., about 56 images on CIFAR-10 and by 0.704%, i.e., about 70 images on CIFAR-100 datasets on an average. Res-SE-Net-110 has achieved the maximum improvement in accuracy of 0.87% on CIFAR-10 and 1.6% on CIFAR-100 over Res-110. Similarly, Res-SE-Net outperforms SE-ResNet by 0.124% on CIFAR-10 and by 1.392% on CIFAR-100 datasets,

Table 4.6 Performance improvement from baseline ResNet.

Architecture	CIFAR-10 (%)		CIFAR-100 (%)	
	Top-1	Top-5	Top-1	Top-5
Res-SE-Net-20	0.5	0.01	0.62	−0.03
Res-SE-Net-32	0.47	0.09	0.13	0.7
Res-SE-Net-44	0.51	0.02	0.68	0.55
Res-SE-Net-56	0.48	0.05	0.49	0.46
Res-SE-Net-110	**0.87**	**0.1**	**1.6**	**0.78**
Average Improvement	0.566	0.504	0.704	0.492

Table 4.7 Performance improvement from baseline SE-ResNet.

Architecture	CIFAR-10 (%)		CIFAR-100 (%)	
	Top-1	Top-5	Top-1	Top-5
Res-SE-Net-20	−0.2	0.05	−0.32	0.34
Res-SE-Net-32	−0.29	−0.01	−0.16	−0.17
Res-SE-Net-44	**0.37**	**0.06**	**2.63**	**1.76**
Res-SE-Net-56	0.0	0.11	2.87	2.17
Res-SE-Net-110	**0.74**	**0.13**	**1.94**	**0.77**
Average Improvement	0.124	0.068	1.392	0.974

respectively. Res-SE-Net-110 has achieved maximum overall improvement over SE-ResNet-110 with an increase in accuracy of 0.74% on CIFAR-10 and of 1.94% on CIFAR-100 datasets, respectively.

With the improvement that addition of SE block provides, one might want to add SE blocks to all the skip-connections to make the performance even better. But it has been empirically found that adding an SE block to every identity skip connection degrades the performance on CIFAR-10 and CIFAR-100 datasets as the depth increases. Also, as for the reasons mentioned in Section 4.4, the addition of SE block before downsampling does not give better results either.

The analysis of the training phase of Res-SE-Net is done by plotting training losses for all the aforesaid depths and for both the datasets. From

Figures 4.5 to 4.7, it can be concluded that training of Res-SE-Net has taken place smoothly. There is no abrupt increase in training loss of Res-SE-Net models. This shows that gradient flow has not been hindered by the introduction of an SE block in bridge connections, maintaining the principle of ResNet (base of our Res-SE-Net) that skip-connections facilitate smooth training of deep networks.

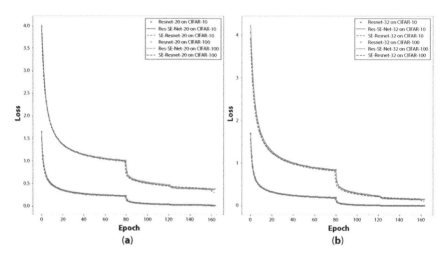

Figure 4.5 (a) Training losses plotted for depth of 20 layers. (b) Training losses plotted for depth of 32 layers.

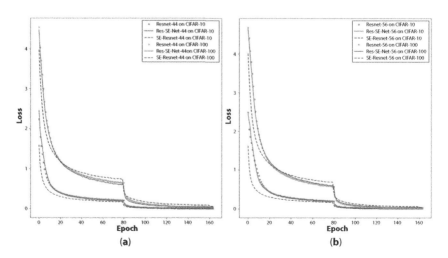

Figure 4.6 (a) Training losses plotted for depth of 44 layers. (b) Training losses plotted for depth of 56 layers.

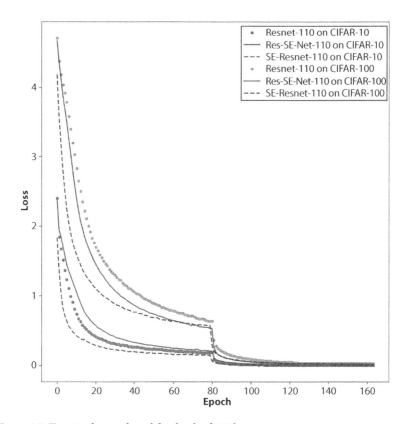

Figure 4.7 Training losses plotted for depth of 110 layers.

4.7   Conclusion

In this work, a novel architecture named "Res-SE-Net" is proposed, which makes bridge connections in ResNets more influential. This is achieved by incorporating an SE block in every bridge connection. Res-SE-Net surpassed the performances of baseline ResNet and SE-ResNets by significant margins on CIFAR-10 and CIFAR-100 datasets. Further, it has been demonstrated that reasonably sized deep networks with positively contributing bridge connections can outperform very deep networks. It is also illustrated that addition of an SE block does not affect training. In future, other ways of making bridge connections in ResNets influential can be explored to enhance its overall performance.

References

1. Glorot, X. and Bengio, Y., Understanding the difficulty of training deep feed-forward neural networks, in: *Proceedings of the thirteenth international conference on artificial intelligence and statistics*, pp. 249–256, 2010.
2. He, K., Zhang, X., Ren, S., Sun, J., Delving deep into rectifiers: Surpassing human-level performance on imagenet classification, in: *Proceedings of the IEEE international conference on computer vision*, pp. 1026–1034, 2015.
3. He, K., Zhang, X., Ren, S., Sun, J., Deep residual learning for image recognition, in: *Proceedings of the IEEE conference on computer vision and pattern recognition*, pp. 770–778, 2016.
4. He, K., Zhang, X., Ren, S., Sun, J., Identity mappings in deep residual networks, in: *European conference on computer vision*, Springer, pp. 630–645, 2016.
5. Hu, J., Shen, L., Sun, G., Squeeze-and-excitation networks, in: *Proceedings of the IEEE conference on computer vision and pattern recognition*, pp. 7132–7141, 2018.
6. Huang, G., Sun, Y., Liu, Z., Sedra, D., Weinberger, K.Q., Deep networks with stochastic depth, in: *European conference on computer vision*, Springer, pp. 646–661, 2016.
7. Huang, G., Liu, Z., Van Der Maaten, L., Weinberger, K.Q., Densely connected convolutional networks, in: *Proceedings of the IEEE conference on computer vision and pattern recognition*, pp. 4700–4708, 2017.
8. Ioffe, S. and Szegedy, C., Batch normalization: Accelerating deep network training by reducing internal covariate shift. CoRR, International conference on machine learning, 2015.
9. Krizhevsky, A., Hinton, G. *et al.*, *Learning multiple layers of features from tiny images*. Technical report, Citeseer, 2009.
10. Nair, V. and Hinton, G.E., Rectified linear units improve restricted boltzmann machines, in: *ICML*, 2010.
11. Paszke, A., Gross, S., Massa, F., Lerer, A., Bradbury, J., Chanan, G., Killeen, T., Lin, Z., Gimelshein, N., Antiga, L., Desmaison, A., Kopf, A., Yang, E., DeVito, Z., Raison, M., Tejani, A., Chilamkurthy, S., Steiner, B., Fang, L., Bai, J., Chintala, S., Pytorch: An imperative style, high-performance deep learning library, in: *Advances in Neural Information Processing Systems*, vol. 32, H. Wallach, H. Larochelle, A. Beygelzimer, F. d'Alché-Buc, E. Fox, R. Garnett (Eds.), pp. 8024–8035, Curran Associates, Inc., NeurIPS, 2019, URL http://papers.neurips.cc/paper/9015-pytorch-an-imperative-style-high-performance-deep-learning-library.pdf.
12. Srivastava, N., Hinton, G., Krizhevsky, A., Sutskever, I., Salakhutdinov, R., Dropout: A simple way to prevent neural networks from overfitting. *J. Mach. Learn. Res.*, 15, 1, 1929–1958, 2014.
13. Szegedy, C., Liu, W., Jia, Y., Sermanet, P., Reed, S., Anguelov, D., Erhan, D., Vanhoucke, V., Rabinovich, A., Going deeper with convolutions, in:

Proceedings of the IEEE conference on computer vision and pattern recognition, pp. 1–9, 2015.

14. Xie, S., Girshick, R., Dollár, P., Tu, Z., He, K., Aggregated residual transformations for deep neural networks, in: *Proceedings of the IEEE conference on computer vision and pattern recognition*, pp. 1492–1500, 2017.

5

Hitting the Success Notes of Deep Learning

Sakshi Aggarwal[1]*, Navjot Singh[2] and K.K. Mishra[1]

[1]*Department of Computer Science and Engineering, Motilal Nehru National Institute of Technology, Allahabad, India*
[2]*Department of Information Technology, Indian Institute of Information Technology, Allahabad, India*

Abstract

During past decade, the Machine Learning (ML) has been driving with different pace. Nowadays, it is disguised in a novel term that has been a buzzing around market, named as *Deep Learning* (DL). Basically, the concept of DL has been derived from human neurological traits. Humans are the masters of thinking, analyzing, expressing, actions, and, supreme of all, improvisation. These activities are controlled by single neurological unit called brain. Our brain behaves according to chemical and biological computation through neurons. Motivated by the neuron functioning, a unique concept, formally known as Artificial Neural Network (ANN), has been born among the research community. It is an art of inducing artificial brain to machines, making them more reliable, robust, independent, efficient, and self-adaptive. It is a well-established art which really needs a comprehensive review in several aspects. Therefore, the endeavor has been made by us to work out over the subject, consolidate the findings and turn it into a chapter. It will offer an organized view of ANN via DL. Further, we try to interpret the fine line created between ML and DL, understand its variants, current trends, emerging challenges, and future scope.

Keywords: Machine learning, artificial neural network, deep learning, convolutional network

**Corresponding author*: sakshiaggarwal@mnnit.ac.in

Mettu Srinivas, G. Sucharitha and Anjanna Matta (eds.) Machine Learning Algorithms and Applications, (77–98) © 2021 Scrivener Publishing LLC

5.1 Genesis

Suppose you have a tremendous amount of data but you do not know how to make a practical use of it or inferences instead. One approach is to deploy conventional statistical models which involve average, variance, regression, or skewness. But the problem here is that the results are truly dependent on average ignoring the qualitative aspects such as health, intelligence, and so on. Another approach is to use the most influential technology takes hold nowadays, i.e., Machine Learning (ML) [1–5]. The word itself has all the necessary terms required for understanding the concept behind it, but primarily, the science of making machines work with minimal or no human assistance, coined as ML. In the broader and deeper sense, the programs are developed and introduced into the systems in such a way that they can learn themselves through accessing data and revise the way they interact with the end-users.

Numerous ML algorithms are proposed to process data and seek hidden insights without being given explicit instructions. We frequently come across ML without even realizing it. In fact, the extent to which it is being used actively is far than one could have expected. The wide range of applications, explored in almost all domains, encompassing autonomous vehicles, virtual assistants, infotainment, medical imaging, object tracking, computer vision (CV), and much more, is the evidence of its acceptance among programmers. According to one article in Gartner 2019 report [6], ML has been on top priority in organization for past years. In fact, the adoption by leading tech giants for enormous success in business expansion has tripled over the past decade. From Google's endeavor to design driverless cars to using Apple's *Siri* via voice commands to Amazon's on-site product recommendation, ML is touted as key pillar. The area is evolving so fast that business leaders have to shift their focus to deviate from the way they deal with the market challenges. If they do not work swiftly on their business model, they might fall behind or not even exist by 2023, the Microsoft reveals in its report [7].

The rise over the applications from past decade has been certainly correlated with turbulent processing powers of system and intricate data set with increased difficulty to interpret. The objective of applications is often learning the model without being given excessive instructions explicitly and generalising the unlabelled data through acquired intelligence. The intelligence implies here is what we call as self-learning and it truly derives from Artificial Neural Network (ANN) [8–10], a gamut of ML algorithms, where model heavily relies on feature engineering. It is analogous to biological human brain where the neurons are imperative element. They are responsible for information distribution and communication across the human biological system. Neurons are interconnected with each other and constitute a crucial support system of our body. Resembling the human brain, the artificial systems can also improvise their learning that gained from experiences and knowledge and entire functions are exercised with purely minimal or no human interaction.

5.2 The Big Picture: Artificial Neural Network

Before unearthing Deep Learning (DL), let us go slightly deeper and uncover the mechanism of ANN. As name implies, neural network (NN) is layered upon neurons or nodes. It represents the dataset of inputs (varies from images, signals, or texts) along with true answer associated with each observation set. The network tunes to estimate true answers provided the inputs upon which it has been fed. A simple illustration would be a situation where we are given variables such as mileage, brand, production year, acquisition value, and second-hand values for given number of cars. Now, suppose our aim is to develop a model which can predict the second-hand values. In few words, we need to design a network that can best correlate the observations and response. The learning will occur continuously and thoroughly by generating output and compare them with true values. The parameters of model are updated automatically if they are differed by wide margin. It tends to push the prediction closer to true observations. The training is an iterative, automatic process and continues to generate output until average difference converges to small value.

After getting the big picture of ANN, we are now in the position to evaluate its architecture. The NN is employed on several layers, consist of neurons. There are mainly three types of layers, *viz.*, input layer, hidden layer, and output layers. The input layer is for parameter feeding and output layer is obvious for target production. The hidden layers are responsible for processing data and establishing correlation among inputs and outputs. It is carried out using weights assigned to each parameter and pass to the computational units thereafter. Weights are enlarged or reduced according to the relevance of the response. The whole scenario is depicted in Figure 5.1.

Any network-based model and ML-based model emphasize on two tasks, i.e., learning and application. While learning, model tries to extract similarities within training data to accomplish a specific task. It could be understood by an example of Facebook plugin, where learning is incorporated to make blind person describe the photos. On the other hand, application stage sends you the response after employing on utilized data.

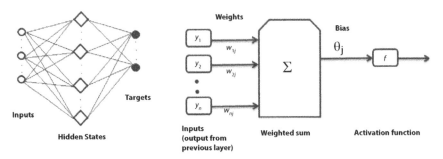

Figure 5.1 Uncovering the network layers for final computation.

For example, a music-app keeps suggesting playlist to a user on weekly basis when it discovers his/her music taste. Both learning and application are integrated to make a way for the systems developing their own intellect and conscience.

5.3   Delineating the Cornerstones

The evolution in the business such as digital marketing is appeared as a part of ML revolution through its direct involvement with the stakeholders. ML is a broader and active area, merely referred to as a branch of science but not its recent state and evolution. It is crucial to understand what makes ML so reputed in the current trend and clarify the misconceptions. Particularly, NNs and DL [11–14] have hyped the ML paradigms and consequently accelerated the mystery around key-notes. In fact, markets and businesses are flourished with the demands of disruptive technologies, yet it brought confusion around terminologies because core concepts of Data Science (DS) (as illustrated in Figure 5.2) are profoundly interweaved and concerned with each other in several aspects.

We have come across several resources like blogs, articles, journals, magazines, chapters, and inferred that preliminaries are impeccably high-lighted but little is known about their differences and it remains uncovered. So, let us shift the focus from palpable discussion towards demarcating and disentangling the threads of DS cornerstones.

5.3.1   Artificial Neural Network vs. Machine Learning

The most significant and encouraging technique for big data processing is ML. It is phenomenal in analysis with experience or newly data addition and reveals the pattern of interest. When we talk about ML, we talk about a

Figure 5.2 Terms attach with DS.

generic term that refers to making systems learn about self-adaption. On the other hand, ANN stems from ML that can frame the algorithms that simulates human brain. It processes the data through multiple layers as mentioned above. Enormous amount of data, normally shared through ubiquitous applications and in unstructured format, is difficult to grasp. But through DL, it becomes least challenging when it comes to unravel this wealth of data. In few words, if ML builds a model around several parameters and triggers the results, those results can be served further to start building ANN model.

5.3.2   Machine Learning vs. Deep Learning

One of the most unprecedented yet least emphasized topics of discussion is ML vs. DL. They are not poles apart; instead, they share the common umbrella of DS. In fact, DL is observed as one of the core facet of ML that sharply works on data semantics. The representation of data in DL is, however, hierarchical, and therefore best suited for unlabelled or unstructured data. It carries out data processing with nonlinear approach enabling machines to translate extracted features effortlessly. It is widely adapted for feature engineering and feature transformation. Thus, it is recommendable for developing major CV applications that can pertain to real-world data such as images, sounds, texts, or languages.

5.3.3   Artificial Neural Network vs. Deep Learning

Both NN and DL are cutting-edge technologies and enjoys special positions among researches. We often use these terms interchangeably without

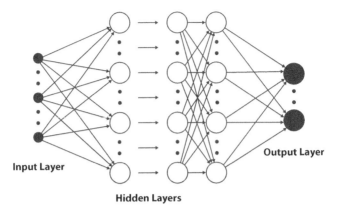

Figure 5.3 ANN serves as a base for DL.

realizing their fine differences. However, they have conceptual similarities yet they are also discrete in their own ways. We must understand there is a fine line between ANN and DL. ANN comes in multitudes and DL is learnt as a more complex form of ANN. The difference is simply lies in the depth of the network which is exhibited in its architecture, shown in Figure 5.3. By saying complex, it attributes to elaborative information that can propagate throughout the model. More complex a model is, more internal layers are used. The increased number of layers is not just for exploiting excess information but also for optimization to achieve better performance.

Finally, the three cornerstones of DS, *viz.*, ML, ANN, and DL are distinguished in one sentence as, DL, a sub-domain of ML, leverages a hierarchical view of ANN to achieve the process of ML.

5.4   Deep Learning Architectures

5.4.1   Unsupervised Pre-Trained Networks

In learning-based models, it would take long or may not efficient to directly put some variants in order to train the network while utilizing supervised learning approach. In fact, it can be alleviated by first "pre-train" using different unsupervised training strategy, followed by fine-tuning with the assistance of supervised learning algorithm. It boosts up the computation process and plummet the data dependency. The results, obtained by unsupervised learning, can serve the purpose to extract high-level attributes for many visual tasks such as classification, detection, or recognition. It rapidly achieves better optimization and convergence, shaping the network

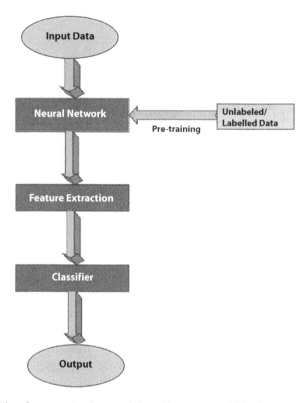

Figure 5.4 Flow for pre-trained network-based learning model [18].

for high-level representation. The researchers use pre-trained learning methodologies in Restricted Boltzmann Machines (RBM) [15] and Auto-Encoders (AE) [16, 17]. Figure 5.4 depicts the absolute flow of pre-training networks.

5.4.2 Convolutional Neural Networks

With the advancement of DL, it elevates the potential of artificial systems. It offers scalability in terms of the functions to look around the world just like humans do, understand it in their own ways, and even cater the knowledge for clusters of tasks such as object detection and recognition and video summarization. The CV domain has achieved new heights, particularly over one algorithm, i.e., Convolutional Neural Network or ConvNet/CNN [32–35, 38–42]. While the conventional CV algorithms are deployed over hand-crafted features, CNN provides wholesome understanding of an image containing more sophisticated features, similarly how humans would. The flow of the CNN

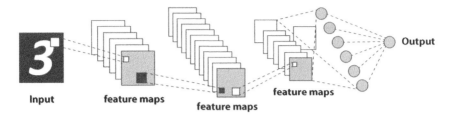

Figure 5.5 Typical CNN process [19].

process is given in Figure 5.5. It consumes less processing time which involves reduced number of observations along with biased reusability.

5.4.3   Recurrent Neural Networks

The aforementioned classes of DL assume all inputs (output as well) reflect least impact on each other. But what happen if we want to form a sentence with enough semantic and grammatical correctness? The words are implicitly dependent on each other just to create a perfect sentence. It requires two-fold process. Firstly, prior knowledge based on how they would likely to occur in real-world and secondly, a state of "memory" to estimate how much information has been calculated so far to predict next word in a sentence. Recurrent Neural Networks (RNN) [20], whose typical architecture is shown in Figure 5.6, is developed for using sequential information

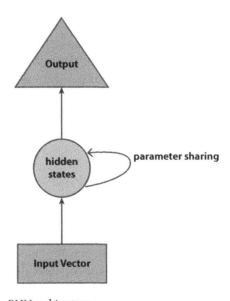

Figure 5.6 Primitive RNN architecture.

like time series. It applies similar task with each element of sequence, and yields output being heavily dependent on past computations. RNNs are capable of constructing language models [21] and text generation might rely on, Natural Language Processing (NLP), or Language Translation Systems (LTSs).

5.4.4   Recursive Neural Network

Recursive Neural Network is more generalized than RNN. This kind of neural network parses data in hierarchical way (Figure 5.7). The primary advantage is to work with patterns represented through trees or graphs as completely contrast to fixed-size vector. The vectors are confined to a particular length that has to be ensued by all data in the set, instead graphs provide flexibility in determining arbitrary number of nodes and edges. It also gaining success in NLP and image analysis [22]. Specifically, the nodes of graph are meant to characterize the vector of variables pertaining to both real and absolute. However, an edge between any two nodes marks the logical association between information structured in the form of nodes.

5.5   Why is CNN Preferred for Computer Vision Applications?

CV [23, 24] is a lobby of science that believes to simulate human visual cortex (HVC) in the computer systems. It processes the images and extracts intrinsic details just like human brain does. When CV was introduced, it was only meant for imitating HVC, but with the revolution of artificial intelligence; now, it found space in various sectors such as banking, surveillance, healthcare, and automotive.

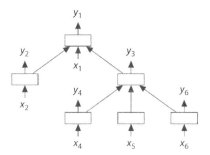

Figure 5.7 Graph-based representation in recursive NN.

Typical ML algorithms are not enough for cumbersome tasks which are difficult to manage. For instance, most of the problem statements deal with object classification, i.e., assigns a label to an object captured in an image based on the saliency. But either it ramps up computation time or system overhead that ends up to low throughput. DL has vast potential for numerous image processing activities such as image analysis, segmentation, classification, and recognition, extensively embedded in CV models and applications. CNN, a class of DL, is globally adopted to assist CV applications via analysing imagery patterns. The motive is to reduce the size of image by carrying multiple convolution layers and pooling layers until it is realized by fully connected layers. The CNN architecture builds around several types of layers which are briefly specified in subsequent headings.

5.5.1 Convolutional Layer

This layer performs convolution operation which is nothing but hovering a small matrix (commonly termed as kernel, filter, or mask) over input image matrix (Figure 5.8). During hovering, it multiplies the values by initial pixel values and finally summing up them to obtain one number. This process reiterates by a number of units to pass across all the pixel values. The idea behind adding this layer is to gain much smaller size of matrix relative to original matrix.

5.5.2 Nonlinear Layer

This layer is followed by convolutional layer to bring non-linearity or inconsistency to data. If the network does not facilitate non-linearity, we do not require multiple layers as incorporating multiple layers become equivalent to single layer. Furthermore, non-linearity strengthens the network that created for complex images which eventually aims to unveil new patterns. To add non-linearity, the most common activation function used is ReLU, though there are varieties of activation functions exist.

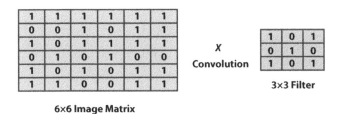

6×6 Image Matrix

Figure 5.8 3×3 filter convolve over 6×6 image matrix.

5.5.3   Pooling Layer

This layer is also helpful in downsizing the image matrix. It is more helpful in reducing the number of parameters and thus, decreasing the computation overhead in the network. The most common method used for pooling is *MaxPooling* (Figure 5.9).

5.5.4   Fully Connected Layer

It works similar to conventional ANN and Multilayer Perceptron (MLP), given in Figure 5.10. However, only difference is that now the image matrix is more simplified, optimized and in shape due to pre-processing offered by early layers of CNN. The classification decision is driven by this layer.

By varying the number of convolutional layer, pooling layer, and fully connected layer, we can maximize the network performance for given image processing task such as restoration or classification. There exist many CNN-based architectures which are developed for accelerating training speed that ultimately leads to high accuracy and low error rate. It is bit hard to conceptualise the architecture thoroughly and beyond the scope of chapter, yet we extract some relevant information and summarize it in Table 5.1.

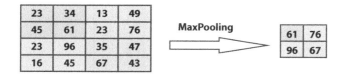

Figure 5.9 Pooling reduces the size of transition matrix.

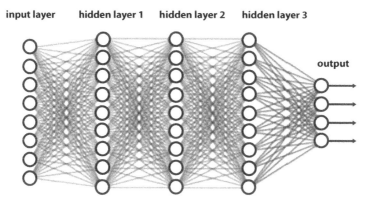

Figure 5.10 Multi-layer neural network.

Table 5.1 CNN-based different architectures.

Architecture	Year	Group/Authors	Error rate (in %)	Activation function used	No. of parameters (in million)
AlexNet [25]	2012	SuperVision	15.3	ReLU	62.3
GoogLeNet [26]	2014	Google	6.67	ReLU	4
VGGNet [27]	2014	Visual Geometry Group	7.32	ReLU	138
ResNet [28]	2015	Kaiming He *et al.*	3.57	ReLU	23

5.6   Unravel Deep Learning in Medical Diagnostic Systems

Nowadays, CV and DL are together conquering greater heights in many areas. The cutting-edge researches influenced by these two frameworks shows promising results in every application, be it agriculture, remote sensing, or autonomous vehicles. Considering the current scenario where the entire globe is grappling with health crisis spread from novel Coronavirus [29], healthcare is emerging as a serious concern among research community. In fact, the virus is not novice for virologists or clinical practitioner, the world has been gone through several zoonotic attacks [30, 31] before 2020 corona pandemic. However, CV and DL in conjunction with simulations gained success in countering the adverse health problems. It was proved effective in aiding doctors and health workers to break the array of misapprehensions. They are widely utilized in developing computer-aided diagnostic (CADS) systems. Therefore, we are leading this section with state-of-the-art techniques stem from image processing and DL in early diagnosis of plausible diseases.

Medical imaging, sometimes, known as diagnostic imaging, such as X-rays, MRIs, CT scans, and mammograms, plays an imperative role in healthcare systems. It is an assortment of techniques and processes to capture visual representations of human parts, organs, or tissues for critical analysis, diagnostics, and clinical treatment. Health disorders like pneumonia, brain tumor, cancer, and Parkinson's disease are being successfully diagnosed with high precision, possible through medical imaging. It thus allows early stage treatment or even nullifying the probability of re-occurring. Not only diagnosis but doctors have embraced the benefits of CV for surgery itself. It has a key role in analysing the damages and loss to body tissues before making any preparation to the surgery. The procedures are positively non-invasive, painless and life-saving. The combination of diagnostic imaging and DL has revolutionized the healthcare sector. It causes researcher and doctor adhere to the patient history, biological data, symptoms, along with microorganism biological cycle or patterns of replication to attain the crucial parameters which are further helpful in drug discovery. Medical imaging also contributes in tracking the effectiveness of patient's on-going treatment and aids the physician to make changes in the dozes, if required. Table 5.2 reviews some state-of-art models for CAD covering relevant diseases.

Table 5.2 Some CAD references driven by deep learning and medical imaging.

Reference	Algorithm(s) used	Performance (in %)	Description
[32]	CNN K-Nearest Neighbor Support Vector Machine	Accuracy = 98 to 99	MRI is used to investigate whether the patient is vulnerable to Alzheimer's disease or not.
[33]	CNN	Accuracy = 97.5	Brain tumor detection by MRI scans
[34]	Deep Neural Network (DNN) Principal Component-Analysis Discrete Wavelet Transform	Accuracy = 96.97 Precision = 97	Classification of brain tumors using MRI
[35]	CNN	Area Under Curve (AUC) = 87 to 94	Chest radiographs are exploited for pathology detection
[36]	DNN Linear Discriminate Analysis	Sensitivity = 96.2 Specificity = 94.2 Accuracy = 94.56	Lung cancer diagnosis using CT scans
[37]	Heterogeneous Modified ANN	Accuracy = 97.5 Prediction ratio = 99.7 AUC = 92.2	Kidney disease diagnosis by utilizing CT scans
[38]	CNN	Sensitivity = 90 above	MRI is used to evaluate brain tumors

(*Continued*)

Table 5.2 Some CAD references driven by deep learning and medical imaging. (*Continued*)

Reference	Algorithm(s) used	Performance (in %)	Description
[39]	Hybridized DL Composite Monte-Carlo Fuzzy-rule	RMSE = 37.77	Devise critical decision process for epidemic by deterministic and non-deterministic data
[40]	CNN	Accuracy = 96.78 Sensitivity = 98.66 Specificity = 96.46	COVID-19 diagnosis using X-rays
[41]	CNN Bayesian optimization	Accuracy = 98.26 Correctness = 98.26 Specificity = 99.13 Completeness = 98.26	Detection model for COVID-19 based on X-rays
[42]	CNN	Accuracy = 87.02 Sensitivity = 85.35 Specificity = 92.18 Precision = 89.96	COVID-19 detection model driven by available X-rays
[43]	Deep Learning	NA	Drug-target interaction model to identify the drug that could work on SARS-CoV-2

(*Continued*)

Table 5.2 Some CAD references driven by deep learning and medical imaging. (*Continued*)

Reference	Algorithm(s) used	Performance (in %)	Description
[44]	Deep Learning Bayesian function	Accuracy = 86.7	Classification of CT images into COVID-19 and other irrelevant groups
[45]	Deep Learning	Category-wise results are mentioned, e.g., Lung cancer: Sensitivity = 62.5 Prostate: Sensitivity = 87 Melanoma = 60	The Bone Scan Index (BSI) is embedded to evaluate different tumors (e.g., prostate cancer, breast cancer, and lung cancer)
[46]	CNN Long short-term memory	Accuracy = 98.5	Exploitation of ECG signals to classify cardiovascular disease
[47]	Deep Learning	Accuracy = 99.5	3D stereophotogrammetry and deep learning are combined to study craniosynostosis condition in infants
[48]	Deep Learning	Accuracy = 72.5 AUC = 81 Specificity = 66.7 Sensitivity = 78.4	To detect appendicitis, a 3D model is developed with pretraining on natural videos

(*Continued*)

Table 5.2 Some CAD references driven by deep learning and medical imaging. (*Continued*)

Reference	Algorithm(s) used	Performance (in %)	Description
[49]	CNN ResNet-50 InceptionResNet-V2 YOLO	Average Accuracy = 94.5, 95.83, 97.5 respectively (for the DDSM dataset) Average Accuracy = 88.74%, 92.55%, 95.32%, respectively (for the INbreast dataset)	A promising breast lesion diagnostic system is proposed from digital mammograms
[50]	CNN	Accuracy = 82.8 Sensitivity = 80.2 Specificity = 83 AUROC = 88.4	CT scan–based diagnosis of cervical lymph node metastasis in patients with thyroid cancer

5.7   Challenges and Future Expectations

In recent years, we have seen an empirical surge in DL deployment. But, as a matter of fact, there are inadequate articles addressing the challenges and expectations owing to data-acquisition, pre-processing, implementation, dataset imbalances, and classifier evaluation. Like, it is quite challenging when working with CNN which requires huge amount of hyper-parameters to tune features. Another issue is dataset imbalance problem which is prominent in medical monitoring. It may be resulted from either distortion or data calibration which affects the DL implementation. As a result, it degrades the performance. Data standards and data interoperability are also major barriers. Since image acquisition is highly varied with sensors and other indicators, it enables poor classification accuracy and learning of model. Different datasets are merged in order to induce diversity and obtain significant volume, but interoperability is still an imaginary aspect. Another deep insight is black-box. It seems building network is not-so-much complicated, but the understanding to reach the output is indeed hefty. DL is continuously offering better results but it is bit hard to answer why and how. Moreover, the privacy and legal issues are also on-board to hinder the process. With the rise in big data, particularly, in health sector where HIPAA (The Health Insurance Portability and Accountability Act of 1996) is prevailed to protect the patient's personal or anonymous information. It restricts the use of such information which could complicate the process of reaching to an individual. Another alternative is differential privacy which limits the use of sensitive data. It prevents the disclosure of person's classified data pertinent to medical history or identifiable information. Unfortunately, all factors contribute to restrict the content that can introduce negative impact on analytical model. It is affected by both legal and ethical perspectives.

From the above discussion, it is learnt that open challenges are present that requires further review and a definite direction in the research. The lack of sufficient data is a biggest challenge in medical research. Ambiguous data or unavailability of adequate medical cases thwarts on-going process addressing rare diseases. It calls for regulatory bodies that defines standards for health dataset and are capable of sharing between providers. An organization should meet these standards while making an opinion on health records.

5.8   Conclusion

Since various cornerstones of DS are deeply engaged with each other, it often takes long discussion to review them individually on the ground level. However, through this article, we are able to underline stark differences among those corners, paying special attention to DL and ANN. While ANN takes the advantage of computational units, *viz.*, neurons to control the flow of information from input units to output units through connections, DL simply looks after feature capturing and transformation that ends up making a relationship with set of stimuli and associated neural results. Depending upon model requirements and objectives, there are numbers of NN architectures available. Moreover, the most trivial class of DL is ConvNet, which influence CV tasks like image pre-processing, object analysis, object detection, and recognition. We provide a generic view of CNN multi-layer architecture and their respective functions. It also comes up with slight variations in layers, proposed by different groups or authors. CNN architectures are highly useful because the time that consumes while training tends to get eliminated as these architectures offer pre-trained networks.

Thereafter, medical applications are discussed that discloses how efficacious DL is in solving the queries associated with medical domain. From Alzheimer's to zoonotic diseases, brain tumor classification to chronic kidney disease diagnosis, DL image processing duo emerges as a silver-line for medical informatics, bioinformatics, or health data analytics. But we should not much celebrate its growth, for there are obstacles that could compromise its flourish. We came forward with quoting major challenges, often we face in NN-based learning specifically in medical domain. We should not consider only one perspective in seeking solutions because there have always been a room for innovation. However, we can keep our eyes out for more researches in the future that nurtures through DL.

References

1. Mohan, S. *et al.*, Effective heart disease prediction using hybrid machine learning techniques. Special Section on Smart Caching, Communications, Computing and Cybersecurity for Information-Centric. *Internet Things*, 7, 81542–81554, 2019.
2. Stephenson, N. *et al.*, Survey of machine learning techniques in drug discovery. *Curr. Drug Metab.*, 9, 20, 185–193, 2019.
3. Hamedan, F. *et al.*, Clinical decision support system to predict chronic kidney disease: A fuzzy expert system approach. *Int. J. Med. Inf.*, Elsevier, 138, 1–9, 2020.
4. Bhatti, G., Machine learning based localization in large-scale wireless sensor networks. *Sensors*, 18, 4179, 2018.
5. Mosavi, A. and Varkonyi-Koczy, A.R., Integration of machine learning and optimization for robot learning. *Adv. Intell. Syst. Comput.*, 519, 349–355, 2017.

6. Smarter with Gartner, Gartner top 10 strategic technology trends for 2019. Homepage https://www.gartner.com/smarterwithgartner.

7. Microsoft Annual report 2019. Homepage www.microsoft.com.

8. Arimura, H., Tokunaga, C., Yamashita, Y., Kuwazuru, J., Magnetic resonance image analysis for brain CAD systems with machine learning, in: *Machine learning. Computer-aided diagnosis: Medical imaging intelligence and analysis*, K. Suzuki (Ed.), pp. 258–296, The University of Chicago, IGI global, USA, 2012.01.

9. El-Dahshan, E.A., Hosny, T., Salem, A.B.M., Hybrid intelligent techniques for MRI brain images classification. *Digital Signal Process.*, 20, 2, 433–441, 2010.

10. Ortiza, A., Gorriz, J.M., Ramırez, Salas-Gonzalez, D., Improving MRI segmentation with probabilistic GHSOM and multi-objective optimization. *Neurocomputing*, 114, 118–131, 2013.

11. Junwei, H. *et al.*, Advanced Deep-Learning Techniques for Salient and Category-Specific Object Detection. *IEEE Signal Process. Mag.*, 35.1, 84–100, 2018.

12. Ajeet, R.P., Manjusha, P., Siddharth, R., Application of deep learning for object detection. *Proc. Comput. Sci.*, 132, 1706–1717, 2018.

13. Liu, *et al.*, Deep learning for generic object detection: A survey. *Int. J. Comput. Vision*, 128, 261–318, 2019.

14. Mohammad, H.H., Wenjing, J., Xiangjian, H., Paul, K., Deep learning techniques for medical image segmentation: Achievements and Challenges. *J. Digit. Imaging*, 32, 582–596, 2019.

15. Hinton, G.E., A practical guide to training restricted boltzmann machines, in: *Neural Networks: Tricks of the Trade*, pp. 599–619, Springer, Berlin, Heidelberg, 2012.

16. Bengio, Y. *et al.*, Learning deep architectures for AI. *Trends® Mach. Learn.*, 2, 1, 1–127, 2009.

17. Liou, C.Y., Cheng, W.C., Liou, J.W., Liou, D.R., Autoencoder for words. *Neurocomputing*, 139, 84–96, 2014.

18. Rehman, S.U. *et al.*, Unsupervised pre-trained filter learning approach for efficient convolution neural network. *Neurocomputing*, 365, 171–190, 2019.

19. Zhang, *et al.*, A new JPEG image steganalysis technique combining rich model features and convolutional neural networks. *Math. Biosci. Eng.*, 16, 5, 4069–4081, 2019.

20. Guan, Y. and Ploetz, T., Ensembles of deep LSTM learners for activity recognition using wearables. *Proceedings of the ACM on Interactive, Mobile, Wearable and Ubiquitous Technologies*, 1.2, 1–28.

21. Majumder, N., Poria, S., Gelbukh, A., Cambria, E., Deep learning-based document modeling for personality detection from text. *IEEE Intell. Syst.*, 32, 2, 74–79, 2017.

22. Baldi, P. and Pollastri, G., The Principled Design of Large-Scale Recursive Neural Networks Architectures-DAG-RNNs and the Protein Structure Prediction Problem. *J. Mach. Learn. Res.*, 4, 575–602, 2003.

23. Ponti, M. A., *et al.* Everything you wanted to know about deep learning for computer vision but were afraid to ask. *2017 30th SIBGRAPI conference on graphics, patterns and images tutorials (SIBGRAPI-T)*. IEEE, 2017.

24. IEEE Computational Intelligence Society, https://cis.ieee.org.

25. Krizhevsky, A., Sutskever, I., Hinton, G.E., Imagenet classification with deep convolutional neural networks. *Adv. Neural Inf. Process. Syst.*, 25, 1097–1105, 2012.

26. Dong, Y. and Bryan, A., Evaluations of deep convolutional neural networks for automatic identification of malaria infected cells, in: *IEEE EMBS International Conference on Biomedical & health informatics (BHI)*, pp. 101–104, 2017.

27. Simonyan, K. and Zisserman, A., Very deep convolutional networks for large-scale image recognition. *International Conference on Learning Representations*, 2015, pp. 1–14, arXiv preprint arXiv:1409.1556, 2014.

28. He, K., Zhang, X., Ren, S., Sun, J., Deep residual learning for image recognition, in: *Proceedings of the IEEE conference on computer vision and pattern recognition*, pp. 770–778, 2016.

29. Santosh, K.C., AI-driven tools for coronavirus outbreak: Need of active learning and cross-population train/test models on multitudinal/multimodal data. *J. Med. Syst.*, 44, 1–5, 2020.

30. Leligdowicz, A., *et al.* Ebola virus disease and critical illness. *Critical Care*, 20.1, 1–14, 2016.

31. Xu, M. *et al.*, Identification of small-molecule inhibitors of Zika virus infection and induced neural cell death via a drug repurposing screen. *Nat. Med.*, 22, 1101–1107, 2016.

32. Khagi, B., Kwon, G.R., Lama, R., Comparative analysis of Alzheimer's disease classification by CDR level using CNN, feature selection, and machine-learning techniques. *Int. J. Imaging Syst. Technol.*, 29, 1–14, 2019.

33. Seetha, J. and Raja, S.S., Brain tumor classification using convolutional neural networks. *Biomed. Pharmacol. J.*, 11, 3, 1457–1461, 2018.

34. Mohsen, H. *et al.*, Classification using deep learning neural networks for brain tumors. *Future Comput. Inf. J.*, 3, 68–71, 2018.

35. Bar, Y. *et al.*, Chest pathology detection using deep learning with non-medical training. *12th international symposium on biomedical imaging (ISBI)*, pp. 294–297, IEEE, 2015.

36. L.S.K. *et al.*, Optimal deep learning model for classification of lung cancer on CT images. *Future Gener. Comput. Syst.*, 92, 1–31, 2018.

37. Ma, *et al.*, Detection and diagnosis of chronic kidney disease using deep learning-based heterogeneous modified artificial neural network. *Future Gener. Comput. Syst.*, 111, 17–26, 2020.

38. Chang, J. *et al.*, A mix-pooling CNN architecture with FCRF for brain tumor segmentation. *J. Vis. Commun. Image R*, 58, 1–23, 2018.

39. Fong, S.J. *et al.*, Composite Monte Carlo decision making under high uncertainty of novel coronavirus epidemic using hybridized deep learning and fuzzy rule induction. *Appl. Soft Comput. J.*, 93, 1–27, 2020.

40. Apostolopoulos, I.D. and Mpesiana, T.A., Covid19: automatic detection from Xray images utilizing transfer learning with convolutional neural networks. *Phys. Eng. Sci. Med.*, 43, 1–6, 2020.

41. Ucar, F. and Korkmaz, D., COVIDiagnosis-Net: Deep Bayes-SqueezeNet based diagnosis of the coronavirus disease 2019 (COVID-19) from X-ray images. *Med. Hypotheses*, 140, 1–12, 2020.

42. Ozturk, T. *et al.*, Automated detection of COVID-19 cases using deep neural networks with X-ray images. *Comput. Biol. Med.*, 121, 1–11, 2020.

43. Beck, B.R. *et al.*, Predicting commercially available antiviral drugs that may act on the novel coronavirus (SARS-CoV-2) through a drug-target interaction deep learning model. *Comput. Struct. Biotechnol. J.*, 18, 784–790, 2020.

44. Xu, X. *et al.*, A Deep Learning System to Screen Novel Coronavirus Disease 2019 Pneumonia. *Engineering*, 6, 1–11, 2020.

45. Wuestemann, J. *et al.*, Analysis of Bone Scans in Various Tumor Entities Using a Deep-Learning-Based Artificial Neural Network Algorithm—Evaluation of Diagnostic Performance. *Cancers*, 12, 1–13, 2020.

46. Lih, O.S. *et al.*, Comprehensive electrocardiographic diagnosis based on deep learning. *Artif. Intell. Med.*, 108, 1–8, 2020.

47. Jong, G.D. *et al.*, Combining deep learning with 3D stereophotogrammetry for craniosynostosis diagnosis. *Sci. Rep.*, 10, 1–6, 2020.

48. Rajpurkar, P. *et al.*, AppendiXNet: Deep Learning for Diagnosis of Appendicitis from A Small Dataset of CT Exams Using Video Pretraining. *Sci. Rep.*, 10, 1–7, 2020.

49. Al-antari, M.A. and Kim, T.S., Evaluation of Deep Learning Detection and Classification towards Computer-aided Diagnosis of Breast Lesions in Digital X-ray Mammograms. *Comput. Methods Programs Biomed.*, 196, 1–38, 2020.

50. Lee, J.H. *et al.*, Application of deep learning to the diagnosis of cervical lymph node metastasis from thyroid cancer with CT: External validation and clinical utility for resident training. *Eur. Radiol.*, 29, 1–7, 2020.

6

Two-Stage Credit Scoring Model Based on Evolutionary Feature Selection and Ensemble Neural Networks

Diwakar Tripathi[1*]**, Damodar Reddy Edla**[2]**, Annushree Bablani**[2] **and Venkatanareshbabu Kuppili**[2]

[1]*Thapar Institute of Engineering & Technology Patiala, Punjab, India*
[2]*National Institute of Technology Goa, Ponda, India*

Abstract

Credit scoring is a progression to estimate the risk accompanying with a credit merchandise. Nowadays, huge number of credit application data with different features set is available of various credit products, as credit industries are issuing various credit product. So, key challenge is to discover insight on how to improve the performance ahead of time using data mining techniques, as it directly effects to viability of that industry. Foremost emphasis of this article is to improve the analytical performance of credit scoring model. Toward that, this article introduces a two-stage credit scoring model. First stage focuses for reduction of irrelevant and noisy features because they may affect model's performances. In second stage, ensemble of neural networks is utilized for categorizing credit applicant. For feature selection, an evolutionary approach by utilizing "Hybrid Binary Particle Swarm Optimization and Gravitational Search Algorithm (BPSOGSA)" is proposed and correlation coefficient is considered as criteria function to compute the fitness value against each search agent generated by BPSOGSA algorithm. Further, proposed credit scoring model is validated on four different credit applicants' real-world credit scoring datasets.

Keywords: Correlation coefficient, neural networks, ensemble learning, feature selection

Corresponding author: diwakarnitgoa@gmail.com

Mettu Srinivas, G. Sucharitha and Anjanna Matta (eds.) Machine Learning Algorithms and Applications, (99–116) © 2021 Scrivener Publishing LLC

6.1   Introduction

Credit scoring is a risk approximation approach associated with credit products such as credit card and loans and is estimated based on applicants' historical data [1]. As specified by Thomas *et al.* [2], "Credit scoring is a set of decision models and their underlying techniques that aid credit lenders in the granting of credit" [3]. Credit scoring efforts to isolate the consequence of diverse applicants' characteristics dependent on unlawful conduct and non-payments. The essential point of convergence of credit scoring is to preference whether an applicant has a place with financially sound group or not. Credit denotes to amount acquired by an applicant from a monetary foundation as "credit limit to an applicant is estimated by system on the basis of customer's credentials like annual income, property and etc". Numerous advantages of credit scoring for monetary foundation incorporate "ascertaining and diminishing credit risk", "making managerial decisions", and "cash flow improvement" [4, 5] and its performance is responsible for the profitability of credit industries. It is not a single step progression, every so often, monetary foundations succeed it in several steps some of them are as follows [4]:

- Application Scoring: It is employed for estimating the genuineness and mistrustfulness of new applicant. That estimation is conducted on basis of societal, economic, and supplementary evidence collected while submitting the application.
- Behavioral Scoring: It is relative as preceding case, nevertheless "it is for the present clients to examine their personal conduct standards and to help dynamic portfolio administration processes".
- Collection Scoring: Similar to step, it tries to classifies clients into several clusters on the basis of change in their behaviors and accordingly monetary foundation pays attention on those clusters' clients, for example, more, moderate, no etc.

6.1.1   Motivation

According to the statistics [7] given by Reserve Bank of India (RBI), the users of credit cards during 2012–2016 are shown in Figure 6.1.

- The number of credit card holders are 24.50, 21.11, and 19.18 million in the financial year 2015–2016, 2014–2015, and 2013–2014, respectively, in India [7].
- Total number of home loan account in the financial year 2009–2010 were 57.38 lakhs in India [8].

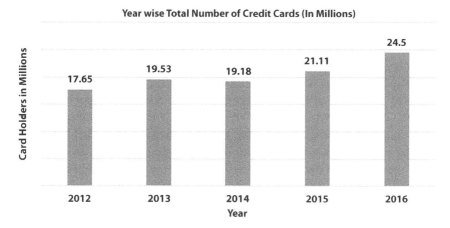

Figure 6.1 Rise in issuing of credit cards during 2012–2016.

Together with credit cards, various credit products such as various types of loan and mortgage and mini and micro finance are also obtainable from various monetary foundations. Attributable to excessive number of new candidates and existing clients, credit scoring is quite difficult to do manually or it necessitates massive amount of authorities with expertise in domain knowledge and customer's behaviors. At present "credit scoring is not restricted to banking or credit industries only, many other domains such as telecommunication, real estate, etc., are also applying credit score calculation models for investigation of clients' conduct". Consequently, "Artificial intelligence may overwhelm the problem of manual credit scoring". Enlightening the predictive performance of model specially applicants with mistrustfulness group will have excessive influence for monetary foundation [9, 10]. This article emphasizes to boost the classification performance of model by dropping the extraneous and noisy features.

Remainder of the article is organized as follows: Section 6.2 designates a brief literature analysis. Section 6.3 presents "proposed credit scoring model". Section 6.4 demonstrates the investigational outcomes of proposed approach followed by the concluding remarks based on obtained investigational outcomes.

6.2 Literature Survey

Most of the scholars have measured the credit risk estimation as a binary class classification problem as creditworthy or non-creditworthy and found it to be reliable to discover hidden patterns in the credit scoring data. These systems help experts to upgrade their insight for credit risk estimation. In this context, various Machine Learning (ML) methods are employed to model the risk estimation systems. Various classification approaches such as "Artificial Neural Network (ANN)" and "Support Vector Machine (SVM)" have efficiently applied for credit risk prediction model.

SVM [11] has "superior features of generalization" and "global optimization". So, many researchers have employed it as classification tool not only in credit scoring but in other domains also. Li *et al.* [12] have presented a credit risk assessment model by considering SVM as classification approach with data pre-processing to distinguish probable applicants for consumer mortgages. Gestel *et al.* [13] have employed "Least Squares Support Vector Machine (LS-SVM)" to evaluate the creditworthiness of probable corporate clients. West [14] has presented a survey of various classification methods and evaluated the performances of classifiers on credit scoring datasets. Xiao and Fei [15] have offered a method based on "SVM with optimal parameters' values". Kuppili *et al.* [16] have applied Extreme Learning Machine for credit scoring data analysis with aggregation of spiking neuron model. Similarly, another approach by considering "weighted SVM" for credit scoring model is presented by Zhou *et al.* [17].

An amalgamation of various approaches is a dynamic arrangement that syndicate the steps of various approaches toward to enhancement of a specific conclusion. In credit scoring dataset, it has various features related to applicants' credentials such as societal and financial status, and these features are heterogeneous features such as categorical, minor range numerical, and wide range numerical. So, there is chance that some the features may be redundant or irreverent which may reduce the model's performance. Accordingly, several scientists have considered various data-preprocessing steps such as "feature selection" and "outlier detection" as prominent way to enhance the predictive performance of credit scoring and inclusive descriptions of those methods are presented as follows.

Hybrid credit scoring models with aggregation of SVM as classification approach and feature selection approaches based on "Multivariate Adaptive Regression Splines (MARS)" and "F-score" are assessed in article [18]. Similarly, feature selection approaches "Stepwise Regression (SR)" and "MARS" aggregated with ANN as classification approaches for credit scoring are applied in article [19] and [20], respectively. A hybrid model based on "Genetic Algorithm (GA)" for opting the valuable features and further aggregated with classification approach is presented by Oreski and Oreski [21]. Similarly, Wang *et al.* [22] and Huang and Dun [23] have applied "Rough Set and Tabu search" and "Binary Particle Swarm Optimization

(BPSO)" for optimizing the set valuable features and further aggregated with SVM for classification, respectively.

From the literature, it is detected that feature selection is a prominent way to improve the predictive performances of classification approaches and is a combinatorial optimization problem. Bio-inspired algorithms suitable for optimization on continuous search spaces. So, for feature optimization, first conversion of continuous to binary search is needed. Ensemble is an association the outputs of base learners together to estimate the final conclusion and in many studied it have been demonstrated that it is more stable and accurate than single models. With consideration of aforementioned advantage of feature selection and ensemble approach, this article presents a "Two-stage Credit Scoring Model based on Evolutionary Feature Selection and Ensemble Neural Networks" with objective to extract the knowledge from the credit scoring dataset using ML algorithms and to improve performance by considering the valuable features.

6.3   Proposed Model for Credit Scoring

This section presents the proposed two-stage credit scoring model as depicted in Figure 6.2. The proposed model combines evolutionary feature selection in stage-1 and ensemble classification in stage-2 for credit scoring and are discussed in the following subsections. Before feature selection, datasets are preprocessed because as in credit scoring datasets have heterogeneous data type. In this work, we have utilized neural network as classification tool which consider the data in vector format. So, datasets are preprocessed which includes data cleaning (eliminating the missing values), data transformation (converting the categorical values in numerical

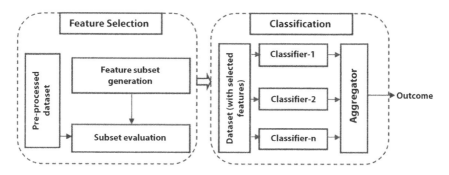

Figure 6.2 Proposed two-stage credit scoring model.

values) and data discretization (converting long range numerical values in small range).

6.3.1   Stage-1: Feature Selection

In this paper, an evolutionary approach BPSOGSA [24] is utilized for selecting a set of valuable features. Authors in [29] have presented PSOGSA, a hybrid approach by combining social thinking (gbest) capability of swarm-based Particle Swarm Optimization (PSO) and exploitation capability of evolutionary-based Gravitational Search Algorithm (GSA). PSOGSA performs better than PSO and GSA toward to exploration and exploitation capabilities [24].

In PSOGSA [29], all search agents move from one position to another in each iteration at the continuous search space and are represented by position vectors. Here, PSOGSA is used for feature selection in which position vector should be presented in binary format, where 0 present corresponding feature is not present else is present in position vector. In order to change the continuous to corresponding binary position vector, a transfer function is expected to adjust position, with the likelihood velocity [25] of search agents. Various transfer functions are available in literature and fall under two categories, i.e., S and V shaped [26]. V-shaped transfer functions are superior to S-shaped transfer functions toward the convergence rate [27]. V-shaped transfer functions are shown as in Equations (6.1)–(6.4) [26].

$$V_1 \rightarrow S\left(V_{ij}^k\right) = \left| \mathrm{erf}\left(\frac{\sqrt{\pi}}{2} V_{ij}^k(t) \right) \right| \tag{6.1}$$

$$V_2 \rightarrow S\left(V_{ij}^k\right) = \left| \mathrm{Tanh}\left(V_{ij}^k(t) \right) \right| \tag{6.2}$$

$$V_3 \rightarrow S\left(V_{ij}^k\right) = \left| \frac{2}{\pi} \mathrm{arktan}\left(\frac{\pi}{2} V_{ij}^k(t) \right) \right| \tag{6.3}$$

$$V_4 \rightarrow S\left(V_{ij}^k\right) = \left| \frac{V_{ij}^k(t)}{\sqrt{1 + \left(V_{ij}^k(t)\right)^2}} \right| \tag{6.4}$$

where V_i^k represents the velocity of search agent i at iteration k.

All aforementioned transfer functions are utilized for adjusting veloci-ties of search agents in BPSOGSA to probabilities of flipping their position vector's elements. Further, probabilities of search agents' position vectors are considered to convert it in binary format and are updated by the rules as presented in Equation (6.5).

$$X_{ij}^k(t+1)=\begin{cases} X_{ij}^k(t) & \text{If } rand \geq S\left(Vl_i^k(t+1)\right) \\ X_{ij}^k(t)^{-1} & \text{If } rand < S\left(Vl_i^k(t+1)\right) \end{cases} \qquad (6.5)$$

where X_i represents the position of ith search agent.

6.3.2   Proposed Criteria Function

Correlation coefficient (Corr) measures the relationship between two vari-ables [28–30] and it can be calculated by Equation (6.6). Corr values may in the range from -1 to $+1$, where $+1$ demonstrates the strongest potential agree-ment, -1 demonstrates the strongest potential disagreement, and 0 demon-strates that there is no linear relationship between those features. Proposed criteria function is as in Equation (6.9), which depends on the proportion of inter class correlation ($Inter_{ccc}$) and intra class correlation ($Intra_{ccc}$) coeffi-cient of features in search agent. $Inter_{ccc}$ represents the correlation between feature and class label and $Intra_{ccc}$ represents the correlation between two feature and are calculated by the Equations (6.7) and (6.8), respectively.

$$Corr = \frac{n*\sum P*Q - \sum P*\sum Q}{\sqrt{n*\sum P^2 - (\sum P)^2} * \sqrt{n*\sum Q^2 - (\sum Q)^2}} \qquad (6.6)$$

where P and Q indicate the features, and n designates the number of values in these features.

$$Inter_{ccc} = \frac{1}{n}\sum_{i=1}^{n} Corr(F_i, Y) \qquad (6.7)$$

$$Intra_{ccc} = \frac{2}{n*(n-1)}\sum_{i=1}^{n}\sum_{j=1}^{n} Corr(F_i, F_j) \qquad (6.8)$$

Here, F_i and Y denote i[th] the feature and target label, respectively.

$$\text{fitness} - \text{value i} = \frac{\text{Inter}_{ccc}}{\text{Intra}_{ccc}} \tag{6.9}$$

where fitness value$_i$ represents the fitness value against i[th] search agent.

6.3.3 Stage-2: Ensemble Classifier

Broad research has been led on data classification and various classification approaches are available in literature. However, there is no specific process to recognize which classifier will have the finest results on a specific dataset. A specific classifier may be more suitable to others for a specific dataset, yet alternative classifier might accomplish superior to that on another dataset. "Ensemble of classifiers has the ability to deliver the close to optimal outcomes on each dataset". The fundamental intention behind utilizing the ensemble classifier system is that, when classifiers make a decision, instead of using single classifier's decision and different base learners may view the same pattern differently, thereby complementing the predicted information of each other and use various classifiers' decision for decision-making process. All participating classifiers for decision-making process are known as base classifiers.

Most common way to aggregate the decisions of base classifiers are as Unanimous Voting (UV), Majority Voting (MV), and Weighted Voting (WV). In case of UV, for a given class let, class-1, if all classifier classifies data as class-1, then UV takes decision as class-1 as final outcome against a sample. In case of MV, final output of ensemble is the class which have the highest or majority of votes. With WV "final output is the weighted sum of the outputs of base classifiers". Weight to respective base classifiers depends and is proportional on its classification performance such as classification accuracy. Ensemble of classifiers can be formed in two ways as homogeneous (base classifiers of same type) or heterogeneous (base classifiers of different type) frameworks. In case of homogeneous and heterogeneous framework with MV and UV, prediction ability is good toward the particular class label [31].

ANNs are powerful classification approach motivated from human mind capabilities like information processing and learning because of their high capability to learn and recognize composite non-linear associations of input-output data [32]. In stage-2, three neural network–based heterogeneous classifiers, namely, "Multi-layer Feed Forward Neural Network (MLFN) [6, 33]", "Time Delay Neural Network (TDNN) [34, 35]", and "Redial Basis Functional Neural Network (RBFN) [36, 37]", are aggregated by WV approach.

6.4   Results and Discussion

This section offers the explanation of datasets together with performance measures utilized to validate the proposed approach and comprehensive outcome investigation on four credit scoring datasets.

6.4.1   Experimental Datasets and Performance Measures

Two-stage credit scoring model is experimented on four credit scoring datasets, *viz.*, "Australian credit approval (AUS)", "German-categorical loan approval (GCD)", "Japanese credit screening (JPD)", and "German-numerical loan approval (GND)". All aforementioned datasets are obtained from the "UCI Machine Learning Repository [38]" and comprehensive descriptions are as tabularized in Table 6.1. All datasets are binary class datasets in which positive and negative classes signify as accepted not accepted applications.

Here, accuracy and G-measure are utilized to measure and compare the performances of proposed approach with other approaches. Accuracy [as in Equation (6.10)] shows the "predictive performance of classifier", and it is not sufficient as a performance measure, if there is noteworthy class disproportion on the way to a class in the dataset. G-measure [as in Equation (6.11)] is a measure which takes "both the positive and negative classes accuracies" in account to calculate the score, where specificity (Spe) and

Table 6.1 Description about experimental datasets.

S. no.	Dataset	Instances	+ve/−ve	No. of features
1	AUS	690	307/383	14
2	GCD	1,000	700/300	20
3	JPD	690	307/383	15
4	GND	1,000	700/300	24

sensitivity (Sen) represent the predictive performance toward the positive and negative class, respectively.

$$Accuracy\,(ACC) = \frac{TP+TN}{TP+TN+FP+FN} \qquad (6.10)$$

$$G-measure(G-M) = \sqrt{Sen * Spe} \qquad (6.11)$$

where "TP", "FP", "TN", and "FN" indicate as "True Positive", "False Positive", "True Negative", and "False Negative", respectively, and $Spe = \frac{TP}{TP+FP}$, $Sen = \frac{TN}{TN+FN}$.

6.4.2   Classification Results With Feature Selection

Pre-processing is the initial and most significant phase in data mining. For pre-processing the data, data cleaning, transformation, and discretization

Table 6.2 Performances of MLFN, RBFN, DTNN, and ensemble approaches with features selection on Australian datasets.

Classifier	Measure	ALL	CFS	V1	V2	V3	V4
MLFN	ACC	83.12	84.35	84.34	82.13	85.57	83.31
	G-M	83.41	84.93	84.32	830.1	85.66	84.41
DTNN	ACC	89.16	90.57	91.81	91.53	91.43	91.04
	G-M	90.39	91.08	92.11	92.05	92.09	91.25
RBFN	ACC	85.59	87.23	87.6	86.48	87.76	87.39
	G-M	86.19	88.36	87.74	87.59	88.06	87.96
MV	ACC	89.43	90.56	91.88	91.86	91.58	91.63
	G-M	89.15	90.93	92.33	92.48	92.23	92.29
WV	ACC	90.02	90.86	91.92	91.89	91.79	91.69
	G-M	90.67	91.26	92.36	92.54	92.46	92.61
UV	ACC	89.11	89.61	89.88	89.92	90.06	89.62
	G-M	90.29	90.58	91.06	91.12	91.09	90.02

processes are applied. Toward the data-cleaning, data samples with missing value are eliminated. Toward the data-transformation distinct nominal values of an attribute is replaced by a unique integer number. Because, neural network-based classifiers require the data samples as a vector of real numbers. Numerical feature value is rescaled in a predefined interval respectively. With the purpose of anticipating to the features with wide-ranging numeric values overlook the features with narrow-ranging numeric values, features are rescaled between a range using discretization procedure by applying Boolean Reasoning Algorithm [39].

As per the proposed two-stage model, in first stage, pre-processed datasets are fed for feature selection, as mentioned in earlier section that a transfer function is required to convert the search space from continuous to binary. Because feature section is binary optimization problem, where 0 and 1 represent that corresponding feature is present and absent respectively in that search agent. From the literature, it is clear that V-shaped functions are better than S-shaped function.

In literature, various V-shaped functions are available and it is not clear that which function may perform well in case of feature selection. So, in this

Table 6.3 Performances of MLFN, RBFN, DTNN, and ensemble approaches with features selection on German-categorical datasets.

Classifier	Measure	ALL	CFS	V1	V2	V3	V4
MLFN	ACC	70.53	72.22	72.58	72.63	72.69	72.36
	G-M	58.23	59.63	61.23	61.36	61.53	60.88
DTNN	ACC	80.36	81.22	82.03	82.36	82.65	82.33
	G-M	69.35	70.22	70.99	71.06	71.77	70.89
RBFN	ACC	74.64	76.25	76.35	76.55	76.83	76.22
	G-M	63.77	64.96	65.23	65.96	66.36	65.84
MV	ACC	81.25	82.36	83.11	83.26	83.69	83.06
	G-M	78.32	79.53	79.65	79.89	79.58	78.98
WV	ACC	81.25	82.36	83.11	83.26	83.69	83.06
	G-M	79.02	79.56	79.99	80.13	80.24	79.36
UV	ACC	80.13	81.19	81.66	81.63	81.81	81.21
	G-M	77.69	78.64	78.59	78.69	78.49	79.07

paper, four V-shaped transfer function, namely, V1, V2, V3, and V4, are applied for converting the continuous to binary search space. Feature selected by proposed approach is compared with state-of-the-art approach for feature selection "Correlation-based Feature Selection (CFS) [40]". Further, the datasets with selected feature are forwarded to next stage for classification and outputs predicted by MLFN, RBFN, and TDNN are aggregated by WV approach. In case of WV approach, weights are required to the base classifiers. For calculating the weights to base classifier, classifiers accuracy is used as parameter and initially equal weights are allocated to all classifier. Further, weights to classifiers are updated by Equation (6.12) based on its classification performances throughout to the iterations [41]. Same procedure is continued n iterations and at last iteration weights are assigned to respective classifier.

$$W_{iu} = W_{io} \frac{1}{2} Log\left(\frac{Acc_i}{1 - Acc_i}\right) \tag{6.12}$$

where w_{io} and w_{iu} indicate the old and updated weights to i^{th} classifier at n^{th} iteration and acc_i indicates accuracy of ith classifier.

Table 6.4 Performances of MLFN, RBFN, DTNN, and ensemble approaches with features selection on Japanese datasets.

Classifier	Measure	ALL	CFS	V1	V2	V3	V4
MLFN	ACC	84.36	85.89	85.79	86.27	86.83	86.42
	G-M	84.53	86.16	86.09	86.13	86.88	86.39
DTNN	ACC	87.16	88.86	88.84	88.78	89.56	89.13
	G-M	88.86	89.38	89.36	89.2	89.93	88.96
RBFN	ACC	84.83	85.02	85.36	85.39	86.07	85.86
	G-M	85.31	86.69	86.83	86.91	87.32	87.09
MV	ACC	88.53	89.77	89.91	89.86	90.08	90.12
	G-M	89.21	89.96	90.01	90.14	90.68	90.13
WV	ACC	88.76	89.65	89.89	89.93	90.06	89.26
	G-M	90.67	90.15	89.79	90.39	90.61	89.97
UV	ACC	88.06	89.16	89.15	89.12	89.31	88.77
	G-M	88.69	89.74	90.11	90.24	90.17	89.44

For comparative results, analysis mean of 10-Fold Cross-Validation (10-FCV) is used and is compared in terms of Accuracy (ACC) and G-measure (G-M) with all features, features selected by CFS and features selected by aforementioned V-shaped transfer functions. Here, three classifiers MLFN, TDNN, and RBFN along with three aggregation approach MV, WV, and UV are also used for comparative analysis. Tables 6.2 to 6.5 present the results on AUS, GDC, JCD, and GND datasets, respectively, and comparative graph of various feature selection approaches by considering the accuracy measure is depicted as in Figure 6.3. As proposed approach for feature selection is an evolutionary approach, so, in order to show the its stability, feature selection is repeated 10 times with all V-shaped function. Further, 10-FCV is applied in each iteration and mean of 10-FCV with each iteration is used for comparative analysis.

In Tables 6.2 to 6.5, V1, V2, V3, and V4 present the performance of the respective classifier and aggregation approach on features selected by respective transfer function, CFS and with all features. From the experimental outcomes, it is observed that proposed feature selection technique has better classification performance as compared to CFS and it improve

Table 6.5 Performances of MLFN, RBFN, DTNN, and ensemble approaches with features selection on German-numerical datasets.

Classifier	Measure	ALL	CFS	V1	V2	V3	V4
MLFN	ACC	73.72	75.87	75.93	75.27	74.89	74.68
	G-M	69.36	71.92	71.36	70.89	71.25	69.83
DTNN	ACC	81.16	82.03	82.85	83.18	83.47	83.15
	G-M	70.73	71.62	72.43	72.48	73.21	72.3
RBFN	ACC	75.38	77.01	77.11	77.31	77.59	76.98
	G-M	65.04	66.25	66.53	67.27	67.68	67.15
MV	ACC	82.87	84.01	84.77	84.92	85.36	84.72
	G-M	79.1	80.32	80.44	80.68	80.37	79.76
WV	ACC	82.87	84.01	84.77	84.92	85.36	84.72
	G-M	80.6	81.15	81.58	81.73	81.84	80.94
UV	ACC	81.73	82.81	83.29	83.26	83.44	82.83
	G-M	79.24	80.21	80.16	80.26	80.05	80.65

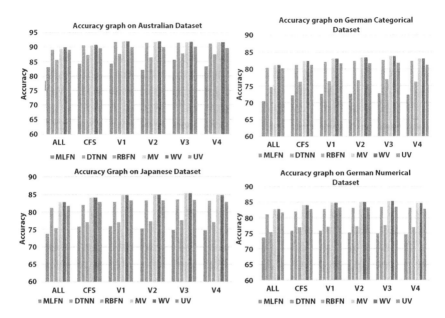

Figure 6.3 Comparative graph on various credit scoring datasets.

the classification performance of RBFN, MLFN, and TDNN with all afore-mentioned credit scoring datasets. From the results as in Tables 6.2 to 6.5, it is also observed that V3 transfer function has better performances in most of the cases and it also improves the classification performance as compare to same with all features. WV has the best performance as compared to MV and UV and it makes significant improvement on classification performances as compared to its base classifiers utilized for construction of same ensemble framework. Final conclusion is that BPSOGSA-based feature selection with V3 transfer function and WV has the best performances on all four credit scoring datasets.

6.5 Conclusion

In this article, a two-stage credit scoring model has been offered as this is a prominent research challenge for various credit industries and it directly affects to viability of that industry. In first stage, we have applied an evolutionary approach by utilizing BPSOGSA that is proposed, and in second stage, ensemble of neural networks, namely, MLFN, TDNN, and RBFN, is assembled by WV approach. Further, proposed credit scoring model is validated on four diverse domain such as credit card and loan applicants' real-world datasets. Further, the results are compared with well-known CFS-based feature selection approach in terms of accuracy and G-measure of MLFN, TDNN, and RBFN along with MV-, WV-, and UV-based aggregation approaches. From the investigational results, it is visible that BPSOGSA based feature selection with V3 transfer function and WV has the best performances on all four credit scoring datasets.

References

1. Mester, L.J., What's the point of credit scoring? *Bus. Rev.*, 3, Sep/Oct, 3–16, 1997.

2. Thomas, L., Crook, J., Edelman, D., Credit scoring and its applications. *Soc. Ind. Appl. Math.*, 2017. https://catalog.princeton.edu/catalog/10425155

3. Louzada, F., Ara, A., Fernandes, G.B., Classification methods applied to credit scoring: Systematic review and overall comparison. *Surv. Oper. Res. Manage. Sci.*, *21*, 2, 117–134, 2016.

4. Paleologo, G., Elisseeff, A., Antonini, G., Subagging for credit scoring models. *Eur. J. Oper. Res.*, *201*, 2, 490–499, 2010.

5. Tripathi, D., Edla, D.R., Cheruku, R., Kuppili, V., A novel hybrid credit scoring model based on ensemble feature selection and multilayer ensemble classification. *Comput. Intell.*, *35*, 2, 371–394, 2019.

6. Svozil, D., Kvasnicka, V., Pospichal, J., Introduction to multi-layer feedforward neural networks. *Chemometr. Intell. Lab. Syst.*, *39*, 1, 43–62, 1997.

7. Saha, M., Credit cards issued. http://www.thehindu.com/business/Industry/Credit-cards-issued-touch-24.5-million/article14378386.ece (2017 (accessed October 1, 2019)).

8. Fulwari, A., *Issues of housing finance in Urban India A symptomatic study* (Doctoral dissertation), Maharaja Sayajirao University of Baroda, 2013. http://shodhganga.inflibnet.ac.in/handle/10603/28192

9. Wang, G., Ma, J., Huang, L., Xu, K., Two credit scoring models based on dual strategy ensemble trees. *Knowledge-Based Syst.*, *26*, 61–68, 2012.

10. Tripathi, D., Edla, D.R., Cheruku, R., Hybrid credit scoring model using neighborhood rough set and multi-layer ensemble classification. *J. Intell. Fuzzy Syst.*, *34*, 3, 1543–1549, 2018.

11. Vapnik, V., *The nature of statistical learning theory*, Springer science & business media, 2013.

12. Li, S.T., Shiue, W., Huang, M.H., The evaluation of consumer loans using support vector machines. *Expert Syst. Appl.*, *30*, 4, 772–782, 2006.

13. Van Gestel, T., Baesens, B., Suykens, J.A., Van den Poel, D., Baestaens, D.E., Willekens, M., Bayesian kernel-based classification for financial distress detection. *Eur. J. Oper. Res.*, *172*, 3, 979–1003, 2006.

14. West, D., Neural network credit scoring models. *Comput. Oper. Res.*, *27*, 11–12, 1131–1152, 2000.
15. Wen-bing, X., II and Qi, F.E., II, A Study of Personal Credit Scoring Models on Support Vector Machine with Optimal Choice of Kernel Function Parameters [J]. *Syst. Eng.-Theory Pract.*, *10*, 73–79, 2006.
16. Kuppili, V., Tripathi, D., Reddy Edla, D., Credit score classification using spiking extreme learning machine. *Comput. Intell.*, *36*, 2, 402–426, 2020.
17. Zhou, L., Lai, K.K., Yen, J., Credit scoring models with AUC maximization based on weighted SVM. *Int. J. Inf. Technol. Decis. Mak.*, *8*, 04, 677–696, 2009.
18. Chen, W., Ma, C., Ma, L., Mining the customer credit using hybrid support vector machine technique. *Expert Syst. Appl.*, *36*, 4, 7611–7616, 2009.
19. Wongchinsri, P. and Kuratach, W., SR-based binary classification in credit scoring, in: *2017 14th International Conference on Electrical Engineering/Electronics, Computer, Telecommunications and Information Technology (ECTI-CON)*, IEEE, pp. 385–388, 2017, June.
20. Lee, T.S. and Chen, I.F., A two-stage hybrid credit scoring model using artificial neural networks and multivariate adaptive regression splines. *Expert Syst. Appl.*, *28*, 4, 743–752, 2005.
21. Oreski, S. and Oreski, G., Genetic algorithm-based heuristic for feature selection in credit risk assessment. *Expert Syst. Appl.*, *41*, 4, 2052–2064, 2014.
22. Wang, J., Guo, K., Wang, S., Rough set and Tabu search based feature selection for credit scoring. *Proc. Comput. Sci.*, *1*, 1, 2425–2432, 2010.
23. Huang, C.L. and Dun, J.F., A distributed PSO–SVM hybrid system with feature selection and parameter optimization. *Appl. Soft Comput.*, *8*, 4, 1381–1391, 2008.
24. Mirjalili, S., Wang, G.G., Coelho, L.D.S., Binary optimization using hybrid particle swarm optimization and gravitational search algorithm. *Neural Comput. Appl.*, *25*, 6, 1423–1435, 2014.
25. Rashedi, E., Nezamabadi-Pour, H., Saryazdi, S., BGSA: binary gravitational search algorithm. *Natural Comput.*, *9*, 3, 727–745, 2010.
26. Mirjalili, S. and Lewis, A., S-shaped versus V-shaped transfer functions for binary particle swarm optimization. *Swarm Evol. Comput.*, *9*, 1–14, 2013.
27. Mirjalili, S., Mirjalili, S.M., Yang, X.S., Binary bat algorithm. *Neural Comput. Appl.*, *25*, 3–4, 663–681, 2014.
28. Cohen, J., Cohen, P., West, S.G., Aiken, L.S., *Applied multiple regression/correlation analysis for the behavioral sciences*, Routledge, 2013.
29. Bluman, A.G., *Elementary statistics: A step by step approach*, McGraw-Hill Higher Education, New York, NY, 2009.
30. Tripathi, D., Edla, D.R., Kuppili, V., Bablani, A., Dharavath, R., Credit scoring model based on weighted voting and cluster-based feature selection. *Proc. Comput. Sci.*, *132*, 22–31, 2018.
31. Tsai, C.F., Lin, Y.C., Yen, D.C., Chen, Y.M., Predicting stock returns by classifier ensembles. *Appl. Soft Comput.*, *11*, 2, 2452–2459, 2011.

32. Haykin, S., *Neural networks: a comprehensive foundation*, Prentice-Hall, Inc., 2007.

33. Hornik, K., Stinchcombe, M., White, H., Multilayer feedforward networks are universal approximators. *Neural Networks*, 2, 5, 359–366, 1989.

34. Edla, D.R., Tripathi, D., Cheruku, R., Kuppili, V., An efficient multi-layer ensemble framework with BPSOGSA-based feature selection for credit scoring data analysis. *Arab. J. Sci. Eng.*, 43, 12, 6909–6928, 2018.

35. Waibel, A., Sawai, H., Shikano, K., Modularity and scaling in large phonemic neural networks. *IEEE Trans. Acoust. Speech Signal Process.*, 37, 12, 1888–1898, 1989.

36. Kala, R., Vazirani, H., Khanwalkar, N., Bhattacharya, M., Evolutionary Radial Basis Function Network for Classificatory Problems. *IJCSA*, 7, 4, 34–49, 2010.

37. Broomhead, D.S. and Lowe, D., *Radial basis functions, multi-variable functional interpolation and adaptive networks* (No. RSRE-MEMO-4148), Royal Signals and Radar Establishment Malvern (United Kingdom), 1988.

38. UCI machine learning repository (Last Accessed 2019/09/25), https://archive.ics.uci.edu/ml/index.php.

39. Nguyen, H.S., *Dicretization of Real Value Attributes: Boolean Reasoning Approach* [Ph. D Dissertaion], Warsaw University, Polland, 1997.

40. Hall, M.A., Correlation-based feature selection of discrete and numeric class machine learning, University of Waikato, Department of Computer Science, 2000.

41. Tripathi, D., Cheruku, R., Bablani, A., Relative performance evaluation of ensemble classification with feature reduction in credit scoring datasets, in: *Advances in Machine Learning and Data Science*, pp. 293–304, Springer, Singapore, 2018.

7

Enhanced Block-Based Feature Agglomeration Clustering for Video Summarization

Sreeja M. U.* and Binsu C. Kovoor

Department of Information Technology, Cochin University of Science and Technology, Kerala, India

Abstract

Video summarization is the process of automatically extracting relevant frames or segments from a video that can best represent the contents of the video. In the proposed framework, a modified block-based clustering technique is implemented for video summarization. The clustering technique employed is feature agglomeration clustering which results in dimensionality reduction and makes the system an optimized one. The sampled frames from the video are divided into varying number of blocks and clustering is employed on corresponding block sets of all frames rather than clustering frames as a whole. Additionally, image compression based on Discrete Cosine Transform is applied on the individual frames. Results prove that the proposed framework can produce optimum results by varying the block sizes in a computationally efficient manner for videos of different duration. Moreover, the division of frames into blocks before applying clustering ensures that maximum information is retained in the summary.

Keywords: Feature agglomeration, block based, hierarchical clustering, video abstraction, key frames, static summaries, shot boundaries, video summarization

---

Corresponding author: kishan.sreeja@gmail.com

Mettu Srinivas, G. Sucharitha and Anjanna Matta (eds.) Machine Learning Algorithms and Applications, (117–140) © 2021 Scrivener Publishing LLC

7.1   Introduction

Video summarization plays a crucial role in effective information exploitation. The growing amount of video data being created and uploaded on the Internet has resulted in an exploding amount of digital information. Availability and ease of access to all sorts of recording devices has led to an increased pace at which videos are generated. The amount of video information being shared and processed on a day to day basis has substantially increased due to which the demand for video processing techniques has become a growing concern. Video summarization, a highly relevant branch of video processing techniques, aims at automatically generating an abstract view of the video so the user can go through the main events of the video in less time. Video summaries aim at providing a gist of the original video in a short duration of time.

Video summaries are typically of two types which are static and dynamic. Static summaries are generated by combining stationary key frames, whereas dynamic summaries are formed by combining key segments from the original video. Strategies adopted to identify and extract the key frames or segments from videos vary among different categories of videos. Similarly, the type of output summary suitable for different categories of videos also varies accordingly. The most effective and computationally efficient technique for video summarization is by employing clustering. Clustering is an unsupervised machine learning technique used for naturally grouping information based on similarity or dissimilarity metrics that differ according to the clustering method. The most common forms of clustering techniques utilized in video summarization are k-means, DBSCAN (density-based spatial clustering of applications with noise), hierarchical, and nearest neighbor algorithm. The distance metric or similarity computation is the factor that changes with each clustering method. The clustering algorithm adopted for summarizing videos vary significantly among applications. The importance of clustering algorithms in video summarization is well emphasized in the literature [1–3]. The various types of clustering methods used along with its effectiveness in different video summarization applications can also be examined. The effectiveness of various clustering techniques and how it varies according to each category of videos can also be observed in the existing works which further substantiates the relevance of conventional clustering approaches in all categories of video summarization [4].

For video summarization to be successful, it is essential to capture the details of the individual frames to a minute level so that information loss is minimal. Apart from minimizing information loss, it is necessary to ensure that the computational cost incurred is also minimal. Hence, in the proposed system, a modified block-based clustering approach is proposed where the clustering algorithm used is feature ag-glomeration. Each of the input frames of the video are divided into a set of blocks and clustering is performed on the respective sets of blocks from all the frames. This ensures that maximum information from the video is captured in the summary. Similarly, the procedures are conducted in compressed domain by performing DCT compression on the individual frames, thereby reducing computational cost. A comprehensive evaluation on the basis of quantitative parameters and qualitative parameters generally found in video summarization has been performed on the popular VSUMM dataset and the results are analyzed. Additionally, a block-based comparative analysis for finding the optimum block size is also conducted.

The major highlights of the proposed framework are as follows:

1. A hierarchical framework that utilizes modified block clustering approach for key frame detection coupled with histogram approach for shot boundary detection.
2. A discrete summarization framework using feature agglomeration clustering technique as opposed to traditional clustering approaches.
3. An optimized video summarization framework implemented in a compressed domain using Discrete Cosine Transform (DCT).

Section 7.2 summarizes the recent works done in video summarization with clustering as the major technique. Section 7.3 provides an introduction to feature agglomeration clustering technique. Methodology of the proposed system is detailed in Section 7.4 with the various stages and algorithms used. Section 7.5 analyzes in detail the results of quantitative and qualitative evaluations followed by conclusion and future scope in Section 7.6.

7.2   Related Works

A highlight of the recent works in video summarization using clustering as the major technique has been outlined below. De Avila *et al.* [5] propose a video summarization framework using k-means clustering. The HSV color features from individual frames are extracted and k-means clustering is performed. The cluster centers are chosen as the final key frame from each cluster. The disadvantage of k-means clustering is that number of clusters has to be determined earlier. Kumar *et al.* [6] implement another framework using k-means clustering. Here, K means clustering is applied onto the video in a two-stage process. In the first stage, the video as a whole is clustered into key frame groups, whereas in the second stage, frames are divided into equal size partitions and then clustering is applied. Mundur *et al.* [7] use Delaunay triangulation clustering for summarization as opposed to the traditional clustering approaches. Delaunay triangulation leads to clusters of different size based on the content significance and the advantage is that number of clusters need not be set in advance. A video summarization framework with spectral clustering is described by Cirne and Pedrini [8]. Spectral clustering utilizes spectrum (Eigen values) for clustering. Spectral approaches for clustering has shown better performance in all domains. Mishra and Singh [9] perform event summarization in videos by finding an optimal clustering algorithm. Frames closer to the cluster heads are chosen as key frames. A video summarization framework where summary is obtained by employing graph theoretic divisive clustering and by constructing minimum spanning tree to select key frames rather than segmenting to shots is implemented by Guimaraes and Gomes [10]. Sachan [11] proposes a framework where framesets are formed by grouping small number of similar contiguous, frames and then, agglomerative clustering is applied to group similar framesets. The importance of cluster is obtained from the number of frames in a cluster. Gharbi *et al.* [12] implement a framework where candidate frames for summarization are selected using a windowing rule. As a next stage, SURF [13] features from frames in candidate set are selected. A repeatability table is constructed which is viewed as a video similarity graph and clustering is performed on graph modularity. The framework implemented by Wu *et al.* [14] bases video representation on high density peak search clustering algorithm [15]. Majumdar *et al.* [16] uses Expectation-Maximization clustering for video summarization. Here, shot boundaries are detected by deploying a modified color layout descriptor [17]. A framework for video summarization in surveillance domain is designed using Density-based Spatial Clustering of Applications with Noise (DBSCAN) clustering technique and background subtraction by Zhao *et al.* [18]. HSV color features are utilized for the same. Background subtraction is performed after clustering for identifying the key frames. A detailed analysis of various clustering techniques used in video summarization currently is surveyed by John *et al.* [19].

Fei *et al.* [20] put forth a key frame extraction model combining sparse frame selection and agglomerative hierarchical clustering. Sparse frame selection is applied initially to obtain the first set of key frames. The criteria for clustering are content loss minimization and representativeness ranking. The clustering algorithm incorporated is also known as an improved mutual information-based agglomerative hierarchical clustering. Sony *et al.* [21] builds a video summarization framework based on clustering similar frames using Euclidean distance. The length of the summary is governed by user defined criteria. A fraction of frames with a comparatively larger Euclidean distance from each cluster is extracted to form the summary sequence. Iterative node segmentation algorithm is used for summarizing the video. Lv and Huang [22] extract key frames from personal videos using nearest neighbor clustering algorithm. Clustering is performed on frames based on the nearest neighbor algorithm which has the additional advantage of not setting the number of clusters beforehand. The clustering is not perfect but compared to other unsupervised clustering methods it performs better. Majumdar *et al.* [23] put forth a novel clustering algorithm named CURE (clustering using representativeness) hierarchical clustering. Cure clustering algorithm is applied for video summarization in healthcare application and big data and the extracted summaries are used for disease analysis and prediction. Chamasemani *et al.* [24] develop a video summarization framework using density-based clustering algorithm for surveillance videos. Global features such as color, texture, and energy, as well as local SURF features extracted for applying the clustering algorithm. The combined approach has resulted in a more informative summary compared to the state of the art. Kuanar *et al.* [25] propose a multi-view video summarization framework preferably for surveillance videos based on graph theory approach. Features are extracted on the basis of bag of words as well as color, texture, and shape before applying Gaussian entropy-based filtering. Clustering is performed by optimum path forest algorithm. The results prove that the summaries demonstrate the effectiveness of the semantic feature set extracted and the clustering employed. On a similar note, several works have emphasized the significance of hybrid clustering approaches. Srinivas and Mohan [26] put forth such a model where two clustering models based on incremental and hierarchical principles are combined. A novel cohesion metric is introduced for computing the inter-cluster distance. The significance of similarity measures for content-based image and video analysis is also described by Srinivas and Mohan [27] where efficient medical image classification is performed on the basis of a combined feature set with three different types of similarity measures.

7.3   Feature Agglomeration Clustering

Hierarchical clustering is a general family of clustering algorithms that build nested clusters by merging or splitting them successively. The root of the tree is the unique cluster that gathers all the samples, the leaves being the clusters with only one sample data. Hierarchical clustering algorithms can be divided into two classes: top-down approach and bottom-up approach. Bottom-up approach progresses by viewing each sample of data as one single cluster and continuously agglomerate or combine pairs of clusters until all the clusters have been combined into a single cluster. This single cluster consists of all the sample data. Hence, bottom-up hierarchical clustering is also termed as hierarchical agglomerative clustering. The Agglomerative clustering object performs a hierarchical clustering by starting in its own cluster, and clusters are successively merged together. A tree representation of this hierarchy of clusters is known as dendrogram. In feature agglomeration, instead of samples, features are merged. It is a dimensionality reduction tool. The prime difference between standard agglomeration and feature agglomeration is that, instead of clustering the samples in the received data matrix as done in standard agglomeration clustering, feature agglomeration performs clustering on the transpose of the standard matrix, thereby actually clustering the features rather than the samples. Euclidean distance is the default distance metric used for performing clustering on the features which are the sample data in the standard matrix. The linkage criterion determines the metric used for the merge strategy. The various linkage criteria are single, complete, average, ward's, etc. One main advantage of hierarchical clustering is that the number of clusters need not be specified beforehand. It can also be specified according to the application requirements. The choice of distance metric also does not influence the performance of the clustering as it is seen that all the metrics almost perform equally well. The choice of distance metric is crucial in other clustering algorithms. Hierarchical clustering is more preferable when the underlying dataset has a hierarchical structure which needs to be exploited for best results.

7.4   Proposed Methodology

The detailed framework of the proposed system is shown in Figure 7.1. The proposed framework performs video summarization in two phases, namely, (a) pre-processing and shot boundary detection and (b) modified

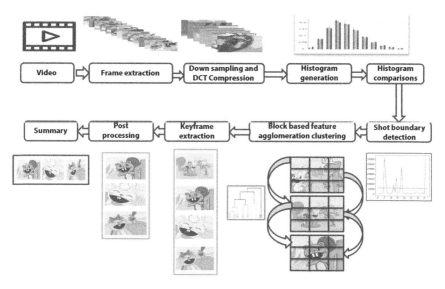

Figure 7.1 Proposed framework.

block clustering using feature agglomeration technique for summarization. The latter phase involves three stages, namely, (a) modified block clustering, (b) key frame extraction, and (c) post-processing and summary generation.

7.4.1 Pre-Processing

Video pre-processing is an essential step in every video processing application. The pre-processing stage in the proposed model consists of down sampling the frames, converting the extracted frames to compressed domain and identifying the shot boundaries.

Down sampling and frame compression. A video comprises of a set of frames which when put together gives the user a notion of continuity and motion. It is evident that majority of the time there is not much difference between the consecutive frames. Hence, not all the frames need to be processed and analyzed for its possibility of being a key frame. Instead, the video is typically down sampled so that it reduces the chances of processing redundant frames thereby making the model computationally efficient. The strategy for down sampling varies for different application. In the proposed model, once the input video is divided into individual frames, the frames are down sampled as one frame in frame rate of the video and compression is performed on the down sampled frames. The compression technique applied is DCT. The DCT transforms a frame from the spatial domain to frequency domain as in Equations (7.1) and (7.2).

$$F(u,v) = \frac{2}{\sqrt{MN}} C(u)C(v) \sum_{x=0}^{M-1} \sum_{y=0}^{N-1} (x,y)\cos\left[\frac{(2x+1)\mu\pi}{2M}\right]\cos\left[\frac{(2y+1)\mu\pi}{2N}\right]$$

(7.1)

$$f(x,y) = \frac{2}{\sqrt{MN}} \sum_{x=0}^{M-1} \sum_{y=0}^{N-1} C(u)C(v)F(u,v)\cos\left[\frac{(2x+1)\mu\pi}{2M}\right]\cos\left[\frac{(2y+1)\mu\pi}{2N}\right]$$

(7.2)

where $u, v, x, y = 0,1,2, \ldots N-1$ and

$$C(u), C(v) = \begin{cases} \dfrac{1}{\sqrt{2}} \ for \ u,v = 0 \\ 1 \quad for \ u,v > 0 \end{cases}$$

x,y and u,v are coordinates in the spatial and frequency domain, respectively. M and N are the size of the frame that the DCT is done. The equation calculates one entry $(x,y)^{th}$ of the transformed image from the pixel values of the frame matrix.

Shot boundary detection. Shot boundary detection is a crucial step for majority of the video summarization frameworks. However, there are certain categories of videos where it is not an essential requirement. A shot is detected when there is a major change in the background and foreground of consecutive frames are detected. Shot boundaries can be detected using various techniques like histogram comparisons and clustering. In the proposed model, shot boundaries are detected by comparing the histograms of the consecutive down sampled frames.

Once, the DCT of the down sampled frames are obtained, color histograms of the individual frames are computed. The distance between consecutive histograms is calculated using histogram comparison methods. The distance measure used is Bhattacharya distance from Equation (7.3).

$$d(H_1, H_2) = \sqrt{1 - \frac{1}{\sqrt{H_1 H_2 N^2}} \sum_I \sqrt{H_1(I).H_2(I)}}$$

(7.3)

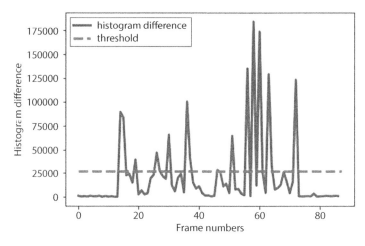

Figure 7.2 Plot of histogram comparison for shot boundary detection.

where N is the number of bins in the histogram and H_1 and H_2 are the histograms compared. The frames that have distance values higher than the threshold are identified as shot boundaries and the number of shot boundaries is retrieved. Figure 7.2 shows the detection of shot boundaries using histogram comparisons for a sample video named "Jumps.mp4". The red line represents the threshold, and the frame numbers corresponding to the peak points above the threshold are the frames where the histogram differences are maximum. This represents a scene or shot change since it can be deciphered that there is an overall change in the color distribution between the consecutive frames at that point. These frames can be identified as the shot boundaries. The threshold value for detecting a shot boundary is computed as the sum of mean and standard deviation of the histogram differences. The X axis shows the frame numbers and Y axis shows the histogram difference values for consecutive frames of the video.

7.4.2 Modified Block Clustering Using Feature Agglomeration Technique

Block clustering in compressed domain. The sampled and compressed frames are divided into $m*m$ blocks where m is the number of blocks into which the frame has to be divided. Histograms based on RGB color model for respective blocks from consecutive frames are computed. The ith clustering operation is defined on the set of histograms formed from the ith blocks of all frames. Histograms are the simplest classifier in use that can differentiate images based on color distribution.

The clustering approach used is Feature Agglomeration clustering as described in Section 7.3. The linkage criterion used is Wards criterion. Here, the objective function for which the optimal value has to be attained is the variance of the clusters under consideration. Ward's minimum variance method is implemented by the Lance Williams formula for disjoint clusters C_i, C_j, and C_k with sizes n_i, n_j, and n_k, respectively, as in Equation (7.4).

$$d(C_i \cup C_j, C_k) = \frac{n_i + n_k}{n_i + n_j + n_k} d(C_i, C_k)$$

$$+ \frac{n_j + n_k}{n_i + n_j + n_k} d(C_j, C_k) - \frac{n_k}{n_i + n_j + n_k} d(C_i, C_j) \tag{7.4}$$

The distance measure used is Euclidean distance from Equation (7.5).

$$d(x, y) = \sqrt{\sum_{i=1}^{n} (x_i - y_i)^2} \tag{7.5}$$

Respective blocks from frames are clustered separately as a result of which $m*m$ sets of clusters are formed. A representative frame from each cluster set, known as the candidate frame, has to be chosen. Suppose, for the ith block of a frame, the sets of clusters formed are represented as in Equation (7.6).

$$X_i = \left[[x_{i1}], [x_{i2}], [x_{i3}], \ldots [x_{ik_i}] \right] \tag{7.6}$$

where k_i is the number of clusters formed in the ith block.

The number of cluster sets formed will be m*m. Suppose that the representative frame chosen from the X_{il}^{th} cluster is x_{il}. Then, the candidate frames from each cluster for each block can be represented as in Equation (7.7).

$$X_i = \left[x_{i1}, x_{i2}, x_{i3}, \ldots x_{ik_i} \right] \tag{7.7}$$

where x_{ij} is the representative frame in the ith block j^{th} cluster and $i = 1$ to $m*m$ and $j = 1$ to k_i. The candidate frame chosen from each cluster is the frame with the maximum index in a cluster. The sets of candidate frames formed from each cluster will have overlapping frames. Hence, it is necessary to develop a strategy with which the key frames can be extracted from these sets.

Key frame extraction. The next phase is to extract the key frames from the representative sets of candidate frames from each cluster. Since the number of cluster sets is $m*m$, it can be clearly stated that if a frame appears in more than half of the count of sets, the corresponding frame can be identified as a key frame. Equation (7.8) shows the representation of key frames.

$$Keyframes = \left\{ x_{i,j} \text{ such that the frequency of } x_{i,j} \geq \frac{m*m}{2} \right\}, \quad (7.8)$$

where $m*m$ is the number of blocks to which the frame is divided.

7.4.3   Post-Processing and Summary Generation

Post-processing. In order to eliminate similar frames in the resulting key frame set, a final post-processing has been performed in the model. The goal is to find the highly similar frames and to discard them to avoid redundancy. Several metrics can be adopted to achieve the same. The similarity computation metric which when experimented in the proposed model and gave best results is Structural Similarity Index [28], as in Equation (7.9).

$$SSIM(x, y) = \frac{(2\mu_x\mu_y + c_1)(2\sigma_{xy} + c_2)}{\left(\mu_x^2 + \mu_y^2 + c_1\right)\left(\sigma_x^2 + \sigma_y^2 + c_2\right)} \quad (7.9)$$

where
$\quad \mu_x$ and μ_y are the respective averages of x and y.
$\quad \sigma_x^2$ and σ_y^2 are the respective variances of x and y.
$\quad \sigma_{xy}$ is the covariance and c_1 and c_2 are constants.

The SSIM between frames in the key frame set is computed. The SSIM value ranges between -1 and 1 where 1 indicates perfect similarity. If the SSIM value is approximately 1, then only either of the frames is kept as key frame. The SSIM index is set to 0.5, greater than which the frames are treated as similar and discarded. The key frames extracted by the proposed framework before and after post-processing for a sample video "v11.flv" from cartoons category with duration less than 1 minute, is depicted in Figures 7.3a and b, respectively. It is evident from Figure 7.3b that the redundant frames have been eliminated after the post-processing stage.

Figure 7.3 Key frames extracted by the proposed framework: (a) before post-processing and (b) after post-processing.

Summary generation. The final key frame set is combined to form the final static summary. The summary generated by the proposed system and VSUMM [5] framework for a sample video "v100.avi" from news category with duration between 1 and 3 minutes is shown in Figures 7.4a and b, respectively. It is obvious from the comparison that the proposed framework could retrieve majority of the relevant frames, but the total number of key frames identified by the system is comparatively high. This results in a drop in precision of the system but it significantly improves the quality of the summary in terms of enjoyability and continuity. A step-by-step algorithm of the work flow of the proposed model is detailed in Algorithms 7.1 and 7.2.

Algorithm 7.1 Pre-processing and shot boundary detection.

Input: Video to be summarized, V
Output: Shot boundaries, S

---

1. Down sample video V as $V=\{F_j\}$, if i mod fps ==0 and i=1,2..number of frames.
2. $F = DCT(F)$ and $H=histogram(F)$
3. $C = \{$histogram comparison$(F_1...F_{n-1})$ $\}$
4. Threshold, $t=$sum(mean(C)+std(C))
5. Shot Boundaries, $S=\{F[i-1]$ where $C[i]>t\}$, $i = 1,2,...$n.

Figure 7.4 (a) Proposed system summary. (b) VSUMM summary.

Algorithm 7.2 Modified block clustering in compressed domain and summarization.

Input: Compressed frame set F, Number of shot boundaries c, and Number of blocks m.
Output: Video Summary

Stage 1: Modified block clustering in compressed domain

1. Divide F to m^*m blocks.
2. Perform Feature Agglomeration clustering on k^{th} block of frameset F with $k=1,2,..m$.
3. $[[Xij]]$ = set of clusters formed for i^{th} block j^{th} cluster, $i=1,..m$ and $j=1,2...m^*m$.
4. Candidate frames x_{ij} = max{indices from each cluster}
5. $[x_{ij}]$ = representative frames from each cluster set corresponding to each block

Stage II. Key frame extraction

1. $K= \{x_{ij}, \text{if } |x_{ij}|>=m^*m/2\}$ for all m^*m sets of frames.

Stage III. Post-processing and summary generation

1. If SSIM $(x,y)>0.5$, frame is discarded where x and y are frames in K,
2. Summary = Final key frame set $\{K\}$

7.5   Results and Analysis

The various experiments conducted to analyze the efficiency of the proposed model is elaborated in this section. The quantitative and qualitative performance metrics used for the evaluation is detailed followed by the comparison of results obtained in the evaluation section.

7.5.1   Experimental Setup and Data Sets Used

The framework is implemented and experimented in python Spyder IDE on Intel i5 processor with 4GB RAM and 64bit OS. The videos experimented belong to different categories including cartoons, news and documentaries, TV shows, etc., of varying duration from the benchmark

VSUMM database. The evaluation criteria and the results obtained for the proposed framework is detailed in the following sections.

7.5.2   Evaluation Metrics

There is currently no existing standard evaluation criterion for video summarization frameworks. Evaluations are generally based on either quantitative measure, qualitative measures, or a combination of both. The proposed framework has been evaluated based on the combination of quantitative and qualitative parameters.

Quantitative parameters. The various quantitative parameters used for performance evaluation are computation time (CT), compression ratio (CR), precision, recall, and f-score. Additionally, the framework applies varying block sizes on frames for clustering. Hence, a detailed evaluation on the basis of varying block sizes has also been included in the quantitative analysis.

CT is defined as the time taken from inputting the video to summary generation. It is also known as the running time of the system for processing a video for automatic summary generation. CR is defined as the fraction of frames that are retrieved as the key frames for the final summary. It is the ratio of the count of final key frames to the total number of frames in the source video. It is computed based on Equation (7.10).

$$CR = 1 - \frac{Number\ of\ key\ frames}{Total\ number\ frames\ in\ the\ video} \tag{7.10}$$

Precision is defined as the fraction of relevant frames among the retrieved frames and is evaluated from Equation (7.11).

$$Precision = \frac{|\{Relevant\ frames\} \cap \{retrieved\ frames\}|}{|\{retrieved\ frames\}|} \tag{7.11}$$

Recall is the fraction of relevant instances that have been retrieved over the total amount of relevant instances and is evaluated from Equation (7.12).

$$Recall = \frac{|\{Relevant\ frames\} \cap \{retrieved\ frames\}|}{|\{relevant\ frames\}|} \tag{7.12}$$

F-score is the harmonic mean of precision and recall and trades off the drawbacks of precision and recall and is evaluated from Equation (7.13).

$$F\_score = \frac{2 * Precision * Recall}{Precision + Recall} \qquad (7.13)$$

It is noteworthy that for all the above metrics, a higher value denotes ideal performance except for CT where a lower value is desirable.

Qualitative parameters. The various qualitative parameters used for performance evaluation are informativeness, enjoyability, continuity, diversity, coverage, and overall score which are defined below.

Informativeness. Informativeness is the measure of how well the generated summary provides information about the original video.

Enjoyability. Enjoyability measures the extent to which the generated summary covers the frames that provide entertainment particularly in movie genre.

Coverage. Coverage evaluates how well the generated summary encompasses the important events in the original video.

Continuity. Continuity is defined as the extent to which the maintenance of consistency or unbroken flow in scenes is maintained while combining the key frames.

Diversity. Diversity is the measure which evaluates the extent to which the summary includes variety of events or scenes and ensures minimal redundancy in frames.

Overall score. Overall score is the combined score of all the above subjective parameters.

Similar to quantitative metrics, a higher value in all the qualitative metrics is desirable for an ideal video summarization framework.

7.5.3   Evaluation

Quantitative analysis. Quantitative analysis based on varying block size, CT, CR, precision, recall, and f-score are detailed in the following sections.

Varying block size. The clustering performed in the proposed model is a block-based approach where frames are divided into blocks and corresponding blocks from consecutive frames in the shots are clustered. Experiments are conducted by varying the block size to identify the perfect block size in order to achieve the optimum results. Table 7.1 shows the key frame count (KF#), CT, and CR achieved for a sample set of videos by varying the block sizes in the range 1 to 6 where TF is the total frame count

Table 7.1 Comparison based on varying block size.

Sl. no.	Sample video	Duration	TF#	Block size m	m*m	KF#	CR	Average CT (seconds)
1	S1	46s	1,155	1	1	12	1.4	1.195
				2	4	11	0.96	2.105
				3	**9**	**9**	**0.8**	**2.905**
				4	16	10	0.9	3.605
				5	25	8	0.7	4.205
				6	36	8	0.7	5.095
2	S2	1m12s	2,180	1	1	18	0.83	3.2
				2	4	10	1.3	5.1
				3	9	9	0.5	5.8
				4	16	8	0.5	6
				5	**25**	**8**	**0.5**	**7.2**
				6	36	8	0.5	7.3

(Continued)

Table 7.1 Comparison based on varying block size. (Continued)

Sl. no.	Sample video	Duration	TF#	Block size m	m*m	KF#	CR	Average CT (seconds)
3	S3	38s	950	1	1	10	1.1	2.57
				2	4	9	1	3.44
				3	**9**	**8**	**0.9**	**3.86**
				4	16	6	0.7	4.78
				5	25	6	0.5	5.47
				6	36	5	0.5	6.47
4	S4	3m55s	5,875	1	1	60	1	5.658
				2	4	99	1.7	11.04
				3	9	87	1.5	14.2
				4	16	65	1.2	17
				5	**25**	**55**	**1.1**	**22**
				6	**36**	**52**	**1**	**33**

(Continued)

Table 7.1 Comparison based on varying block size. (*Continued*)

Sl. no.	Sample video	Duration	TF#	Block size m	m*m	KF#	CR	Average CT (seconds)
5	S5	1m49s	3,291	1	1	48	1.5	5.51
				2	4	48	1.5	9.2
				3	9	36	1.1	9.5
				4	16	36	1.1	11.9
				5	25	20	0.7	13.9
				6	36	19	0.5	17.9

of the video. Sample videos represented by S1, S2, S3, S4, and S5 are v11. flv, v100.avi, Jumps.mp4, v103.avi, and greatwebofwater.mpg, respectively. The block sizes for which optimum results are achieved are highlighted in bold. It can be observed that for videos with duration less than 1 minute, the optimum block size was reached by 3 after which there was no major change in the summary generated. But for videos with longer duration, the best summary achieved was for higher block sizes. It can be seen that for the sample video S5 with duration more than 3 minutes, the optimum summary was achieved with block sizes 5 and 6. It is evident from these facts that for videos with even longer duration, the increase in block size will result in better quality summaries whereas for shorter videos, increase in block size might just increase the computational overhead rather than producing better results.

Computation time (CT) and compression ratio (CR). The average CR achieved and CT taken by the proposed framework for videos of different duration is plotted in Figures 7.5a and b, respectively. The presence of DCT compression stage has led to significant reduction in CT. The reduction in CT can also be attributed to the adoption of a variant of conventional widely accepted clustering technique for summarization. Even when the duration of videos is longer the CT taken has not drastically increased. The results for CR are also promising. The summaries extracted are less than 5 percentage of the original video which is a desirable property of video summaries.

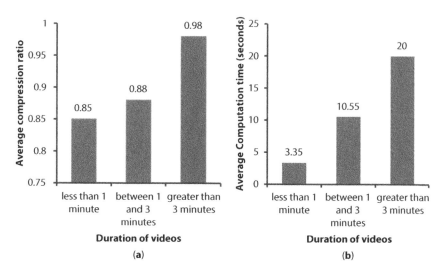

Figure 7.5 Performance of proposed framework based on (a) average compression ratio and (b) average computation time.

Precision, recall, and f-score. Precision, recall, and f-score are computed by comparing the generated summaries of the proposed framework with ground truth summaries for the sample videos in the dataset. The average results obtained for precision, recall, and f-scores for the proposed system and existing frameworks are plotted in Figure 7.6. The existing frameworks with which the performance of the proposed framework is compared are VSUMM [5], Delaunay Triangulation [7], and VRCVS [14]. The average f-score obtained for the proposed system is 72% which is relatively high compared with the previous systems. A higher f-score is always a desirable factor in the performance of video summarization frameworks. F-score trades off the drawbacks of using precision and recall alone for information retrieval systems. However, it can be observed that the average precision value obtained is not the best. This is due to the fact that number of key frames retrieved by the proposed framework is comparatively higher than the compared models. Since precision is the fraction of relevant frames in the retrieved key frames, when the number of retrieved frames is slightly higher, it is quite obvious that the precision value tends to be on the lower side as they are inversely proportional. On the other hand, there is a spike in the value of recall compared to other models. Since, recall is the fraction of relevant frames retrieved among total relevant frames, a higher value indicates that the number of relevant frames retrieved as key frames by the proposed model is on the higher side. It can be observed that the average recall value obtained is 88% which substantiates that the proposed system

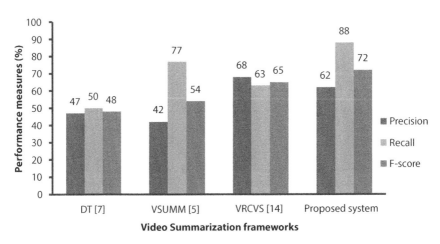

Figure 7.6 Comparison of proposed system with existing systems based on quantitative metrics.

was capable of identifying and retrieving a higher share of the relevant frames from the ground truth. On the whole, the results of quantitative analysis prove that the model shows superior performance considering the minimal complexities involved.

Qualitative analysis. Qualitative evaluation is performed on a set of 20 users. The qualitative parameters considered for evaluation are informativeness, enjoyability, diversity, continuity, and overall score each of them ranging from 1 to 5 where 5 is the best. The users were asked to provide a score for each parameter based on the generated summary and the results are averaged. The performance of the system based on the qualitative parameters is plotted in Figure 7.7. It can be observed that the informativeness parameter obtained, which measures the informative content present in the summary compared to original video, is high for all categories of videos. The results for enjoyability parameter are also promising. This shows that in commercial videos like cartoons, the model is capable of extracting frames that not only provides useful information but also provides entertaining details too. Diversity and continuity results are also satisfactory but are not the best. Diversity tends to be on the lower side because the number of key frames retrieved is slightly high for the proposed system. Similarly, since the output generated is static summary, continuity which measures the unobstructed flow of information is also on the lower side. However, the overall score obtained for the proposed framework is high for all categories of videos which substantiates the acceptability of the model.

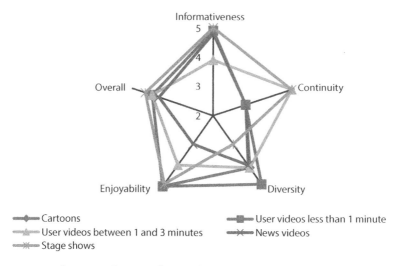

Figure 7.7 Performance of proposed system based on qualitative measures.

7.6   Conclusion

Video summarization aims at providing a gist of the video to the user by automatically identifying relevant frames or segments from a video. An ideal video summary should be informative, representative, and at the same time concise. The proposed system implements a key frame–based video summarization framework based on feature agglomeration clustering. The clustering is applied on sets of individual blocks of the sampled frames. The results prove that the system is computationally efficient due to the clustering technique used and the compression stage incorporated. Additionally, it can be seen that when clustering is applied on varying block sizes, extraction of maximum information from the video is ensured. In quantitative analysis, the framework achieves a relatively high f-score than the existing systems. The results can be improved by modifying the block size based on duration of videos. Qualitative analysis also demonstrates that the system is capable of producing summaries that are diverse, informative, and enjoyable. Enhancing the system by making it real time is yet to be realized which can further make the computation efficient in terms of space and time. Likewise, employing deep learning techniques which has gained high popularity these days due to its amazing performance in all domains is also a prospective future concern.

References

1. Ajmal, M., Ashraf, M.H., Shakir, M., Abbas, Y., Shah, F.A., Video summarization: techniques and classification, in: *International Conference on Computer Vision and Graphics*, Springer, Berlin, Heidelberg, pp. 1–13, 2012.
2. Kaur, P. and Kumar, R., Analysis of video summarization techniques. *Int. J. Res. Appl. Sci. Eng. Technol., (IJRASET)*, 6, 1, 1157–1162, 2018.
3. Moses, T.M. and Balachandran, K., A classified study on semantic analysis of video summarization, in: *2017 International Conference on Algorithms, Methodology, Models and Applications in Emerging Technologies (ICAMMAET)*, IEEE, pp. 1–6, 2017.
4. Sreeja, M.U. and Kovoor, B.C., Towards genre-specific frameworks for video summarization: A survey. *J. Visual Commun. Image Represent.*, 62, 340–358, 2019.
5. De Avila, S.E.F., Lopes, A.P.B., da Luz Jr., A., de Albuquerque Araújo, A., VSUMM: A mechanism designed to produce static video summaries and a novel evaluation method. *Pattern Recognit. Lett.*, 32, 1, 56–68, 2011.
6. Kumar, K., Shrimankar, D.D., Singh, N., Equal partition based clustering approach for event summarization in videos, in: *Signal-Image Technology*

& Internet-Based Systems (SITIS), 12th International Conference on, IEEE, pp. 119–126, 2016.

7. Mundur, P., Rao, Y., Yesha, Y., Keyframe-based video summarization using Delaunay clustering. *Int. J. Digit. Libr.*, 6, 2, 219–232, 2006.

8. Cirne, M.V.M. and Pedrini, H., A Video Summarization Method Based on Spectral Clustering, in: *Iberoamerican Congress on Pattern Recognition*, pp. 479–486, Springer, Berlin, Heidelberg, 2013.

9. Mishra, D.K. and Singh, N., Parameter Free Clustering Approach for Event Summarization in Videos, in: *Proceedings of International Conference on Computer Vision and Image Processing*, Springer, Singapore, pp. 389–397, 2017.

10. Guimarães, S.J.F. and Gomes, W., A static video summarization method based on hierarchical clustering, in: *Iberoamerican Congress on Pattern Recognition*, pp. 46–54, Springer, Berlin, Heidelberg, 2010.

11. Sachan, P.R., Frame clustering technique towards single video summarization, in: *Cognitive Computing and Information Processing (CCIP), Second International Conference on*, IEEE, pp. 1–5, 2016.

12. Gharbi, H., Bahroun, S., Massaoudi, M., Zagrouba, E., Key frames extraction using graph modularity clustering for efficient video summarization, in: *Acoustics, Speech and Signal Processing (ICASSP), IEEE International Conference on*, pp. 1502–1506, 2017.

13. Bay, H., Ess, A., Tuytelaars, T., Van Gool, L., Speeded-up robust features (SURF). *Comput. Vision Image Understanding*, 110, 3, 346–359, 2008.

14. Wu, J., Zhong, S.H., Jiang, J., Yang, Y., A novel clustering method for static video summarization. *Multimed. Tools Appl.*, 76, 7, 9625–9641, 2017.

15. Rodriguez, A. and Laio, A., Clustering by fast search and find of density peaks. *Science*, 344, 6191, 1492–1496, 2014.

16. Majumdar, J., Kumar, K.S., Venkatesh, G.M., Analysis of video shot detection using color layout descriptor and video summarization based on expectation-maximization clustering, in: *Cognitive Computing and Information Processing (CCIP), International Conference on*, IEEE, pp. 1–5, 2015.

17. Cvetkovic, S., Jelenkovic, M., Nikolic, S.V., Video summarization using color features and efficient adaptive threshold technique. *Prz. Elektrotech.*, 89, 2, 247–250, 2013.

18. Zhao, Y., Lv, G., Ma, T., Ji, H., Zheng, H., A novel method of surveillance video Summarization based on clustering and background subtraction, in: *Image and Signal Processing (CISP), 8th International Congress on*, IEEE, pp. 131–136, 2015.

19. John, A.A., Nair, B.B., Kumar, P.N., Application of Clustering Techniques for Video Summarization–An Empirical Study, in: *Computer Science On-line Conference*, Springer, Cham, pp. 494–506, 2017.

20. Fei, M., Jiang, W., Mao, W., Song, Z., New fusional framework combining sparse selection and clustering for key frame extraction. *IET Comput. Vision*, 10, 4, 280–288, 2016.

21. Sony, A., Ajith, K., Thomas, K., Thomas, T., Deepa, P.L., Video summarization by clustering using Euclidean distance, in: *2011 International Conference on Signal Processing, Communication, Computing and Networking Technologies*, IEEE, pp. 642–646, 2011.

22. Lv, C. and Huang, Y., Effective Keyframe Extraction from Personal Video by Using Nearest Neighbor Clustering, in: *2018 11th International Congress on Image and Signal Processing, BioMedical Engineering and Informatics (CISP-BMEI)*, IEEE, pp. 1–4, 2018.

23. Majumdar, J., Udandakar, S., Bai, B.M., Implementation of Cure Clustering Algorithm for Video Summarization and Healthcare Applications in Big Data, in: *Emerging Research in Computing, Information, Communication and Applications*, pp. 553–564, Springer, Singapore, 2019.

24. Chamasemani, F.F., Affendey, L.S., Mustapha, N., Khalid, F., Video abstraction using density-based clustering algorithm. *Vis. Comput.*, 34, 10, 1299–1314, 2018.

25. Kuanar, S.K., Ranga, K.B., Chowdhury, A.S., Multi-view video summarization using bipartite matching constrained optimum-path forest clustering. *IEEE Trans. Multimedia*, 17, 8, 1166–1173, 2015.

26. Srinivas, M. and Mohan, C.K., Efficient clustering approach using incremental and hierarchical clustering methods. *International Joint Conference on Neural Networks (IJCNN)*, Barcelona, pp. 1–7, 2010.

27. Srinivas, M. and Mohan, C.K., Medical Image Indexing and Retrieval Using Multiple Features, in: *International Conference on Computational Intelligence and Information Technology*, October 2013.

28. Wang, Z., Bovik, A.C., Sheikh, H.R., Simoncelli, E.P., Image quality assessment: from error visibility to structural similarity. *IEEE Trans. Image Process.*, 13, 4, 600–612, 2004.

Part 2

MACHINE LEARNING FOR HEALTHCARE SYSTEMS

8

Cardiac Arrhythmia Detection and Classification From ECG Signals Using XGBoost Classifier

Saroj Kumar Pandeyz*, Rekh Ram Janghel and Vaibhav Gupta

Department of Information Technology, National Institute of Technology, Raipur, India (C.G.) India

Abstract

In this paper, we propose an effective electrocardiogram (ECG) signal classification method using XGBoost classifier. The ECG signals are passed through four phases of data acquisition, noise filtering, feature extraction, and classification. In first phase, dataset is collected from the MIT-BIH arrhythmia database. In second phase, noise is removed using baseline wandering removal filter. In next phase, 45 descriptors from four prominent features which showed good results in previous work, namely, wavelets, higher order statistics (HOS), morphological descriptors, and R-R intervals, are being employed. Using these features as an input to the XGBoost classifier, the signals are being classified into four classes (N, S, V, and F) as per the ANSI-AAMI standards; of all the classifiers, XGBoost shows best result with an accuracy of 99.43%.

Keywords: Arrhythmia, XGBoost, ECG, wavelet, morphology, R-R interval

8.1 Introduction

Arrhythmia is defined as an abnormality in normal heart rate; it is a general indication of cardiovascular diseases which can be severe in most cases if left unattended. It signifies that the heart is not beating at its normal rate or it is beating with an irregular pattern [1]. Timely detection of this

---

*Corresponding author: skpandey.phd2016.it@nitrr.ac.in

Mettu Srinivas, G. Sucharitha and Anjanna Matta (eds.) Machine Learning Algorithms and Applications, (143–158) © 2021 Scrivener Publishing LLC

irregularity is helpful in curing it and saving the patient from cardiovascular diseases [2].

Electrocardiogram (ECG) signal, which is the result of electrical activity in the heart due to its depolarization and repolarization, is used. It is measured by putting electrodes at various points of the body and is recorded when the heart goes through its cardiac cycle. ECGs from healthy persons have a characteristic natural shape; any kind of abnormality can change the electrical activity of the heart which, in turn, leads to change in ECG shape. Diseases like abnormal heart rhythms, heart attack can be detected using arrhythmia detection. Classification of ECG signals as normal or arrhythmic is a challenging task and, if done manually, can lead to a lot of errors and wrong detection. This is why a lot of work is needed in this field of arrhythmia detection [3].

Different papers have taken the ECG signals from different databases; two of the most common ones are MIT-BIH and ECG-ID arrhythmia database. The dataset from these sources are not completely pure as they have various high frequency noises. These are unwanted and can affect our results if not removed. So, the dataset is made to go through the process of de-noising. Generally, noises include power line interference of 50/60 Hz that is caused by electromagnetic interference of power line, electromyography (EMG) noise that comes at the time of muscle activity and baseline wandering which is the low-frequency component is present in ECG system. To get rid of these noises, different filters have been employed in different papers like digital Infinite Impulse Response (IIR) filter, which is a type of notch filter capable of removing power line interference, along with that Finite Impulse Response (FIR) filters, which have also been used [4].

After getting the dataset noise free from the databases, the next step is feature extraction; features are the descriptors which basically define the condition of the datasets. Many different feature extraction techniques have been used in different papers; most of them are based on frequency and time techniques. The extracted features of time domain are heart-beat intervals, duration parameters (PR, QT, and QRS), amplitude features (ST and QRS). The features extracted from time domain are not very good discriminant. In place of time domain features, frequency domain methods are a better alternative; therefore, techniques like power spectral density (PSD) and Fourier transform are popular in this field, but the problem with frequency methods is that they do not provide the temporal information of the ECG signals. Out of all the frequency domain methods, wavelet transform is the most widely used one [5].

Mahmoud *et al.* [6] proposed a technique where a set of non-fiducial features, fiducial features, and a fusion of non-fiducial and fiducial features has been used, for classification three classifiers Artificial Neural Network (ANN), K-Nearest Neighbour (KNN), and Support Vector Machine (SVM) have been used. Rajagopal *et al.* [7] used a set of features including 1) temporal features of heartbeat such as P-Q interval, the QRS interval, the S-T interval, the Q-R interval, and the R-R interval between adjacent heartbeats; 2) amplitude-based features; 3) wavelet transform–based features like Harr wavelets and Daubechies wavelets; 4) Stockwell transform–based features and for classification a model that employs collaborative decision from KNN and SVM, has been used. Mondejarr-Guerra *et al.* [8] presented classification using features such as wavelets, higher order statistics (HOS), 1D local binary pattern, morphological descriptors, and R-R intervals were employed; for classification, an ensemble of SVM has been used as classifier where each feature is provided to an SVM and its result are taken and then combined by One-Versus-One (OVO) voting strategy, to get the output class.

Mathews *et al.* [9] dealt with classification using Deep Belief Network (DBN) and Restricted Boltzmann Machine (RBM) that have been used for the classification of supraventricular and ventricular heartbeats. Sannino *et al.* [10] proposed Deep Neural Network; it compared to 11 other WEKA tool and gives better accuracy. Diker *et al.* [12] used pan Tompkins and discrete wavelet transform (DWT) methods were used for extracting critical points, which are then fed to traditional extreme machine learning algorithm.

This paper discusses ECG classification and is organized as follows: Section 8.2 discusses the features selected for the ECG classification and overview of theoretical background. Section 8.2 also presents the main classifiers used in this paper involving its architecture. Section 8.3 focuses on the experimental results obtained and comparison with other existing works. Conclusion extracted from this work is mentioned in Section 8.4.

8.2 Materials and Methods

The dataset has been taken from MIT-BIH database and is pre-processed first to remove the noises. Then, features are extracted from the dataset which are used by the classifier to classify the signals into four classes (N, S, V, and F) as per the ANSI-AAMI standard. Different steps involved in the process can be summarized by the following workflow diagram Figure 8.1.

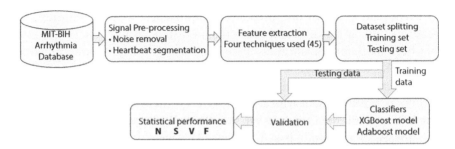

Figure 8.1 Workflow diagram describing the approach to ECG classification used in the paper.

8.2.1   MIT-BIH Arrhythmia Database

The database contains ECG signals from 47 patients of about 30 minutes which is sampled at 360 Hz at 11-bit resolution. There are two signals in each record modified-lead II (ML II), and one of V1, V2, V4, or V5. As ML II is common in all the records, only it is considered while doing the classification, and there are approximately 110,000 beats. These beats have been classified into five classes [11]. There are certain records that contain paced beats which are not considered for the process of classification. The database is highly imbalanced with majority of beats belonging to Normal (N) class. The database distribution is presented in Table 8.1. The unknown beat (Q) class has been ignored in this work as it is practically non-existent with very rare samples belonging to this class [12, 13]. The database has been used using the intra-patient's scheme where the dataset is taken together and from that collection some are used for training and some for testing. In this work, only out of signals from all the other electrodes only lead II are taken into consideration [14].

Table 8.1 Classes present in MIT-BIH database with their percentage.

Classes	Records (%)
N	90
SVEB	3
VEB	6
F	1

8.2.2   Signal Pre-Processing

Pre-processing is the step in which we filter the signals so that the features extracted from the signal are pure and without any noise and disturbances. This is crucial as this directly affects the classification results. Median filter are useful in reducing random noise using the median value in the segmented window. In this paper, baseline wandering removal using the median filter with a local window size of kernel size 180 has been proposed.

8.2.3   Feature Extraction

In this paper, for the purpose of extraction of features, symmetric window of size 180 was taken around the R-peak and features were extracted from the window. The features extracted were as follows.

Wavelets: Wavelets are the descriptor of the waveform of the ECG signal so they contain information of the time as well as frequency domain, Daubechies wavelet function (db1) with 3 levels of decomposition has been applied here. It provides in total 23 descriptors. This is proved to give relevant information by different authors [15].

RR-Interval: The highest point in the amplitude of the ECG signal is the R-peak, distance between the successive R-peaks can give useful information about the state of ECG signals, and it is categorized into four types, namely, Pre-RR, which is the distance between current and preceding R peak, Post-RR, that is the distance between current and following R peak, local RR, which is the mean value of previous 10 pre-RR values, and global-RR, which I the mean value of the pre-RR values of last twenty minutes. In addition to these, their normalized values are also used so total 8 features are extracted from the RR-Interval [16].

Higher Order Statistics (HOS): HOS is particularly useful in estimation of the shape parameters such as skewness and kurtosis; here, the functions uses third or higher powers unlike the lower order statistics which uses zeroth, linear, and quadratic functions. Skewness refers to the asymmetry of the probability distribution about the mean, while kurtosis is a measure of tailenders of the probability distribution. Here, each beat is divided into five intervals and from each interval a 10-dimensional feature is created; now, from these intervals, skewness and kurtosis values are calculated [17].

Morphological descriptor: The signal is segmented to a window size of 180 and values from this segment is taken. It is the Euclidean distance of the R-peaks and four different points taken from the beats. Four amplitude values are considered which are 10 maximum from beat [0,40], minimum from beat [75, 85], minimum from beat (95,105), and maximum from beat (150, 180).

8.2.4 Classification

Two prominent classifiers, namely, XGBoost and AdaBoost have been used for the classification of the MIT-BIH Arrhythmia database. The working of XGBoost classifier and AdaBoost classifier is mentioned/given in the following.

8.2.4.1 XGBoost Classifier

XGBoost classifier is an implementation of gradient boosted decision tree that uses ensemble machine learning algorithm. It gives good classification by boosting the weak learners using the gradient descent architecture. Boosting is an ensemble technique where new models are added to correct the errors made in previous models. It is generally faster than other implementation of gradient boosting and also gives dominates other classifiers on structured or tabular datasets [17]. XGBoost is an ensemble based machine learning classifier originally constructed from a set of classification and regression trees (CART). When XGBoost is applied to the classification of the dataset, the model uses a training dataset x to predict the output $\hat{Y}_{out}$, which is as follows:

$$\hat{Y}_{out} = \sum_{i=1}^{I} f_i(x_i), f_i \in A \tag{8.1}$$

where I denotes the total trees, and f_i is a function in the functional space A for i^{th} tree, and A is a set having all possible CARTs. In the training model, each of the trained CARTs will attempt to supplement the far-flung residual. The objective function (D) been optimized at $(n+1)^{th}$ CART is as follows:

$$D = \sum_{k=1}^{t} l\left(y_k, \hat{y}_k^{(n)}\right) + \sum_{k=1}^{n} \Omega(f_k) \tag{8.2}$$

where $l()$ is the training loss function, y_k is the actual output value, and $\hat{y}_k^{(n)}$ is the predicted values at time step n. The function $\Omega()$ is a regularization term and described as follows:

$$\Omega(f) = \gamma L + \frac{1}{2}\lambda \sum_{l=1}^{L} w_l^2 \qquad (8.3)$$

where L denotes the number of leaves and w_i is the score on l^{th} leaf. When Equation (8.3) is optimized, the gradient descent can work for the differential loss function because it uses a Taylor expansion. In addition, the XGBoost model has no need for feature selection, as good features will be selected as nodes in the tree. In this study, we use Python programming with a scikit learn library for the XGBoost classifier. The input sample of each heartbeat has a total of 45 features and classifies the output into four distinct classes. It is configured with a learning rate of one, and the number of boosting stages, i.e., n-estimator is fixed at 50.

8.2.4.2   AdaBoost Classifier

AdaBoost is a machine learning meta algorithm, which was developed by Robert Schapire and Yoavfreund. It is the short form of Adaptive Boosting algorithm and basically works on the principle of combining the weak classifiers to a weighted sum that represents the final output, thus this model converges to strong learner [18]. The main purpose of this classifier is to reduce the error rate of weak classifiers by introducing a new classifier. Adaboost is the most sensitive algorithm described as noise data:

$$F(x) = sign\left(\sum_{m=1}^{M} \theta_m f_m(x)\right) \qquad (8.4)$$

Where
$\quad$ f_m: The mth weak classifier.
$\quad$ θ_m: The corresponding weight.

8.3   Results and Discussion

Following the AAMI specifications, confusion matrix has been used for the purpose of performance evaluation. Confusion matrix, also called as error matrix, is a specific table layout that helps in visualization of performance of an algorithm. It completely describes the classification performance. Various parameters are computed from the confusion matrix that helps in performance analysis. In this work, three measurements are used to evaluate the performance of our approaches; these are accuracy, specificity, and sensitivity.

$$Accuracy = \frac{TP + TN}{TP + TN + FP + FN} \tag{8.5}$$

$$Sensitivity = \frac{TP}{TP + FN} \tag{8.6}$$

$$Specificity = \frac{TN}{TN + FN} \tag{8.7}$$

The below experiments have been performed in system with processor of core i5 with 1.6-GHz main frequency and 8-GB main memory under ubuntu 18.04.03 LTS 64-bit operating system. Intra-patient scheme has been used here for obtaining the training and testing dataset from the MIT-BIH database; in this, we split the database in a certain ratio such that one part of it is used for training the classifier and the other part for testing it; the following table [8.2–8.6] shows the result obtained on splitting the database in different ratio.

Table 8.2 shows the results obtained on splitting the arrhythmia database in 60-40 ratio. Approximately, 60,414 records are used for training the classifier, and approximately, 40,277 are used for testing its predictions. This gives an overall accuracy of 99.26% and a precision of 99.36%.

It is clear from Table 8.2 that the XGBoost model classifies the MIT-BIH arrhythmia database into four distinct classes according to ANSI-AAMI standards and achieves an average accuracy of 99.81%, average sensitivity of 99.07% and average precision of 99.36%.

Table 8.3 shows the results obtained on splitting the database in 50-50 train-test ratio. Approximately, 50,345 records are used for training the classifier, and approximately, 50,346 are used for testing its predictions. The overall accuracy achieved in this method is 99.24%. The precision achieved here is 99.35%.

Table 8.4 shows the results obtained on splitting the database in 70-30 train-test ratio. Approximately, 70,483 records are used for training the

Table 8.2 XGBoost model performance for heartbeat classification using MIT-BIH arrhythmia dataset with train-test ratio 60:40.

Heartbeat types	Evaluation parameters		
	Accuracy	Sensitivity	Precision
Normal (N)	99.66	99.84	99.72
SVEB (S)	99.95	99.61	99.85
VEB (V)	99.93	99.44	99.61
Fusion (F)	99.70	97.40	98.27
Mean	99.81	99.07	99.36
Overall accuracy	99.26		

Table 8.3 XGBoost model performance for heartbeat classification using MIT-BIH arrhythmia dataset with train-test ratio 50:50.

Heartbeat types	Evaluation parameters		
	Accuracy	Sensitivity	Precision
Normal (N)	99.63	99.83	99.69
SVEB (S)	99.94	99.39	99.85
VEB (V)	99.94	99.44	99.80
Fusion (F)	99.68	97.44	98.04
Mean	99.80	99.025	99.35
Overall accuracy	99.24		

classifier, and approximately, 30,208 are used for testing its predictions. The overall accuracy here is 99.28% and precision is 99.45%.

Table 8.5 shows the results obtained on splitting the database in 80-20 train-test ratio. Approximately, 80,552 records are used for training the classifier, and approximately, 20,139 are used for testing its predictions. The overall accuracy achieved by this technique is 99.33% and precision is 99.55%.

Table 8.6 shows the results obtained on splitting the database in 90-10 ratio. Approximately, 90,261 records are used for training the classifier, and approximately, 10,070 are used for testing its predictions. The overall accuracy achieved here is 99.43%, and precision is 99.60%.

Table 8.4 XGBoost model performance for heartbeat classification using MIT-BIH arrhythmia dataset with train-test ratio 70:30.

Heartbeat types	Evaluation parameters		
	Accuracy	Sensitivity	Precision
Normal (N)	99.68	99.86	99.72
SVEB (S)	99.96	99.68	99.80
VEB (V)	99.94	99.44	99.76
Fusion (F)	99.72	97.46	98.52
Mean	99.82	99.11	99.45
Overall accuracy	99.28		

Table 8.5 XGBoost model performance for heartbeat classification using MIT-BIH arrhythmia dataset with train-test ratio 80:20.

Heartbeat types	Evaluation parameters		
	Accuracy	Sensitivity	Precision
Normal (N)	99.73	99.92	99.74
SVEB (S)	99.97	99.70	99.94
VEB (V)	99.95	99.72	99.58
Fusion (F)	99.72	97.67	98.95
Mean	99.84	99.25	99.55
Overall accuracy	99.33		

Table 8.7 shows comparison of results obtained from AdaBoost model and XGBoost model. In this study, we have also used the AdaBoost classifier to classify the MIT-BIH arrhythmia database into four different classes using different train test ratios like the XGBoost classifier. The overall accuracy obtained by the AdaBoost and XGBoost models is summarized in the following table using different train-test ratios.

The results clearly indicate that XGBoost completely outperformed AdaBoost at all the splitting ratios. AdaBoost gives its best result at train-test split of 70-30 and that is 93.29%, while XGBoost gives best results in train-test split of 90-10 which is 99.43%. The following figure shows a comparison of

Table 8.6 XGBoost model performance for heartbeat classification using MIT-BIH arrhythmia dataset with train-test ratio 90:10.

Heartbeat types	Evaluation parameters		
	Accuracy	Sensitivity	Precision
Normal (N)	99.77	99.90	99.80
SVEB (S)	99.99	99.88	100
VEB (V)	99.97	99.71	99.86
Fusion (F)	99.79	97.98	98.74
Mean	99.88	99.36	99.60
Overall Accuracy	99.43		

Table 8.7 Comparison of the overall accuracy achieved by the XGBoost and AdaBoost classifiers using different train-test ratios of the MIT-BIH arrhythmia database.

Train-test split	Accuracy (%)	
	XGBoost	AdaBoost
50-50	99.24	89.55
60-40	99.26	87.22
70-30	99.28	93.29
80-20	99.33	91.12
90-10	99.43	90.60

accuracy between the XGBoost and AdaBoost classifiers using different train-test ratios on the MIT-BIH arrhythmia database as shown in given Figure 8.2.

Table 8.8 compares the state-of-art techniques used in automatic ECG classification with the proposed work. U Rajendra *et al.* [19] proposed an 11-layer deep convolution neural network that was used to detect congestive heart failure and it gave its best results with accuracy of 98.97%, specificity of 99.01%, and sensitivity of 98.87%. Nahian *et al.* [20] dealt with ECG signal that are decomposed through empirical mode decomposition (EMD) and higher order Intrinsic Mode Functions (IMFs) are combined to form modified ECG signal, and then, one-dimensional convolution neural network is used for classification, and it gives a maximum accuracy

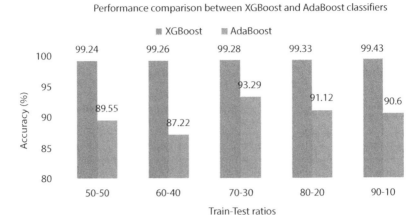

Figure 8.2 Classification accuracies comparison between XGBoost and AdaBoost classifiers.

Table 8.8 Comparison of classification accuracy of proposed work and other state-of-the-art techniques.

Authors	Accuracy (%)
U Rajendra *et al.* [19]	98.97
Nahian *et al.* [20]	97.7
Hamidofujita *et al.* [21]	97.78
Kachuee *et al.* [22]	93.4
Yang *et al.* [23]	97.94
Shadman *et al.* [24]	97
Proposed work	99.43

of 97.70%. Hamidofujita *et al.* [21] proposed a six-layer deep convolution neural network that is used for automatic ECG pattern classification; this model obtains a maximum accuracy of 97.78%. Further, Pandey *et al.* [25] proposed machine learning algorithms for classification of ECG heartbeat according to the patient's specific plans and achieved an overall accuracy of 94.40%. The following graph Figure 8.3 shows a comparison between the proposed XGBoost classifier and other existing work in the literature.

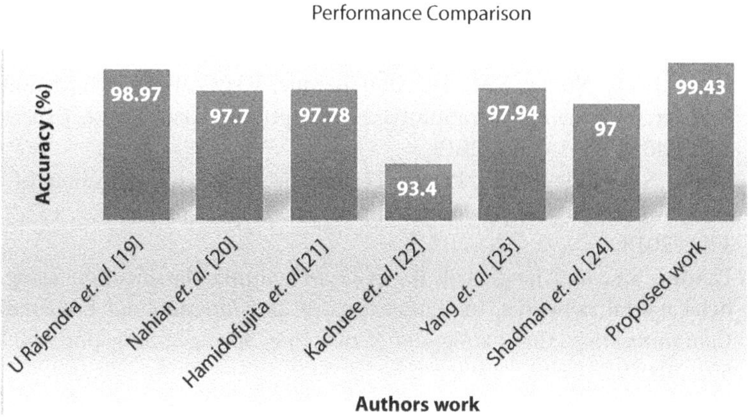

Performance Comparison

Figure 8.3 Comparison between proposed work and other existing literature.

8.4 Conclusion

This paper proposes the classification of ECG signals to four classes: Normal (N), Supraventricular Ectopic Beat (SVEB), Ventricular Ectopic Beat (VEB), and Fusion (F) using XGBoost classifier. The data pre-processing has been done through baseline wandering removal, and then, features are extracted using segmentation of the signals.

The experiments performed here are done on the MIT-BIH database and for the record selection scheme intra-patient scheme is adopted. The features taken into consideration for the classification purpose are R-R intervals, wavelet, HOS, and our own morphological descriptor. The method proposed here only takes data from the single lead (lead 2) and uses segmentation for feature extraction, which is better as compared to other state-of-the-art methods that require more than one lead for the input data and have more sophisticated segmentation step like the computation of P, QRS, and T waves. Introducing more complexity in the segmentation step generally leads to higher error probability. The results by the XGBoost classifier is better than many state-of-the-art methods, on 90-10 split of database we are getting the best results with an overall accuracy of 99.43%. Due to these, the proposed methodology of ECG classification is better than other state-of-the-art methods.

Future scope of the paper will focus on getting better result in interpatient database scheme where data is split by records of patients into two groups, one group of patient's records is used for training and the classifier is tested on the other set of records.

References

1. Luz, E.J.D.S., Nunes, T.M., De Albuquerque, V.H.C., Papa, J.P., Menotti, D., ECG arrhythmia classification based on optimum-path forest. *Expert Syst. Appl.*, 40, 9, 3561–3573, 2013.

2. Singh, S., Pandey, S.K., Pawar, U., Janghel, R.R., Classification of ECG arrhythmia using recurrent neural networks. *Proc. Comput. Sci.*, 132, 1290–1297, 2018.

3. Pandey, S.K. and Janghel, R.R., ECG arrhythmia classification using artificial neural networks, in: *Proceedings of 2nd International Conference on Communication, Computing and Networking*, Springer, Singapore, pp. 645–652, 2019.

4. Thalkar, S. and Upasani, D., Various techniques for removal of power line interference from ECG signal. *Int. J. Sci. Eng. Res.*, 4, 12, 12–23, 2013.

5. Elhaj, F.A., Salim, N., Harris, A.R., Swee, T.T., Ahmed, T., Arrhythmia recognition and classification using combined linear and nonlinear features of ECG signals. *Comput. Methods Programs Biomed.*, 127, 52–63, 2016.

6. Bassiouni, M.M., El-Dahshan, E.S.A., Khalefa, W., Salem, A.M., Intelligent hybrid approaches for human ECG signals identification. *Signal Image Video Process.*, 12, 5, 941–949, 2018.

7. Rajagopal, R. and Ranganathan, V., Design of a hybrid model for cardiac arrhythmia classification based on Daubechies wavelet transform. *Adv. Clin. Exp. Med.: Official Organ Wroclaw Medical University*, 27, 6, 727–734, 2018.

8. Mondéjar-Guerra, V., Novo, J., Rouco, J., Penedo, M.G., Ortega, M., Heartbeat classification fusing temporal and morphological information of ECGs via ensemble of classifiers. *Biomed. Signal Process. Control*, 47, 41–48, 2019.

9. Mathews, S.M., Kambhamettu, C., Barner, K.E., A novel application of deep learning for single-lead ECG classification. *Comput. Biol. Med.*, 99, 53–62, 2018.

10. Sannino, G. and De Pietro, G., A deep learning approach for ECG-based heartbeat classification for arrhythmia detection. *Future Gener. Comput. Syst.*, 86, 446–455, 2018.

11. Arlington, V. A. N. S., Testing and reporting performance results of cardiac rhythm and ST segment measurement algorithms. *ANSI-AAMI EC57*, 1998.

12. Diker, A., Avci, D., Avci, E., Gedikpinar, M., A new technique for ECG signal classification genetic algorithm Wavelet Kernel extreme learning machine. *Optik*, 180, 46–55, 2019.

13. Moody, G.B. and Mark, R.G., The impact of the MIT-BIH arrhythmia database. *IEEE Eng. Med. Biol. Mag.*, 20, 3, 45–50, 2001.

14. De Chazal, P., Detection of supraventricular and ventricular ectopic beats using a single lead ECG, in: *Conference proceedings:.. Annual International Conference of the IEEE Engineering in Medicine and Biology Society. IEEE Engineering in Medicine and Biology Society. Annual Conference*, vol. 2013, p. 45, 2013.

15. Mar, T., Zaunseder, S., Martínez, J.P., Llamedo, M., Poll, R., Optimization of ECG classification by means of feature selection. *IEEE Trans. Biomed. Eng.*, 58, 8, 2168–2177, 2011.
16. Luz, E.J.D.S., Schwartz, W.R., Cámara-Chávez, G., Menotti, D., ECG-based heartbeat classification for arrhythmia detection: A survey. *Comput. Methods Programs Biomed.*, 127, 144–164, 2016.
17. Osowski, S. and Linh, T.H., ECG beat recognition using fuzzy hybrid neural network. *IEEE Trans. Biomed. Eng.*, 48, 11, 1265–1271, 2001.
18. Torlay, L., Perrone-Bertolotti, M., Thomas, E., Baciu, M., Machine learning–XGBoost analysis of language networks to classify patients with epilepsy. *Brain Inform.*, 4, 3, 159–169, 2017.
19. Li, X., Wang, L., Sung, E., AdaBoost with SVM-based component classifiers. *Eng. Appl. Artif. Intell.*, 21, 5, 785–795, 2008.
20. Acharya, U.R., Fujita, H., Oh, S.L., Hagiwara, Y., Tan, J.H., Adam, M., San Tan, R., Deep convolutional neural network for the automated diagnosis of congestive heart failure using ECG signals. *Appl. Intell.*, 49, 1, 16–27, 2019.
21. Hasan, N., II and Bhattacharjee, A., Deep Learning Approach to Cardiovascular Disease Classification Employing Modified ECG Signal from Empirical Mode Decomposition. *Biomed. Signal Process. Control*, 52, 128–140, 2019.
22. Kachuee, M., Fazeli, S., Sarrafzadeh, M., Ecg heartbeat classification: A deep transferable representation, in: *2018 IEEE International Conference on Healthcare Informatics (ICHI)*, 2018, June, IEEE, pp. 443–444.
23. Yang, Z.M., He, J.Y., Shao, Y.H., Feature selection based on linear twin support vector machines. *Proc. Comput. Sci.*, 17, 1039–1046, 2013.
24. Shadmand, S. and Mashoufi, B., A new personalized ECG signal classification algorithm using block-based neural network and particle swarm optimization. *Biomed. Signal Process. Control*, 25, 12–23, 2016.
25. Pandey, S.K., Janghel, R.R., Vani, V., Patient Specific Machine Learning Models for ECG Signal Classification. *Proc. Comput. Sci.*, 167, 2181–2190, 2020.

9

GSA-Based Approach for Gene Selection from Microarray Gene Expression Data

Pintu Kumar Ram* and Pratyay Kuila†

Department of Computer Science and Engineering, National Institute of Technology, Ravangla, Sikkim, India

Abstract

Selection of gene is the most effective method that plays a vital role to detect the cancers. Due to non-redundant data set, it is very difficult to extract the optimal features or genes from microarray data. In this paper, we have proposed a new model to extract the best features subset with high accuracy based on Gravitational Search Algorithm (GSA) with machine learning classifiers. An extensive simulation is performed to evaluate the performance of the proposed algorithm. Simulation results are compared with the Particle Swarm Optimization Algorithm (PSO). The superiority of the proposed algorithm has been observed.

Keywords: Microarray, GSA, Signal-to-Noise Ratio (SNR), machine learning classifier

9.1 Introduction

Nowadays, it has been found that almost 1.8 million cases of cancer have to be diagnosed in the USA [1]. Normally, cancer is caused due to the abnormal growth of cell and damaged the DNA (Deoxyribo Nucleic Acid) [2]. It is necessary to detect the abnormal cell at initial stage to prevent the cancers. Microarray technology is the great invention in the molecular biology to address this issue. This technology focuses on identification of cancerous cell by gene expressed data and draws an enormous attention of the

---

Corresponding author: rampintu570@gmail.com
†*Corresponding author*: pratyay_kuila@yahoo.com

Mettu Srinivas, G. Sucharitha and Anjanna Matta (eds.) Machine Learning Algorithms and Applications, (159–174) © 2021 Scrivener Publishing LLC

researchers and computer scientist to classify the cancers from microarray gene expressed data. However, it is a challenging issue for the researcher to classify or detect the cancers from large microarray gene expressed data. Many computer researchers have been developing different types of models or approach to classify the features or gene from gene expression data [3].

Microarray is a 2D array matrix, where row represents the samples and column represents the genes. Formation of microarray technology is shown in Figure 9.1. Few samples are taken from both the cell (normal cell and tumor cell). Both samples are hybridized with different color. Then, hybridized samples are put in a silicon chip (also known as microarray chip). Normally, gene expression is the process where DNA holds the codes that determine which genes will be expressed to make a cell specialized. For an example, if the switch of light is on, then gene is expressed to perform the specialized cell, and in case of off, it is not. Some factors can influence which genes are turned on or off. These factors can be internal or external. External factors are effected by the human body. If the cell is not expressed, then it may be formed as diseases as shown in Figure 9.2.

In this paper, we propose a Gravitational Search Algorithm (GSA)–based approach to develop a model that can extract the optimal features from microarray data for cancer detection. Our main contributions in this paper are as follows:

1. We have used Signal-to-Noise Ratio (SNR) technique to extract the N number of features from microarray data.
2. A GSA-based approach is used to extract the subset of optimal features from training data.

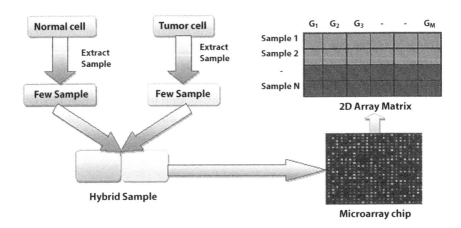

Figure 9.1 Microarray technology.

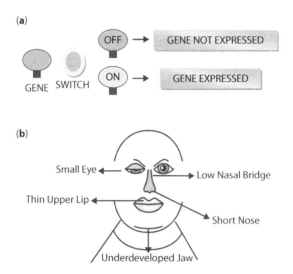

Figure 9.2 Basic information for gene expression, (a) how gene is expressed, and (b) external effect by gene expression to produced diseases.

3. Derived an efficient fitness function to evaluate the features obtained by GSA.
4. Efficient agents are represented with real values.
5. An extensive simulation is performed and results are compared with PSO.
6. Biological behavior of selected features is analyzed by the heat map.

The rest of this paper is organized as follows. In Section 9.2, we have explored the literature. An overview of GSA is given in Section 9.3. In Section 9.4, the proposed model has been depicted. The simulation results are shown in Section 9.5. Finally, we conclude the research in Section 9.6.

9.2   Related Works

Feature selection from high dimension of data is getting interest for the academician, researchers, and industrialist. Best features are provides the appropriate solutions. Hence, classification of feature from microarray gene expression data is the challenging issue for the researchers [4]. It is necessary to identify the behavior of features from small subset of features because it gives the approximate solution [5, 6] in terms of different domain. Many researchers have used different number of subset of features that have taken to analysis the experimental performance. In [7, 8], authors have used 100, 150, and 500 features that are selected to perform the analysis. In [9], the feature has been selected based on qualitative mutual information from gene expression data. Also, in [10], the feature has been selected from high dimension imbalanced microarray data based on rough set feature selection. In [11], genes have been selected based on recursive feature selection. Tang *et al.* [12] have used to select the best feature by using mutual information. In [13], the features have been selected based on rough set method from microarray gene expression data. In [14], recursive model has been used to select the feature. Moreover, the authors have tried to find out the best feature by applying mRMR method in [15]. In [16], the authors have used information gain method to select the features. Authors have used fisher ratio to analyze the features in [17]. Moreover, in [18], co-relation–based feature selection has been used. Zhu *et al.* [19] employed Markov blanket model to get the redundant feature. The implementation of the model is difficult in practice.

Many researchers have used some hybrid (combining of filter and wrapper) approach with meta-heuristic algorithm. In [20], PSO- and ACO-based hybrid approach has been used to select the number of features. In [21], authors have introduced the model with combination of PSO and k-means.

9.3 An Overview of Gravitational Search Algorithm

GSA is based on Newton's second law of motion. It follows the moving of particles with certain masses in the search space. These particles (also called agent) are attracted toward each other by the gravitational force. Each particle is attracted by the other particles and moves in the direction of forces. Also, it produces the acceleration by mutual attraction between two particles. The particles with smaller masses are moving toward the higher masses of the particle. Mass of a particle is represented by its fitness value. So, the optimal solution will be obtained by the higher masses of the particles as in Figure 9.3. Mainly, GSA [22] is based on two fundamental aspects which are exploration and exploitation. Exploration is expanding the search space and exploitation is to deal with the finding of such optima around better solution. With the usage of threshold upon mass (to avoid the over fitting), GSA helps us to avoid trapping in local optima by exploring the search space more efficiently and thus providing faster convergence toward optimal solution.

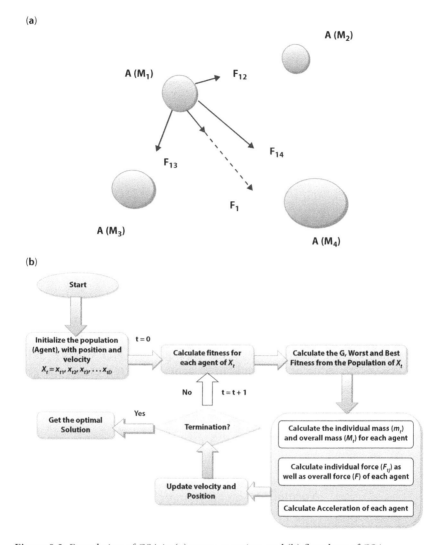

Figure 9.3 Foundation of GSA in (a) mass attraction, and (b) flowchart of GSA.

9.4   Proposed Model

In our proposed model as shown in Figure 9.4, the following phases are as follows.

9.4.1   Pre-Processing

In this phase, we explore the redundant data to obtain the non-redundant feature set. We use the SNR technique to get the best feature set from

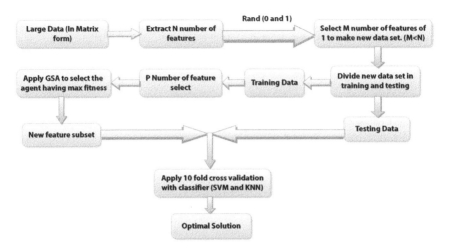

Figure 9.4 Proposed model.

microarray gene expression data. By using Equation (9.1), where μ and σ represent the mean and standard deviation of classes say (c_1, c_2), respectively. We select the N number of features with higher SNR value. Then, we normalize these feature subsets by using Equation (9.2), where g_{st} is the gene expression value of sth sample in t^{th} gene and g_t represents the gene expression value of tth gene over all the samples.

$$SNR = \frac{\mu(c_1) - \mu(c_2)}{\sigma(c_1) + \sigma(c_2)} \tag{9.1}$$

$$Normalize = \frac{g_{st} - \min(g_t)}{\max(g_t) - \min(g_t)} \tag{9.2}$$

9.4.2   Proposed GSA-Based Feature Selection

Initialization of Agent: We have encoded the agent by random number between [0 and 1]. The position of the agents is defined by $A_i = \{a_i^1, a_i^2, ..., a_i^d\}$, which is the position of the ith agent and a_i^d is the position of ith agent in d_{th} dimension. Agent with heavy mass moves slowly in the search space, hence creating and adaptive learning rate in the process of moving toward optimal solution.

Calculation of Mass: Each agent has its mass, $Mass_i$. The mass is calculated based on the fitness value of the agent itself, best fittest agent and worst fittest agent. It is calculated by the following equation:

$$mass_i(t) = \frac{fitness_i(t) - worst\_fitness(t)}{best\_fitness(t) - worst\_fitness(t)} \qquad (9.3)$$

where $fitness_i(t)$ is the fitness of the ith agent at t^{th} iteration, $best\_fitness(t)$ be the best fitness value and $worst\_fitness(t)$ be the worst fitness value among the population.

Calculation of Gravitational Force: We calculate the force from A_i to A_j on d^{th} dimension with Equation (9.4)

$$F_{ij}^d = G(t) \times \frac{mass_i(t) \times mass_j(t)}{R_{ij}(t) + \in} \times a_j^d(t) - a_i^d(t) \qquad (9.4)$$

The gravitational constant is calculated as $G(t) = G_0 \times e^{\frac{-\propto t}{T}}$, where $G_0 = 10$, $\propto = 20$. The maximum iteration is T and we set the $\in = 0.5$, $R_{ij} = \|A_i(t), A_j(t)\|$, be the Euclidean distance between two agents at t^{th} generation. Then, we need to find out the individual force as well as overall force at d^{th} dimension by using Equation (9.5)

$$Force_i^d(t) = \sum_{j=1, j \neq 1} rand_j \times F_{ij}^d(t) \qquad (9.5)$$

Calculation of Acceleration: After evaluation of the force, we calculate acceleration by $ac_i^d(t) = \frac{Force_i^d(t)}{mass_i(t)}$.

Update Position and Velocity: In each iteration, the position and velocity of the agents are updated by using Equations (9.6) and (9.7), respectively.

$$v_i^d(t+1) = rand_i \times v_i^d(t) + ac_i^d(t) \qquad (9.6)$$

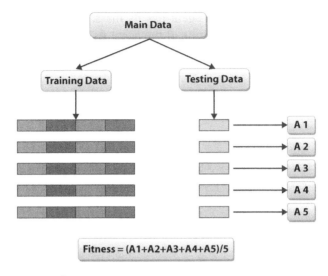

Figure 9.5 Fitness evaluation.

$$a_i^d(t+1) = a_i^d(t) + v_i^d(t+1) \tag{9.7}$$

Derivation of Fitness Function: To evaluate the fitness of the agents, five-fold cross-validation technique is used with Support Vector Machine (SVM). In Figure 9.5, the data has been partitioned into five subsets, where four subsets are used as training set and one subset is used as a test set. Thus, for every dataset, the model is built using tanning set over the test set data. Then, the accuracy is calculated.

9.5   Simulation Results

In this work, five real-life gene datasets (Prostate, DLBCL, Child All, Gastric, and Lymphoma and Leukemia) are used. Respective datasets are easily access from www.biolab.si/supp/bi-cancer/projections/info/, which contain the following genes and samples as follows:

Prostate: It contains the total number of genes is 12,533. It includes two samples: normal sample which contains 50 sample and tumor sample which contain 52 sample.

DLBCL (Diffuse Large B-cell Lymphoma): In this dataset, 7,070 number of total genes are observed. In addition, it contains two samples [DLBCL = 58 and FL (Follicular Lymphomas) = 19].

Child All: It includes 8,280 genes and 110 samples of two class (before therapy = 50 and after therapy = 60).

GSE2685 (Gastric Cancer): This kind of data sets is introduced in two class problem in terms of gastric tumor = 22 and normal cell = 8. Also, it contains the total number of genes is 4,522.

GSE1577 (Lymphoma and Leukemia): It includes total number of genes that is 15,434. It contains the 29 samples, where 9 samples of T-LL (T cell of lymphoblastic lymphoma) in class 1 and 10 samples of T-ALL (T cell of acute lymphoblastic leukemia) in class 2 and additional 10 sample of B-ALL (bone marrow samples of acute lymphoblastic leukemia) cell in class three.

After preprocessing the data set, we divide these selected feature set of training and testing data in the ratio of 80:20. Then, we have applied the GSA over training data. The population size is taken as 50 and compared the proposed algorithm with various classifiers like SVM and KNN (K-Nearest Neighbor) and PSO for the sensitivity, specificity, accuracy, and f-score. It can be observed from Tables 9.1 to 9.5 that the proposed algorithm (GSA with SVM) provides better performance for sensitivity, specificity, accuracy, and f-score than PSO with SVM and KNN based approach.

Table 9.1 Result for prostate cancer data.

Algorithm	Sensitivity	Specificity	Accuracy	F-score
Proposed GSA + SVM	0.94	0.90	0.92	0.94
Proposed GSA + KNN	0.90	0.89	0.90	0.91
PSO + SVM	0.92	0.90	0.90	0.92
PSO + KNN	0.90	0.90	0.89	0.90

Table 9.2 Result for DLBCL data.

Algorithm	Sensitivity	Specificity	Accuracy	F-score
Proposed GSA + SVM	0.92	0.90	0.90	0.89
Proposed GSA + KNN	0.91	0.86	0.89	0.90
PSO + SVM	0.90	0.86	0.90	0.90
PSO + KNN	0.86	0.89	0.89	0.88

Table 9.3 Result for child all data.

Algorithm	Sensitivity	Specificity	Accuracy	F-score
Proposed GSA + SVM	0.91	0.90	0.94	0.90
Proposed GSA + KNN	0.85	0.80	0.89	0.89
PSO + SVM	0.91	0.90	0.90	0.90
PSO + KNN	0.90	0.89	0.89	0.89

Table 9.4 Result for gastric cancer data.

Algorithm	Sensitivity	Specificity	Accuracy	F-score
Proposed GSA + SVM	0.92	0.90	0.92	0.89
Proposed GSA + KNN	0.88	0.86	0.89	0.88
PSO + SVM	0.91	0.90	0.91	0.88
PSO + KNN	0.88	0.89	0.88	0.88

Table 9.5 Result for lymphoma and leukemia.

Algorithm	Sensitivity	Specificity	Accuracy	F-score
Proposed GSA + SVM	0.90	0.89	0.89	0.90
Proposed GSA + KNN	0.89	0.88	0.90	0.89
PSO + SVM	0.90	0.88	0.88	0.88
PSO + KNN	0.90	0.89	0.89	0.86

In Figure 9.6, we have depicted the fitness value with respect to number of iteration of all data set and configured that our method (GSA) performed better than that of PSO. Also, we have presented the bar graph for accuracy with different classifiers as shown in Figure 9.7.

9.5.1   Biological Analysis

Here, we have explored the biological significance of the selected feature. In Figure 9.8, we have introduced the selected features by using a heat map for all data sets. Heat map tells the expression level of the genes in a form

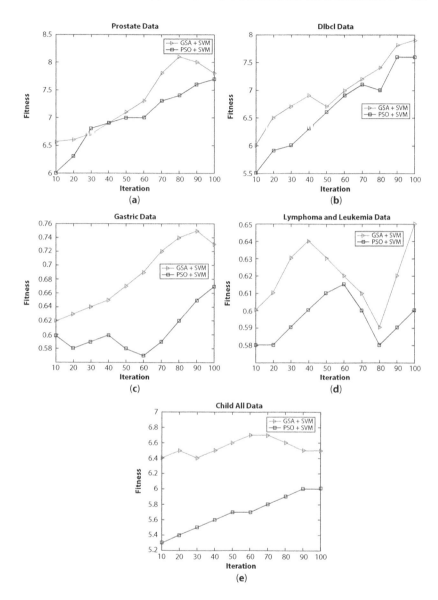

Figure 9.6 Fitness vs. iteration for (a) Prostate data, (b) DLBCL data, (c) Gastric cancer data, (d) Lymphoma and leukemia, and (e) Child all data.

of color. Red indicates the high expression level, i.e., cancerous, green represents the low expression level, i.e., noncancerous and black represent the no expressions of genes. For Prostate Data, we got the five features (39939_at, 41288_at, 38028_at, 37720_at, and 38634_at), where the percentage of

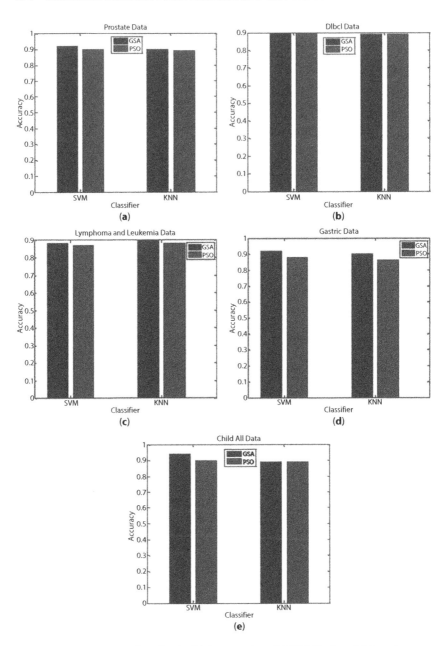

Figure 9.7 Accuracy vs. Classifier for (a) Prostate data, (b) DLBCL data, (c) Lymphoma and leukemia data, (d) Gastric cancer data, and (e) Child all data.

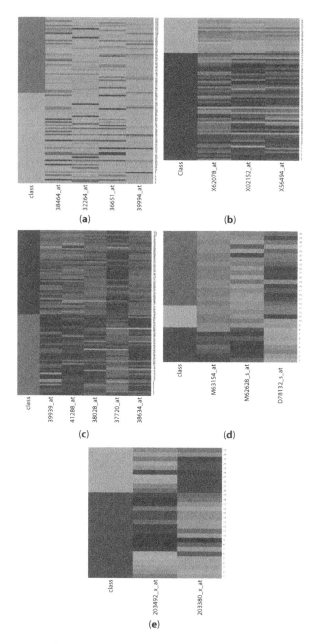

Figure 9.8 Heat map for (a) Child all data, (b) DLBCL data, (c) Prostate data, (d) Gastric cancer data, and (e) Lymphoma and leukemia data.

black color is more in feature 39939_at and the rest four features are having greenish black in color. Therefore, it is quite difficult to analyze the cancerous or non-cancerous features. For DLBCL data, we have got the three features (X62078_at, X02152_at, and X56494_at), where the features (X62078_at and X02152_at) are having lack of expression level of genes because it contains the higher percentage of black color than the rest of colors and the feature (X56494_at) contains the higher percentage of green color than black and red color so it represents the low expression level of gene (it is called the noncancerous or normal feature). Similarly, for Child All Data, we have got the four features (38464_at, 32264_at, and 36651_at and 39994_at), where all the features are having the higher percentage of green color than red or black color. Therefore, it tends the non-cancerous features. Also, for Gastric Cancer Data and Lymphoma and Leukemia Data set, we obtained the three (M63154_at, M62628_s_at, and D78132_s_at) and two (203492_at and 203380_X_at), respectively. Whereas the % of green expression is higher of all the features in Gastric data. So, it represents the non-cancerous. Similarly, in gastric data, feature (203380_x_at) represents the low expression level but the feature (203492_x_at) could not tell the appropriate level.

9.6   Conclusion

Here, we propose the model based on selection of feature from the large amount of gene expression data by the GSA. We have used SNR for feature preprocessing and select few genes for minimum feature selection with maximum accuracy. Also, we have used 5-fold cross-validation technique for fitness evaluation. Moreover, we have applied machine learning classifier (SVM and KNN) with 10-fold cross-validation to get the reduced features and maximize the accuracy. For comparison, we have implemented PSO.

References

1. Islami, F., Sauer, A.G., Miller, K.D., Siegel, R.L., Fedewa, S.A., Jacobs, E.J., McCullough, M.L., Patel, A.V., Ma, J., Soerjomataram, I. *et al.*, Proportion and number of cancer cases and deaths attributable to potentially modifiable risk factors in the united states. *CA: Cancer J. Clin.*, 68, 1, 31–54, 2018.
2. Ruskin, H.J., Computational modeling and analysis of microarray data: New horizons 26, 2016.

3. Ram, P.K. and Kuila, P., Feature selection from microarray data: Genetic algorithm based approach. *J. Inf. Optim. Sci.*, 40, 8, 1599–1610, 2019.

4. Lee, J.W., Lee, J.B., Park, M., Song, S.H., An extensive comparison of recent classi_cation tools applied to microarray data. *Comput. Stat. Data Anal.*, 48, 4, 869–885, 2005.

5. Ding, C. and Peng, H., Minimum redundancy feature selection from micro-array gene expression data. *J. Bioinf. Comput. Biol.*, 3, 02, 185–205, 2005.

6. Hua, J., Tembe, W.D., Dougherty, E.R., Performance of feature-selection methods in the classification of high-dimension data. *Pattern Recognit.*, 42, 3, 409–424, 2009.

7. Yang, C.-S., Chuang, L.-Y., Ke, C.-H., Yang, C.-H., A hybrid feature selection method for microarray classification. *IAENG Int. J. Comput. Sci.*, 35, 3, 2008.

8. Wang, S.-L., Li, X.-L., Fang, J., Finding minimum gene subsets with heuristic breadth-first search algorithm for robust tumor classification. *BMC Bioinf.*, 13, 1, 178, 2012.

9. Nagpal, A. and Singh, V., A feature selection algorithm based on qualitative mutual information for cancer microarray data. *Proc. Comput. Sci.*, 132, 244–252, 2018.

10. Chinnaswamy, A., Srinivasan, R., Poolakkaparambil, S.M., Rough set based variable tolerance attribute selection on high dimensional microarray imbalanced data, in: *Data-Enabled Discovery and Applications*, vol. 2(1), p. 7, 2018.

11. Prasad, Y., Biswas, K.K., Hanmandlu, M., A recursive pso scheme for gene selection in microarray data. *Appl. Soft Comput.*, 71, 213–225, 2018.

12. Tang, J. and Zhou, S., A new approach for feature selection from micro-array data based on mutual information. *IEEE/ACM Trans. Comput. Biol. Bioinform.*, 13, 6, 1004–1015, 2016.

13. Banerjee, M., Mitra, S., Banka, H., Evolutionary rough feature selection in gene expression data. *IEEE Trans. Syst. Man Cybern., Part C (Appl. Rev.)*, 37, 4, 622–632, 2007.

14. Li, F. and Yang, Y., Analysis of recursive gene selection approaches from microarray data. *Bioinformatics*, 21, 19, 3741–3747, 2005.

15. Peng, H., Long, F., Ding, C., Feature selection based on mutual information criteria of max-dependency, max-relevance, and min-redundancy. *IEEE Trans. Pattern Anal. Mach. Intell.*, 27, 8, 1226–1238, 2005.

16. Xing, E.P., Jordan, M., II, Karp, R.M. *et al.*, Feature selection for highdimensional genomic microarray data, in: *ICML*, vol. 1, Citeseer, pp. 601–608, 2001.

17. Guyon, I. and Elissee, A., An introduction to variable and feature selection. *J. Mach. Learn. Res.*, 3, Mar, 1157–1182, 2003.

18. Yu, L. and Liu, H., Feature selection for high-dimensional data: A fast correlation-based filter solution, in: *Proceedings of the 20th international conference on machine learning (ICML-03)*, pp. 856–863, 2003.

19. Zhu, Z., Ong, Y.-S., Dash, M., Markov blanket-embedded genetic algorithm for gene selection. *Pattern Recognit.*, 40, 11, 3236–3248, 2007.

20. Shen, Q., Shi, W.-M., Kong, W., Hybrid particle swarm optimization and tabu search approach for selecting genes for tumor classification using gene expression data. *Comput. Biol. Chem.*, 32, 1, 53–60, 2008.
21. Niknam, T. and Amiri, B., An efficient hybrid approach based on PSO, ACO and k-means for cluster analysis. *Appl. Soft Comput.*, 10, 1, 183–197, 2010.
22. Rashedi, E., Nezamabadi-Pour, H., Saryazdi, S., GSA: a gravitational search algorithm. *Inf. Sci.*, 179, 13, 2232–2248, 2009.

Part 3

MACHINE LEARNING
FOR SECURITY SYSTEMS

10

On Fusion of NIR and VW Information for Cross-Spectral Iris Matching

Ritesh Vyas[1]*, Tirupathiraju Kanumuri[2], Gyanendra Sheoran[2] and Pawan Dubey[2]

[1]Bennett University, Greater Noida, India
[2]NIT Delhi, Delhi, India

Abstract

Iris has been the most promising biometric trait when it comes to personal authentication. But there are certain situations where iris images captured in one spectrum or wavelength must be matched against the templates of feature vectors created from iris images from another spectrum or wavelength. Representation of iris texture using different spectrum is significantly different. Therefore, this paper investigates the application of different fusion strategies in combining the information from near infrared and visible wavelength images to enhance the recognition performance. Two benchmark cross-spectral iris databases are used in the experimentation, namely, PolyU cross spectral database and Cross-Eyed database. Fusion schemes at two different levels, feature level and score level, are adopted to validate the hypothesis of performance improvement through combination of information from different spectrum. Results show that fusion helps in improvement of cross-spectral iris matching.

Keywords: Iris recognition, cross-spectral, near infrared (NIR), visible wavelength (VW), information fusion

10.1 Introduction

Since its inception [1, 2], iris recognition has been the choice of researchers working in the field of biometric authentication. Reasons behind such popularity of iris biometric are the uniqueness, randomness, and stability of iris features. The core steps of any iris recognition system comprise

---

*Corresponding author: ritesh.vyas157@gmail.com

Mettu Srinivas, G. Sucharitha and Anjanna Matta (eds.) Machine Learning Algorithms and Applications, (177–192) © 2021 Scrivener Publishing LLC

of segmentation (i.e., localizing the iris boundaries), normalization (i.e., transforming the nearly circular iris into rectangular templates for achieving the scale invariance), feature extraction (i.e., representing the iris texture in most distinctive manner), and matching (i.e., measuring the similarity between two different feature templates) [3].

Traditionally, iris-dependent biometric applications employ iris images obtained in the near infrared (NIR) wavelength band, as this band is good at revealing the pigmentation of the iris and offers more physical comfort to the user as compared to other illuminations. Moreover, it also works for dark irides, where intensity difference between that of pupil and iris is not much. However, there have been studies like refs. [4, 5] which have explored the potentials of iris recognition in multiple spectra other than traditional NIR spectrum. In recent past, researchers have turned their attention toward efficient iris recognition in visible wavelength (VW; 400–700 nm). Despite various noise factors being added to the iris images due to VW imaging, there exists a firm rationale that endorses its use in iris recognition. First is that VW cameras are cost-effective in providing higher resolution images. Besides, large-scale surveillance/monitoring often incorporates visible range cameras [6]. Extensive application of hand-held devices like smartphones has also drawn the attention of research community toward enhanced iris recognition through VW-based imaging.

Therefore, due to the transfer of iris recognition technology from NIR to VW spectrum, there arise some situations where iris samples captured in one wavelength (NIR/VW) need to be matched against those of acquired in the other (VW/NIR). The most suitable example of such situations is the application of surveillance, where live stream of people is acquired through advanced VW cameras and images from this stream are matched against the stored databases which have NIR-based images. This sort of cross-spectral matching causes decadence in the overall recognition performance, reason behind which is the uncorrelated information present in different wavelengths' images.

10.1.1   Related Works

There have been many efforts in the literature, which have dealt with the challenging issue of cross-spectral iris matchings. Boyce *et al.* [7] reported a phenomenal explication of the iris structure at different wavelengths. Additionally, it was suggested in [7, 8] that the system performance varies inversely with the relative wavelength between two channels being compared. Feature-level fusion using augmentation and ordered weighted average (OWA) was used in [9] to combine the features of NIR and VW images.

Burge and Monaco [10] implemented pixel-level fusion of different spectrum images to extract the features. Furthermore, NIR iris images were predicted based on the features of VW images through multi-stage supervised learning. In the work of Zuo *et al.* [11], the channel information for NIR was predicted from color image by utilizing a nonlinear multivariate adaptive mapping and feed forward neural network. Abdullah *et al.* [12, 13] proposed a substantial cross-spectral iris recognition framework employing three separate descriptors and 1D log-Gabor filter. Nalla and Kumar [6] proposed domain adaptation framework using Markov random fields model. Recently, Vyas *et al.* [14] proposed difference of variance (DoV) utilizing Gabor filtered iris images at multiple scales and orientations.

In this paper, combination of the information furnished by both NIR- and VW-based iris images is investigated. The purpose of this sort of fusion is improvement in the performance of cross-spectral iris matching. The Xor-Sum Code approach, erstwhile developed for NIR-based iris recognition [15], has been expanded to address the cross-spectral iris recognition. Additionally, a more generalized framework is proposed using two benchmark cross-spectral iris databases. Fusion of information is investigated at feature level and score level, respectively. Unlike other works on cross-spectral iris recognition, this work does not require any sort of training or model to combine the NIR and VW information. Rather, this seems the first attempt to achieve huge performance improvements in cross-spectral iris matching through conventional methods of information fusion.

The rest of the chapter is organized as follows. Section 10.2 provides the preliminary details about Xor-Sum Code. Section 10.3 presents the experimental results, and Section 10.4 concludes the paper.

10.2   Preliminary Details

The Xor-Sum Code descriptor uses 2D Gabor filter for revealing the texture patterns of iris template at various orientations (refer to eq. (10.1)). Gabor filter, mathematically expressed as eq. (10.2), is preferred for texture analysis of images because of its ability to model the human visual system effectively [16]. As is evident from the name of the descriptor that it involves two important operations: 1) Exclusive-OR operation (expressed as eq. (10.3)), which is performed to fuse the information from real and imaginary parts of the filtered iris image at one particular orientation, and 2) Sum operation (expressed as eq. (10.4)), which is performed to combine the Xor operations' output for all orientations. Thereafter, the output of Sum operation is encoded into bits to have different planes of binary feature vectors (see eq. (10.5)), corresponding to the input iris template. The four core steps of the Xor-Sum Code approach (Filtering, Exclusive OR, Sum, and Encoding) and their mathematical representations are as follows:

Filtering: $$\bar{I}_n = I * G \tag{10.1}$$

where I and G denote the input iris image and Gabor filter, respectively. $(x, y, \sigma, f, \theta_n)$ are the Gabor filter parameters, respectively, defined as spatial coordinates, scale, frequency, and orientation. Formal definition of Gabor filter G can be expressed as follows:

$$G(x,y,\sigma,f,\theta_n)=\frac{1}{2\pi\sigma^2}\exp\left\{-\frac{x^2+y^2}{2\sigma^2}\right\}\times\exp\{2\pi\,if\,(x\cos\theta_n+y\sin\theta_n)\} \tag{10.2}$$

where $\theta_n = \dfrac{n*\pi}{N}$ and $n = (0,1,...,N-1)$ with N denoting the number of orientations. The optimal parameters used for 2D Gabor filter is given in Table 10.1.

Exclusive OR: $$X_n = Re(\bar{I}_n) \oplus Im(\bar{I}_n) \tag{10.3}$$

Sum: $$S = \sum_{n=0}^{N-1} X_n \tag{10.4}$$

Encoding: $$XSC(b)=\begin{cases} 1\,if\,b\leq S<b+\dfrac{N+1}{2} \\[2mm] 0\,otherwise \end{cases} \tag{10.5}$$

Table 10.1 Optimal parameters for 2D Gabor.

size	f	σ	θ	n	N
15×15	0.1833	2.8090	n*π/N	0, 1, ..., N-1	4

where $b = 1,2,…,B$ *and* $B = [(N + 1)/2]$.

Hamming distance (D_h) is then used to find the similarity score between two templates (say P and Q), as given in the following:

$$D_h(P,Q) = \frac{\sum_{b=1}^{B} XSC_P(b) \oplus XSC_Q(b)}{B} \tag{10.6}$$

10.2.1   Fusion

Fusion of information is performed at two possible levels, at feature level and at score level. Since the extracted feature template is binary in nature, two well-known binary operations (i.e., OR operation and AND operation) are used to combine the features. In brief, OR fusion gives "1" for any bit position if any of the VW or NIR feature templates has "1" at that particular position, while AND fusion produces "1" corresponding to the bit positions which are "1" in both the VW and NIR features. Regarding score-level fusion, SUM and PROD (product) rule of fusion is employed here to show the improvement in performance of cross-spectral iris matching. Mathematically, all four fusion schemes employed in this work can be written as the following equations:

- Feature-level fusion:

$$\textit{Fusion using OR: } F = F_1 + F_2$$

$$\textit{Fusion using AND: } F = F_1 \cdot F_2 \tag{10.7}$$

where F_1 and F_2 represent the XOR-SUM features for VW and NIR illuminated iris images, respectively.
- Score-level fusion:

$$\textit{Fusion using SUM: } S = \frac{(S_1 + S_2)}{2}$$

$$\textit{Fusion using PROD: } S = \sqrt{(S_1 \times S_2)} \tag{10.8}$$

where S_1 and S_2 are the Hamming distance matching scores for VW and NIR features, respectively.

10.3   Experiments and Results

In this section, the databases with which the experiments are carried out, are described first. Afterward, various sorts of matchings are performed to validate the use of fusion in cross-spectral matching.

10.3.1   Databases

Two major cross-spectral iris databases are used here to investigate the idea of information fusion from NIR and VW images. First database is The Hong Kong PolyU cross-spectral database [17], which has 6,270 images from 209 subjects (or 418 classes) at the rate of 30 images per subject (or 15 images per class). Each image in this database has a resolution of 640 × 480. Second cross-spectral database is the Cross-Eyed database [18]. This database contains 1,920 images from 240 classes, i.e., 8 images per class. Each image has a resolution of 400 × 300. Both the employed databases are affluent with registered iris images which confer pixel-to-pixel consistency between VW and NIR channel iris images. Sample images from both the databases are depicted in Figure 10.1. In this paper, 1,050 images from 35 subjects of PolyU database and 1,000 images from 125 subjects of Cross-Eyed database are used. For segmentation purpose, method suggested in [19] is employed.

10.3.2   Experimental Results

Two important measures, namely, equal error rate (EER) and receiver operator characteristic (ROC) curves are employed to assess the proposed approach. Notably, ROC curve is a graph drawn between two metrics called

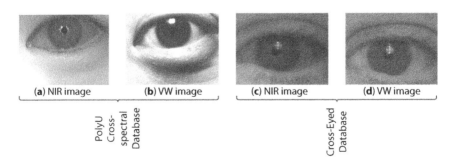

(a) NIR image   **(b)** VW image   **(c)** NIR image   **(d)** VW image

PolyU Cross-spectral Database   Cross-Eyed Database

Figure 10.1 Sample images from both the employed databases.

false acceptance rate (FAR) (on *x*-axis) and genuine acceptance rate (GAR) (on *y*-axis). While, GAR is obtained by subtracting false rejection rate (FRR) from one. Both FAR and FRR denote the falsely accepted and rejected users, respectively, at varying decision thresholds. For investigating the use of fusion strategies to enhance the performance of cross-spectral iris matching system, the following different matching scenarios are considered.

10.3.2.1   Same Spectral Matchings

This section deals with the iris matchings which are performed within the same spectral images. For instance, the features extracted from the red-channel of the VW iris images are matched against those of the same channel only. The ROC curves for these same-spectrum matchings using both the employed feature extraction schemes for both PolyU and

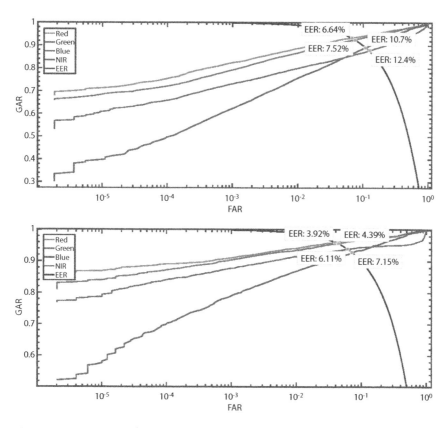

Figure 10.2 ROC curves for same-spectral matchings of (top) PolyU and (bottom) Cross-Eyed.

Cross-Eyed databases are depicted in Figures 10.2 (top) and (bottom). Four different matching cases are exhibited in the ROC curves using red, green, blue, and NIR channels, respectively. The EER values for all same-spectral matchings are also displayed for more clarification. Table 10.2 summarizes all EER values in tabular form.

It can be observed from Figure 10.2 (top) that the best EER of 6.64% is yielded for red channel of VW images from PolyU database, followed by 7.52%, 10.74%, and 12.38% in case of green, blue, and NIR channel matchings, respectively. Consequently, it can be stated that the red channel of the PolyU dataset images provides the most discriminating information when compared to the other channels. Considering Cross-Eyed database [Figure 10.2 (bottom)], the Xor-Sum descriptor again provides best EER in case of red-channel matchings with 3.92%. Unlike PolyU database, NIR images of Cross-Eyed database have greater discrimination than the blue channel of VW images. This fact is supported by the EER value (6.11%) obtained in NIR matching of Cross-Eyed database, which is relatively lower as compared to that obtained in blue channel matchings (7.15%).

10.3.2.2   Cross Spectral Matchings

These sorts of matchings form the core of the present work. The phrase "cross-spectral" beckons toward the comparison of any one spectrum's features with those of another spectra. In present context, cross-spectral matchings include following six matching scenarios: 1) Red-Green matchings, 2) Red-blue matchings, 3) Green-Blue matchings, 4) Red-NIR matchings, 5) Green-NIR matchings, and 6) Blue-NIR matchings. Figures 10.3 (top) and (bottom) depict the ROC curves for cross-spectral matchings using both the databases, respectively. The EER values for all these matchings are displayed in the ROC curves as well as in Table 10.2.

The EER values are in compliance with the fact that the matching performance deteriorates with the rise in difference between the wavelengths of the channels being matched. Among VW channels, largest EER is produced when red channel is matched against blue channel. These EER values are 15.75% and 17.84% for PolyU and Cross-Eyed database, respectively. Whereas, the cross-spectral (VW-NIR) matching between any one channel of VW images against NIR images may lead to even larger values of EER. For illustration, the EER values in VW-NIR matching for PolyU and Cross-Eyed databases fall in the range of 38%–42% and 13%–26%, respectively. These larger values of EER indicate that iris representation using different wavelengths is quite different. Therefore, matching the iris images

Table 10.2 EER (%) values using different channels of the VW images.

Database→	PolyU				Cross-eyed			
Channels	Red	Green	Blue	NIR	Red	Green	Blue	NIR
Red	6.64	8.06	15.75	38.43	3.91	6.11	17.84	13.99
Green	---	7.52	12.49	39.63	---	4.39	9.34	19.28
Blue	---	---	10.74	41.27	---	---	7.15	25.21
NIR	---	---	---	12.38	---	---	---	6.10

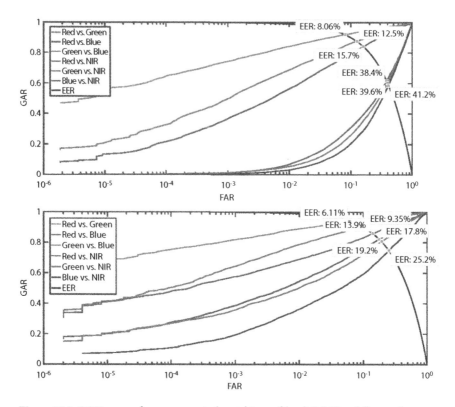

Figure 10.3 ROC curves for cross-spectral matchings of (top) PolyU and (bottom) Cross-Eyed.

across different wavelengths can cause severe problems. These problems can be avoided by combining the information of VW and NIR images, as described in the following subsections. Two different ways of this combination are employed in this paper.

10.3.3   Feature-Level Fusion

As the feature descriptor employed in this work produces binary feature vectors, two binary operators, namely, OR and AND, are used to combine the features extracted from VW and NIR images. Fusion using OR operator results in improved EER values. Table 10.3 displays the EER values for all types of matchings performed after feature-level fusion. After looking into the table, it can be observed that the features of red and NIR channels when fused through OR and matched against NIR yield EER of 15.34% which is less than half of the EER attained when individual NIR

Table 10.3 EER (%) values using feature-level fusion (OR and AND).

Database→		PolyU				Cross-eyed			
Fusion	Channels	Red	Green	Blue	NIR	Red	Green	Blue	NIR
OR Fusion	Red + NIR	10.25	--	--	15.34	5.27	--	--	6.30
	Green + NIR	--	11.23	--	15.68	--	6.24	--	6.98
	Blue + NIR	--	--	15.07	15.82	--	--	2.74	7.88
AND Fusion	Red.NIR	9.45	--	--	15.31	5.51	--	--	6.71
	Green.NIR	--	10.39	--	15.10	--	5.89	--	7.26
	Blue.NIR	--	--	16.05	14.6	--	--	11.21	7.55

and Red channel features are matched. Similarly, AND fusion also results in decrease in EER values in cross-spectral matchings. This fall in EER values after feature-level fusion is more clearly demonstrated in Figure 10.4. In this figure, blue colored bars indicate the EER values achieved in cross-spectral matching without using any feature-level fusion. While green and pink colored bars indicate EER values after feature-level fusion using OR and AND operator, respectively.

EER values are shown with respect to each of the channels of VW images, i.e., red, green, and blue. On an overall basis, for PolyU database, feature fusion using OR operation brings the EER values in the range of 10%–16%. Similarly, fusing the features using AND operation results in EER values falling in the range of 9%–16%, which is also smaller when compared to the EER values of matching without any fusion. Similarly, for Cross-Eyed database, the EER values fall in the range of 5%–13% for fusion using OR and 5%–12% for fusion using AND.

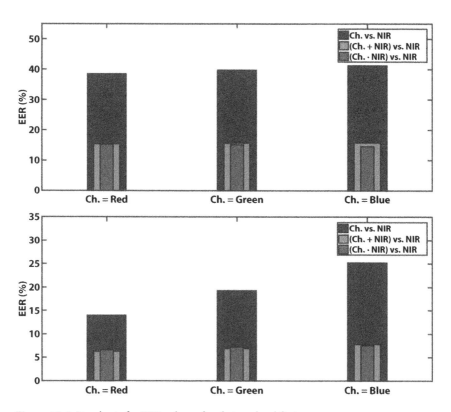

Figure 10.4 Bar charts for EER values after feature-level fusion.

10.3.4   Score-Level Fusion

Another type of fusion employed in this paper is score-level fusion, i.e., combining the matching scores from different channels of VW images and the NIR images. In total, 11 different combinations of scores are experimented using SUM and PROD rule of fusion, to get improved results. These combinations include scores from red, green, and blue channels of VW images and scores from the NIR images. EER values of different combinations of matching scores are listed in Table 10.4. It is observed from Table 10.4 that the best value of EER can be obtained using the combination of red, green, and NIR channels for both PolyU and Cross-Eyed databases. The best values of EER with PolyU database are 4.34% and 4.35%, respectively, using SUM and PROD rule of fusion. While in case of Cross-Eyed database, best EER values are yielded as 2.05% and 2.02% using SUM and PROD fusion, respectively. These values of EER clearly demonstrate that score-level fusion helps in improving the performance of recognition system.

Table 10.4 EER (%) values using score-level fusion.

Database→	PolyU		Cross-Eyed	
Channels↓	SUM	PROD	SUM	PROD
(R,G)	6.32	6.36	3.63	3.64
(R,B)	6.16	6.21	4.38	4.40
(G,B)	7.13	7.10	4.57	4.56
(R,NIR)	4.72	4.53	2.54	2.51
(G,NIR)	4.72	4.71	2.55	2.37
(B,NIR)	5.41	5.19	3.69	3.62
(R,G,B)	6.10	6.16	4.01	3.95
(R,G,NIR)	4.34	4.35	2.05	2.02
(R,B,NIR)	**4.03**	**4.01**	**2.11**	**2.07**
(G,B,NIR)	4.26	4.34	2.32	2.21
(R,G,B,NIR)	4.16	4.16	2.16	2.04

10.4   Conclusions

The feasibility of advancement in cross-spectral iris recognition using fusion of information obtained from NIR and VW images is investigated in this paper. Two databases, PolyU cross-spectral and Cross-Eyed databases, are employed to validate the said purpose. Binary features, from iris images captured in both the spectrum, are extracted using Xor-Sum Code. Feature-level fusion and score-level fusion are implemented to combine the information from different spectrum. Results indicate that AND fusion between binary features of different wavelengths performs better than fusion using OR. Regarding score-level fusion, best results, in terms of EER, are obtained when scores from NIR and red and green channels of VW images are fused together. Finally, the gist of the paper is that if the information from different spectrum is combined, then the performance of cross-spectral iris matching can be significantly improved. In future, sophisticated fusion schemes, like learning-based fusion, can be utilized to further enhance the recognition accuracy.

References

1. Flom, L. and Safir, A., Iris recognition system. U.S. Patent No. 4, 641, 349, 1987.
2. Daugman, J.G., High Confidence Visual Recognition of Persons by a test of statistical independence. *IEEE Trans. Pattern Anal. Mach. Intell.*, 15, 11, 1148–1161, 1993.
3. Bowyer, K.W., Hollingsworth, K., Flynn, P.J., Image understanding for iris biometrics: A survey. *Comput. Vis. Image Underst.*, 110, 2, 281–307, 2008.
4. Ross, A., Pasula, R., Hornak, L., Exploring multispectral iris recognition beyond 900nm, in: *IEEE 3rd International Conference on Biometrics: Theory, Applications and Systems, BTAS 2009*, pp. 1–8, 2009.
5. Ives, R.W., Ngo, H.T., Winchell, S.D., Matey, J.R., Preliminary evaluation of multispectral iris imagery, in: *IET Conference on Image Processing (IPR 2012)*, pp. 1–5, 2012.
6. Nalla, P.R. and Kumar, A., Towards More Accurate Iris Recognition using Cross-Spectral Matching. *IEEE Trans. Image Process.*, 26, 1, 208–221, Jan. 2017.
7. Boyce, C., Ross, A., Monaco, M., Hornak, L., Xin, L., Multispectral iris analysis: A preliminary study, in: *2006 IEEE Conference on Computer Vision and Pattern Recognition Workshop (CVPRW'06)*, pp. 51–51, 2006.

8. Trokielewicz, M., Czajka, A., Maciejewicz, P., Cataract influence on iris recognition performance. *Proc. SPIE - Int. Soc. Opt. Eng.*, vol. 9290, pp. 1–14, 2014.

9. Tajbakhsh, N., Araabi, B.N., Soltanianzadeh, H., Feature Fusion as a Practical Solution toward Noncooperative Iris Recognition, in: *11th IEEE International Conference on Information Fusion*, pp. 1–7, 2008.

10. Burge, M.J. and Monaco, M.K., Multispectral iris fusion for enhancement, interoperability, and cross wavelength matching, in: *Algorithms and Technologies for Multispectral, Hyperspectral and Ultraspectral Imagery*, vol. 7334, pp. 73341D-1-73341D-8, 2009.

11. Zuo, J., Nicolo, F., Schmid, N.A., Cross spectral iris matching based on predictive image mapping, in: *2010 Fourth IEEE International Conference on Biometrics: Theory, Applications and Systems (BTAS)*, pp. 1–5, 2010.

12. Abdullah, M.A.M., Dlay, S.S., Woo, W.L., Chambers, J.A., A novel framework for cross-spectral iris matching. *IPSJ Trans. Comput. Vis. Appl.*, 8, 1, 9, 2016.

13. Abdullah, M.A.M., Al-Nima, R.R., Dlay, S.S., Woo, W.L., Chambers, J.A., Cross-Spectral Iris Matching for Surveillance Applications, in: *Surveillance in Action, Advanced Sciences and Technologies for Security Applications*, P. Karampelas and T. Bourlai (Eds.), pp. 105–125, Springer, Cham, 2018.

14. Vyas, R., Kanumuri, T., Sheoran, G., Cross spectral iris recognition for surveillance based applications. *Multimed. Tools Appl.*, 78, 5, 5681–5699, 2019.

15. Vyas, R., Kanumuri, T., Sheoran, G., Iris recognition using 2-D Gabor filter and XOR-SUM code, in: *2016 IEEE 1st India International Conference on Information Processing (IICIP)*, pp. 1–5, 2016.

16. Lee, T.S., Tai Sing, L., Lee, T.S., Image representation using 2D Gabor wavelets. *IEEE Trans. Pattern Anal. Mach. Intell.*, 18, 10, 959–971, 1996.

17. The Hong Kong Polytechnic University Cross-Spectral Iris Images Database. [Online]. Available: http://www4.comp.polyu.edu.hk/~csajaykr/polyuiris.htm.

18. Sequeira, A.F. *et al.*, Cross-Eyed - Cross-Spectral Iris/Periocular Recognition Database and Competition, in: *5th International conference of the Biometrics Special Interest Group (BIOSIG 2016)*, pp. 1–5, 2016, [Online]. Available: https://sites.google.com/site/crossspectrumcompetition/home.

19. Zhao, Z. and Kumar, A., An accurate iris segmentation framework under relaxed imaging constraints using total variation model, in: *IEEE International Conference on Computer Vision*, pp. 3828–3836, 2015.

11

Fake Social Media Profile Detection

Umita Deepak Joshi[1], Vanshika[2], Ajay Pratap Singh[3], Tushar Rajesh Pahuja[4], Smita Naval[5] and Gaurav Singal[6*]

[1]College of Engineering, Pune, India
[2]Maharaja Surajmal Institute of Technology, Delhi, India
[3]Galgotias University, Greater Noida, India
[4]Thadomal Shahani Engineering College, Mumbai, India
[5]Malaviya National Institute of Technology, Jaipur, India
[6]Bennett University, Greater Noida, India

Abstract

Social media like Twitter, Facebook, Instagram, and LinkedIn are an integral part of our lives. People all over the world are actively engaged in these social media platforms. But at the same time, it faces the problem of fake profiles. Fake profiles are generally human-generated or bot-generated or cyborgs, created for spreading rumors, phishing, data breaching, and identity theft. Therefore, in this article, we discuss fake profile detection models. These differentiate between fake profiles and genuine profiles on Twitter based on visible features like followers count, friends count, status count, and more. We form the models using various machine learning methods. We use the MIB dataset of Twitter profiles, TFP, and E13 for genuine and INT, TWT, and FSF for fake accounts. Here, we have tested different ML approaches, such as Neural Networks, Random Forest, XG Boost, and LSTM. We select significant features for determining the authenticity of a social media profile. As a result, we get the output as 0 for real profiles and 1 for fake profiles. The accuracy achieved is 99.46% by XG Boost and 98% by Neural Network. The fake detected profiles can be blocked/deleted to avoiding future cyber-security threats.

Keywords: Neural Network, Random Forest, XG Boost, social media, fake profile, machine learning, social media

Corresponding author: gauravsingal789@gmail.com

Mettu Srinivas, G. Sucharitha and Anjanna Matta (eds.) Machine Learning Algorithms and Applications, (193–210) © 2021 Scrivener Publishing LLC

11.1   Introduction

Social media has become a vital part of our lives. From sharing attractive extravagant photographs to follow celebrities to chat with close and far away friends, everyone is active on social media. It is a great platform to share information and interact with people. But everything has a downside. As social media is footing a firm spot in our lives, there are instances where it has turned out to be a bigger problem.

There are 330 million monthly active users and 145 million daily active users on Twitter. Facebook also adds about 500,000 new users every day and six new users every second. Loads of information are shared over twitter every single day. From hot trending topics to the latest hash-tags and news to one's most recent trip, you get everything on Twitter. People react, like, comment, share their views, and raise their opinions all through the 280 character limit. The social media users discuss genuine issues; but, sometimes there are some rumors. These rumors lead to conflicts between different sections of society. The concern of privacy, misuse, cyberbullying [1], and false information has come into light in the recent past. Fake profiles perform all these tasks. Fake accounts can be human-generated or computer-generated or cyborgs [2]. Cyborgs are accounts initially created by humans but later operated by computers.

Fake profiles usually get created in false names, and misleading and abusive posts and pictures are circulated by these profiles to manipulate the society or to push anti-vaccine conspiracy theories, etc. Every social media platform is facing the problem of fake profiles these days. The goal behind creating fake profiles is mainly spamming [3], phishing, and obtaining more followers. Malicious accounts have the full potential to commit cybercrimes. The bogus accounts propose a major threat like identity theft and data breaching [4]. These fake accounts send various URLs to people which, when visited, send all the user's data to faraway servers that could be utilized against an individual. Also, the fake profiles, created seemingly on behalf of organizations or people, can damage their reputations and decrease their numbers of likes and followers. Along with all these, social media manipulation is also an obstacle. The fake accounts lead to the spread of misleading and inappropriate information, which, in turn, give rise to conflicts.

These hoax accounts get created to obtain more followers too. Who does not want to be voguish on social media? To achieve a high figure of followers, people tend to find fake followers [5]. Overall, the research findings revealed that fake profiles cause more harm than any other cybercrime. Therefore, it is important to detect a fake profile even before the user is notified. To combat the creation of fake profiles, common defenses are as follows [6]:

1. Methods such as user verification must be incorporated while creating accounts on social media.
2. To detect abnormal activities, user behavior analysis must be employed. Bot detection solution consisting of analyzation based on real-time AI will be beneficial.
3. An automated bot protection tool must be used.

In this context here, we talk about detecting fake profiles on Twitter:

- The dataset of twitter profiles E13 and TFP for genuine, and INT, TWT, and FSF for fake is taken into use.
- As a technical contribution, we designed a multi-layer neural network model [7], a random forest model, an XG boost model, and an LSTM model. The mentioned models have supervised machine learning models.
- Also, the LSTM deep learning model classifies based on tweets; the result can be combined with a convolution neural network in the near future [8].

The paper is organized into various sections. The existing work is summarized in Section 11.2. Data pre-processing and methodology have been shown in Section 11.3 and experimental results in Section 11.4 with the accuracy of models. In the last section, conclusion and future work are described.

11.2   Related Work

Social media: A Boon or Bane, this question has always subsisted. All companies have aimed at providing a platform with the least errors and better experience. Hence, every day new developments and updates are done. Seeing that not enough is done so far for the detection of fake human identities on social media platforms like Twitter [9], we looked toward past research addressing similar problems. Some methods classified profiles based on the activity of the account [1], the number of requests responded, messages sent, and more. The models use a graph-based system. Some methods also aimed at identifying between bots and cyborgs. Some past researches are mentioned below.

If certain words appear in a message, then the message is considered Spam. This concept has been used to detect fake profiles on social media [10]. For the detection of such words on social media, pattern matching techniques were used. But the significant drawback of this rule is that with time, there is the continuous development and use of new words. Also, the use of abbreviations like lol, gbu, and gn is becoming popular on Twitter.

Sybil Guard [11] developed in 2008 aimed at limiting the corrupting influence of Sybil attacks via social media. It had constrained random walk by every node and was based on the occurrence of random-walk interactions. The dataset used was Kleinberg's synthetic social network. Along with Sybil guard, another approach called the Sybil limit [12] was also developed around the same time. Like Sybil guard, it also worked on the assumption that the non-Sybil region is fast mixing. It worked on the approach of multiple random walks by every node, and ranking was based on the occurrence of tails of walk intersection.

Sybil-infer [13] was developed in 2009. It made use of methods like greedy algorithm, Bayesian inference technique, and Monte Carlo sampling with the assumptions like the non-Sybil region is fast mixing, and random walks are fast-mixing. The selection technique is threshold based on probability. Mislove's algorithm, 2010 worked on the Facebook dataset using greedy search and selected profiles based on normalized metric conductance. In 2011, came a new model named Facebook immune system that used random forest, SVM, and boosting techniques. It also used the Facebook dataset, and the feature loop was the selection technique.

An algorithm is used by Facebook to detect bots based on the number of friends which could be either related to tagging or relationship history [14]. The rules stated above can identify bot accounts but are not successful in identifying fake accounts created by humans. Unsupervised ML was used for detecting bots [9]. In this technique, instead of labeling, information was assembled based on closeness. The bots were recognized by grouping functions so admirably because of co-attributes.

Sybil rank [11, 15] designed in 2012, is based on a graph-based system. The profiles were ranked based on interactions, tags, and wall posts. The profiles with a high rank are labeled as real profiles and the ones with lower as fake. But this method was unreliable as there were instances where a real profile was ranked low. Next, there was another model developed called the Sybil frame [12]. It used a multi-stage level classification. It worked in two steps, firstly on a content-based approach and secondly on a structure-based method.

Filtering is also among one of the past approaches [16]. A new threat or malicious activity is detected, and the account is added to the blacklist.

But as far as human-fake accounts are concerned, they tend to adapt and yet somehow avoid the blacklist. Researches were also done to detect fake accounts based on factors like engagement rate and artificial activity [17]. An engagement rate is the percentage of the interaction of the audience with a post. The engagement rate is calculated as (Total number of interactions/Total number of followers) × 100. These interactions could be in the form of likes, shares, or comments.

Artificial activity is based on the number of shares, likes, and comments made by a particular account. Insufficient information and the status of verification of email are also considered as an artificial activity. In previous methods of detecting fake profile, the following features are examined:

- If an account consists of more than 30 followers, then it is declared as malicious. The email linked with the account, contrasted with the user name of the profile. If these two do not show some resemblance, then the user-profile is declared as fake.
- The discrepancy between location set by the user and the location used by the user leads the account to be fake.

11.3   Methodology

For the detection of fake Twitter profiles, we incorporated various supervised methods, all with the same goal yet different accuracy. Each model detects a fake profile based upon visible features only. All these supervised models are fed the same dataset, and corresponding accuracy and loss graphs are plotted. Also, a comparison graph of the accuracy of different models is indicated. The models are trained using appropriate optimizers, loss functions, and activation functions. The used models are mentioned below.

11.3.1   Dataset

We used the dataset available on MIB [18]. The data set consisted of 3,474 genuine profiles and 3,351 fake profiles. The data set selected was TFP and E13 for genuine and INT, TWT, and FSF for fake accounts. The data is stored in CSV file format for easy reading by the machine.

All the labels on the x-axis depict the features used for the detection of the fake profile. These got selected during the pre-processing. The y-axis depicts the number of entries corresponding to each feature available in the dataset as shown in Figure 11.1.

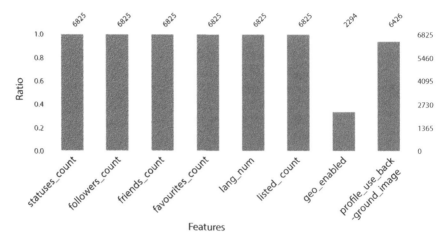

Figure 11.1 Dataset description.

11.3.2   Pre-Processing

Before proceeding for the models, we append one more stride, i.e., pre-processing. The data set is pre-processed before it is fed to a model. For feature extraction, we used the principal component analysis method. It is a dimensionality reduction method used to reduce the dimensionality of a large data set. It transforms a dataset of many variables into smaller ones that contain vital information in the large dataset (Figure 11.2). It is comparatively easy to visualize and analyze small data sets without affecting the accuracy of the original data set.

• The first step of PCA is to standardize the range of initial variables for equal contribution to the analysis. Here, the variables with large ranges will dominate over those with a small range. Mathematically, it is calculated by the given formula.

$$z = \frac{value - mean}{standard\ deviation} \tag{11.1}$$

• The next step of PCA is covariance matrix calculation to understand and analyze the relationship between the variables because dense correlated variables may contain redundant information. From this, we can also understand

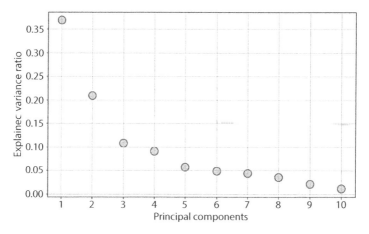

Figure 11.2 Explained variance ratio of fitted principal components.

- variations of input data set variables from the mean with respect to each other.
- And the last step is computing the eigen-vectors and eigen-values of the covariance matrix.

After performing principal component analysis, 96% of the total variance comprises of the seven features: friends count, followers count, status count, listed count, favorite count, geo-enabled, and language number.

Our model aims at detecting a profile as a hoax or legitimate based on the visible characteristics. Henceforth, all the precise aspects are determined. Only the numerical data has been selected, and the categorical features are discarded. The following traits are picked [19]. Then, the data set of fake and genuine users

friends	followers	status count	listed count	fav count	geo enabled	lang num

are merged into one with an additional label for each profile, i.e., "is Fake" that is a Boolean variable. It is then stored in the Y variable that is the response concerning a profile X. Finally, the blank entries or NAN are substituted with zeros.

11.3.3   Artificial Neural Network

Neural network [7] is the deep learning model that works similarly to the neuron network of a human brain. The neural network has layers, and each

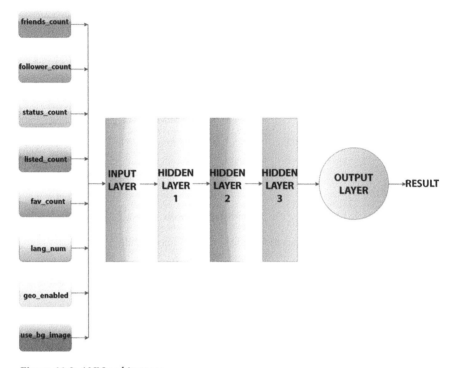

Figure 11.3 ANN architecture.

layer has neurons (nodes). We used the sequential from Keras. The model design with an input layer, three hidden layers, and an output layer has activation function ReLU for all but the output layer. Sigmoid is used as an activation function for the output layer. The model compiled using optimizer: Adam, loss function: binary cross-entropy. In our model (Figure 11.3), ANN of the stated above architecture is used. Sigmoid function finally provides the output between 0 and 1 and based on the prediction of a particular profile, labelled as fake or genuine.

Hyperparameters

1. Rectified Linear Units (ReLU): The rectified linear activation function is a piecewise linear function. ReLU (Figure 11.4) is the default activation function for many neural networks as it is easier to train and produces better results.

$$R(z) = max(0, z) \qquad (11.2)$$

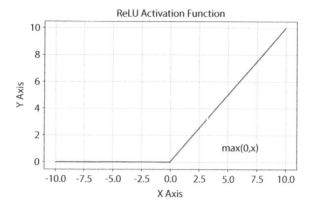

Figure 11.4 Rectified linear units.

2. Sigmoid Function: This is also known as the logistic function. When values between 0.0 and 1.0 are required, sigmoid function (Figure 11.5) is used. It is a non-linear activation function and is differentiable and hence slope can be found at any two points.

$$\sigma(z) = \frac{1}{1+e^{-z}} \qquad (11.3)$$

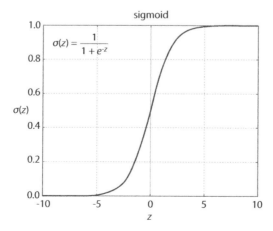

Figure 11.5 Sigmoid function.

- If z is very large, then e^z is close to zero and

$$\sigma(z) = \frac{1}{1+0} \approx 1 \tag{11.4}$$

- If z is very small, then e^z is large and

$$\sigma(z) = \frac{1}{1 + largenumber} \approx 0 \tag{11.5}$$

11.3.4 Random Forest

Random forest also known as random-decision-forest is one of the methods that correspond to the category ensemble learning methods. This method is used in machine learning due to its simplicity in solving regression problems as well as classification (Figure 11.6).

Random forest, unlike the decision tree method, generates multiple decision trees, and the final output is collectively the result of all the decision trees formed. Similarly, we deployed the random forest [20] method for profile detection. The data is fed to the model and corresponding outputs are obtained. While training, the bootstrap aggregating algorithm is applied for the given set of $X = x_1, x_2, \cdots, x_n$ and $Y = y_1, y_2, \cdots, y_n$ responses, repeatedly (B times) random sample is selected and fits the trees (f_b) to the sample. After training, the predictions for a given sample (x') are calculated by the formula specified below:

$$\hat{f} = \frac{1}{B} \sum_{b-1}^{B} f_b(x') \tag{11.6}$$

11.3.5 Extreme Gradient Boost

XG Boost is another ensemble learning method used for regression. This implements the stochastic gradient boosting algorithm. Random forest has a drawback, and it is efficient only when all inputs are available, i.e., there is no missing value. To overcome this, we use a gradient boosting algorithm. As per the boosting algorithm, firstly, $F_0(x)$ is initialized.

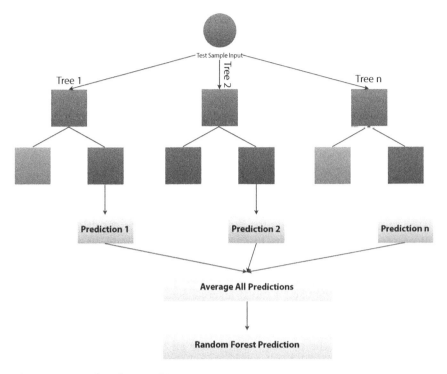

Figure 11.6 Random forest architecture.

$$F_0(x) = argmin_\gamma \sum_{i=1}^{n} L(y_i, \gamma) \qquad (11.7)$$

Then, iterative calculation of gradient of loss function takes place

$$r_{im} = -\alpha \left[\frac{\partial L(y_i, F(x_i))}{\partial F(x_i)} \right] \qquad (11.8)$$

Finally, the boosted model $F_m(x)$ is defined

$$F_m(x) = F_{m-1}(x) + \gamma_m h_m(x) \qquad (11.9)$$

α is the learning rate and γ_m is the multiplicative factor.

11.3.6 Long Short-Term Memory

LSTM is a recurrent neural network architecture. This architecture is capable of learning long-term dependencies. In our work, we have developed a model using LSTM that classifies the profile as fake or genuine based on tweets. Before training the LSTM on the tweets, we pre-processed the data by forming a string of tokens from each tweet.

- We have converted all tokens into lower case.
- We have removed the stop words from tweets.

Then, we have transformed these tokenized tweets into an embedding layer to create word vectors for incoming words. The resulting sequence of vectors is then fed to the LSTM that outputs a single 32-dimensional vector that is then fed forward through sigmoid activated layers to give the output.

In our model, we used a multi-layered neural network, random forest [20] approach, and XG Boost that work on the visible features of a profile. These extracted features are stored in a comma-separated file (CSV) that is easy to read by the model. Finally, after all, training, testing, and evaluating the model can label a profile as legitimate or not. We are considering features like friends, followers, status count, listed count, fav count, geo-enabled, and lang num. If the account is having a very less (or less than moderate) number of all parameters like friends, followers, status count, listed count, fav count along with geo-enabled as 0 or none, and then we are declaring the account as fake.

11.4 Experimental Results

Finally, we arrive at the experimental results. These are the results obtained by running the machine learning models on the chosen dataset. The results obtained are in the form of graphs or comparison charts or ROC curves. Corresponding to every model, we discuss the accuracy or loss trends. The accuracy or loss calculated during training and validation are discussed further. We trained our models on Google Colab because Google provides the use of free GPU. The Google Colab 12GB NVIDIA Tesla K80 GPU that can be used up to 12 hours continuously. All the models were coded down in Python3 language.

After training and testing all the models, the following results were obtained. The model accuracy, model loss vs. the epoch graphs are plotted for neural network LSTM, and model accuracy comparison, and ROC curve for random forest, XG boost and other methods.

Neural Network: The model's accuracy and loss graph have been shown in Figures 11.7 and 11.8 for the trained neural network. After running for 15 epochs, the above accuracy and loss graphs are obtained. Initially, starting from 0.97 the accuracy varies along the path and finally reaches its maximum, i.e., 0.98. Similarly, the loss graph for testing data begins from 1 and for validation data begins from 4 and eventually reaches a minimum

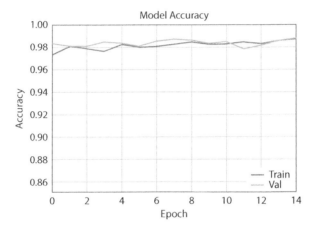

Figure 11.7 Model accuracy.

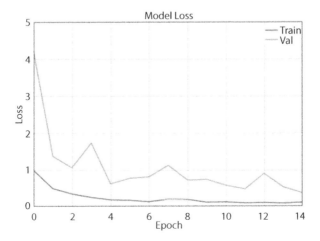

Figure 11.8 Model loss.

point, less than 0.5. To calculate the loss binary cross-entropy function is used. Initially, random weights get assigned to each feature and finally the machine defines a unique weight to each feature.

Random Forest and Other Methods: In the comparison chart (Figure 11.9), we observe accuracy of different models, namely, random forest, xg boost, ada boost, and decision tree. The maximum accuracy is achieved by XG boost that equals to 0.996. Further, we have a decision tree and random forest with approximately similar accuracy of 0.99. The least accuracy of ADA boost model. Histogram for accuracy comparison and the ROC curves have been presented in Figures 11.9 to 11.11.

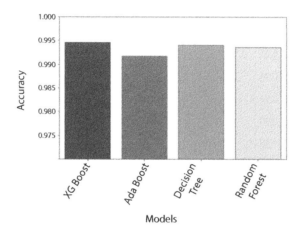

Figure 11.9 Accuracy of different models.

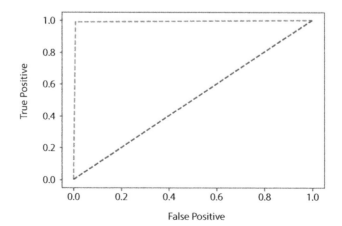

Figure 11.10 ROC curve XG Boost.

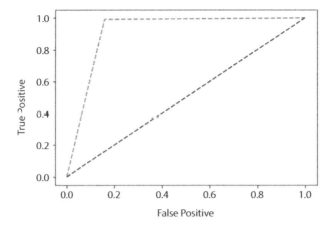

Figure 11.11 ROC curve Random Forest.

11.5   Conclusion and Future Work

Fake profile is a common issue as the demand of social media network increasing day by day. People are harassing others by making a fake profile of a user. In this work, we implemented the Neural Network, Random Forest, and XG Boost machine learning methods to train our system to detect fake Twitter profiles based on visible data. After training, validating, and testing our models on the MIB dataset, we finally arrive at an inference that the maximum accuracy achieved is 99.46% by XG Boost method followed by ANN and random forest as showed in the result analysis.

Further work can be done by combining images of profiles along with the categorical and numeric data and implementation using a CNN. Also, including other hyperparamete rs, combining different models, and assembling a real-time model may achieve better results.

Acknowledgment

We extend our sincere gratitude to the mentors for their patient guidance and useful critiques for this work. Their enthusiastic encouragement helped us to keep the progress on schedule.

References

1. Elyusufi, Y., Elyusufi, Z., Kbir, M.A., Social networks fake profiles detection based on account setting and activity, in: *Proceedings of the 4th International*

Conference on Smart City Applications (SCA '19), Association for Computing Machinery, New York, NY, USA, Article 37, p. 15, 2019.

2. Van Der Walt, E. and Eloff, J., Using machine learning to detect fake identities: Bots vs humans. *IEEE Access*, 6, 6540–6549, 2018.

3. Mitter, S., Wagner, C., Strohmaier, M., A categorization scheme for socialbot attacks in online social networks. arXiv preprint arXiv:1402.6288, 2014.

4. Singh, N., Sharma, T., Thakral, A., Choudhury, T., Detection of fake profile in online social networks using machine learning, in: *2018 International Conference on Advances in Computing and Communication Engineering (ICACCE)*, IEEE, pp. 231–234, 2018.

5. Cresci, S., Di Pietro, R., Petrocchi, M., Spognardi, A., Tesconi, M., Fame for sale: Efficient detection of fake Twitter followers. *Decis. Support Syst.*, Elsevier, 80, 56–71, 2015.

6. Fire, M., Goldschmidt, R., Elovici, Y., Online social networks: threats and solutions. *IEEE Commun. Surv. Tutorials*, 16, 4, 2019–2036, 2014.

7. Likitha, M., Rahul, K., Prudhvi Sai, A., Mallikarjuna Reddy, A., Design and Development of Artificial Neural Networks to Identify Fake Profiles. *Purakala with ISSN 0971–2143 is an UGC CARE Journal*, vol. 31, no. 21, pp. 831–836, 2020.

8. Kudugunta, S. and Ferrara, E., Deep neural networks for bot detection. *Inf. Sci.*, 467, 312–322, 2018.

9. Abokhodair, N., Yoo, D., McDonald, D.W., Dissecting a social botnet: Growth, content and influence in Twitter, in: *Proceedings of the 18th ACM conference on computer supported cooperative work & social computing*, pp. 839–851, 2015.

10. Romanov, A., Semenov, A., Mazhelis, O., Veijalainen, J., Detection of fake profiles in social media-Literature review, in: *International Conference on Web Information Systems and Technologies*, vol. 2, SCITEPRESS, pp. 363–369, 2017.

11. Ramalingam, D. and Chinnaiah, V., Fake profile detection techniques in large-scale online social networks: A comprehensive review. *Comput. Electr. Eng.*, 65, 165–177, 2018.

12. Yu, H., Gibbons, P.B., Kaminsky, M., Xiao, F., Sybillimit: A near-optimal social network defense against sybil attacks, in: *2008 IEEE Symposium on Security and Privacy (sp 2008)*, IEEE, pp. 3–17, 2008.

13. Mulamba, D., Ray, I., Ray, I., Sybilradar: A graph-structure based framework for sybil detection in on-line social networks, in: *IFIP International Conference on ICT Systems Security and Privacy Protection*, Springer, Cham, pp. 179–193, 2016.

14. Romanov, A., Semenov, A., Veijalainen, J., Revealing fake profiles in social networks by longitudinal data analysis, in: *International Conference on Web Information Systems and Technologies*, vol. 2, SCITEPRESS, pp. 51–58, 2017.

15. Hajdu, G., Minoso, Y., Lopez, R., Acosta, M., Elleithy, A., Use of Artificial Neural Networks to Identify Fake Profiles, in: *2019 IEEE Long Island Systems, Applications and Technology Conference (LISAT)*, IEEE, pp. 1–4, 2019.

16. Kharaji, M.Y. and Rizi, F.S., An iac approach for detecting profile cloning in online social networks. arXiv preprint arXiv:1403.2006, 2014.

17. Raturi, R., Machine learning implementation for identifying fake accounts in social network. *Int. J, Pure Appl. Math.*, 118, 20, 4785–4797, 2018.

18. Cresci, S., Di Pietro, R., Petrocchi, M., Spognardi, A., Tesconi, M., The Paradigm-Shift of Social Spambots: Evidence, Theories, and Tools for the Arms Race, in: *In Proceedings of the 26th International Conference on World Wide Web Companion (WWW '17 Companion)*, International World Wide Web Conferences Steering Committee, Republic and Canton of Geneva, CHE, 963972, 2017.

19. Elyusufi, Y. and Elyusufi, Z., Social Networks Fake Profiles Detection Using Machine Learning Algorithms. *The Proceedings of the Third International Conference on Smart City Applications*, Springer, Cham, 2019.

20. Jyothi, V., Hamsini, K., Reddy, G.S., Vasireddy, B.K., Fake Profile Identification Using Machine Learning. *Tathapi with ISSN 2320-0693 is an UGC CARE Journal*, vol. 19(8), pp. 714–720, 2020.

12

Extraction of the Features of Fingerprints Using Conventional Methods and Convolutional Neural Networks

E. M. V. Naga Karthik* and Madan Gopal

Shiv Nadar University, Gautam Buddha Nagar, U.P., India

Abstract

Fingerprints are one of the most common biometric identifiers. Until recently, the conventional image processing methods were being used in extracting the features of the fingerprints for the fingerprint classification problem. However, with the rise of artificial intelligence, deep learning models such as the Convolutional Neural Networks (CNNs) have shown promising results in image classification problems. In this paper, we explain why CNNs are performing better by visualizing the features learned by its convolutional layers, and comparing them with the fingerprints' features extracted by estimating the local orientation map and detecting the singular regions. A 17-layer CNN model is proposed, which obtains a classification accuracy of 92.45% on the NIST-DB4 fingerprint dataset. We conclude that the first two convolutional layers are learning features that are similar to the ones obtained after using the above techniques, while the remaining layers are learning abstract and more complex features that are class-specific. This explains why the deep learning models are performing better. The results are promising as they bring us one step closer in demystifying the inner functioning of the CNNs.

Keywords: Deep learning, CNNs, fingerprints, image processing, feature visualization

Corresponding author: muni-venkata-naga-karthik.enamundram.1@etsmtl.net

Mettu Srinivas, G. Sucharitha and Anjanna Matta (eds.) Machine Learning Algorithms and Applications, (211–228) © 2021 Scrivener Publishing LLC

12.1   Introduction

Biometrics plays an important role in securing user data and maintaining its privacy. Each individual has a unique biometric trait which can be used for quick recognition and easy identification. Fingerprint identification technology has seen tremendous success in recent times due to its low cost of acquisition and the availability of abundant computational resources. Fingerprints are characterized by their continuous ridge and valley patterns that are seen as dark and white regions respectively, in fingerprint images. The Henry system [1] of fingerprint classification consists of five classes of fingerprints: Arch (A), Tented Arch (T), Whorl (W), Left loop (L), and Right loop (R). Figure 12.1 shows the examples of fingerprints from the NIST DB-4 dataset containing those five classes. Each class shows a different visual pattern, and the distribution of these fingerprints, in general, is unequal. This is shown in Table 12.1. The fingerprint distribution shows that the whorl, left loop, and right loop class patterns make upto 93.4%, while the remaining classes comprise only 6.6% of all fingerprints [2].

There are two main levels in fingerprint analysis: the global level and the minutiae level. By using the location of singular points as features, fingerprint classification is done by analysing the global structure of fingerprints. On the other hand, the fingerprint minutiae are used for identification and recognition tasks.

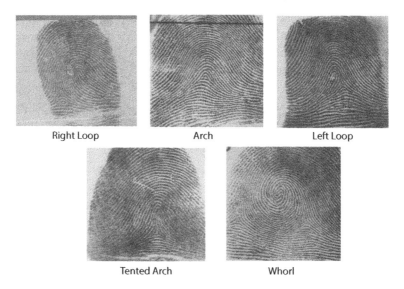

Right Loop   Arch   Left Loop

Tented Arch   Whorl

Figure 12.1 Sample images from the NIST DB-4 dataset showing all five classes.

Table 12.1 The percentage of each class of fingerprints [2].

Whorl	27.9%
Left Loop	33.8%
Right Loop	31.7%
Arch	3.7%
Tented Arch	2.9%

The classification of fingerprints is a two-step process, namely, feature extraction and classification on the basis of the extracted features [3]. First, a pre-processing stage involves division of an image into blocks and a subsequent normalization of each block. This facilitates the feature extraction step. The extracted features are then used for classification using support vector machines (SVMs) or fully connected neural networks (NNs). However, one major limitation of these methods is that manual extraction of the features considers only specific regions of the fingerprint by discarding some subtler features, thereby resulting in a loss of information. Hence, extraction of features using conventional image processing methods is a difficult task.

On the other hand, deep neural networks (DNNs) have gained attention due to their ability to accurately classify datasets containing millions of images. The advantage of using DNNs is that the neurons in each layer have the capability to automatically detect the features implicitly. In Convolutional Neural Networks (CNNs), the images are directly fed as the input, thereby decreasing the additional computation required for converting the image into a one-dimensional vector, which is generally the case in fully connected NNs.

The chapter is structured as follows. A summary of the previous work in the field is discussed in Section 12.2. Section 12.3 presents an overview of the methods proposed and the dataset used. The results from our method along with the comparison of the features of by visualization are shown in Section 12.4, and finally, Section 12.5 presents the conclusion.

12.2   Related Work

Fingerprint classification using conventional methods is based on the global features, namely, the local orientation maps, singular regions, and the ridge-valley structures. The gradient-based methods [4–7] are used for obtaining the orientation maps and the Poincare index method [4, 8, 9] for singular region detection.

Hong et al. [6] normalized the fingerprint images and estimated the orientation maps using the least squares method. Based on fixed criteria of the range of index values as defined in [10], Kawagoe and Tojo [8] and Bo et al. [9] computed the Poincaré index value and located the singular regions in the image. Jain et al. [4] proposed an algorithm called FingerCode to extract the features such that the minutiae details and the global ridge-valley structure are represented effectively. Bay et al. [11] proposed SURF (Speeded-up Robust Features) to automatically detect local image features based on the Hessian matrix for finding the features of interest. Srinivas and Mohan [12] proposed edge and patch-based feature extraction methods for content-based retrieval of medical images. In the context of fine-grained object detection, Srinivas et al. [13] used online dictionary learning sparse and efficient feature representations using CNNs. Wang et al. [14] used a stacked sparse autoencoder for fingerprint classification and obtained a 93.1% accuracy on the NIST DB-4 dataset. The orientation map was used as a feature input to the model. Peralta et al. [3] used CaffeNet for fingerprint classification and compared their results with the accuracies obtained by using SVMs and k-NNs. Both real (NIST-DB-4) and synthetic (SFinGe) fingerprint datasets were used in their study. Simonyan et al. [15] proposed a method, where given a trained CNN and a class of interest, an image that maximizes the corresponding class score is obtained along with a class saliency map that is unique to the image and the class. Zeiler et al. [16] proposed a De-Convolutional Neural Network (DeConvNet) for visualization by mapping the activations back to the input pixel space. By mapping features to input pixels, parts of the image causing an activation in the feature map are obtained.

There are two ways in which we can visualize the learnings of a CNN: (i) by visualizing the layer activations, and (ii) by visualizing the weights of the network at each layer. In this study, we visualized the layer activations and the kernels of the initial convolutional layers. This gave us an insight as to what CNN is learning at each stage from the fingerprint images.

The novelty in our method lies in the fact that there has not been any study, where the learnings of the CNN have been investigated for the fingerprint classification problem. While there are many results in the literature which talk about new methods that result in high classification accuracies, none of them discuss *how* these CNNs are able to produce such high accuracies. Therefore, our work in this paper primarily focuses on comparing the global set of features, namely, the singular regions computed using the Poincare index method [9] and the local orientation maps of the fingerprints using the least squares method [6], with the features learned by CNN. We have visualized the features of the initial convolutional layers of the CNN and have found a correlation between the conventionally extracted features and what the deep network is learning.

12.3   Methods and Materials

12.3.1   Feature Extraction Using SURF

SURF is an automatic feature detection method that uses the Hessian matrix for finding the points of interest. More concretely, the algorithm uses an approximation of the determinant of the Hessian blob detector computed using the integral image. It has three major steps: (i) interest point detection, (ii) local neighbourhood description, and (iii) matching. One of the important applications of the Hessian matrix is that its determinant can be used to accurately measure the local change around a point of interest. The result after applying the SURF algorithm to fingerprint images is shown in Figure 12.2.

It can be observed that across all four images, the detected points of interest are non-uniform. For instance, in the first row, the detected features

Strongest SURF-detected features
overlayed on fingerprints

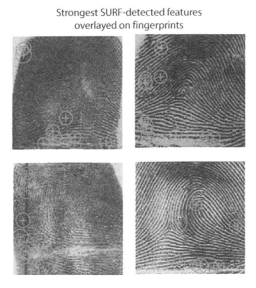

Figure 12.2 Results after applying the SURF algorithm. The green markers show the detected keypoints. Circles are drawn around each keypoint. The size of the circle depends on the relative weight of the detected keypoints. Notice that most of the features are biased toward the corners of the image.

are near the edges of the image, whereas in the bottom-right image, features are spread throughout the image—some at the center and a few near the edges. This non-uniformity does not help in accurately detecting the location of features across all fingerprint classes. This motivated us to use the conventional methods to extract the fingerprints' features.

12.3.2 Feature Extraction Using Conventional Methods

To reduce irregular intensities in the fingerprint image, all fingerprints are normalized such that the ridge-like regions have zero mean and unit standard deviation. An input fingerprint image along with its normalized version is shown in Figure 12.3.

12.3.2.1 Local Orientation Estimation

The angle $\theta(i,j)$ between the pixel coordinate (i,j) and the horizontal axis is defined as the local ridge orientation at that particular pixel. The orientation field of a fingerprint image represents the directionality of the ridges, which explains the pattern of the ridge lines in a fingerprint. The step-wise details of the least squares method proposed in [6] are used for estimating the local orientation.

1. The normalized image $I_{norm}(i,j)$ is divided into blocks of specific sizes.
2. The gradients in x and y directions, $\delta_x(i,j)$ and $\delta_y(i,j)$, respectively, are computed for each pixel in the image.

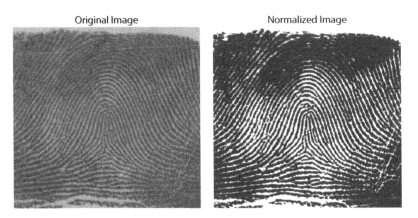

Figure 12.3 Left: Original, raw fingerprint image. Right: Normalized image.

3. The local orientation, $\theta(i,j)$, centered at pixel (i,j) is estimated by $\theta(i,j) = 0.5 * tan^{-1} V_y(i, j)/V_x(i, j))$, where

$$V_x(i, j) = \sum_{u=i-\frac{w}{2}}^{i+\frac{w}{2}} \sum_{v=j-\frac{w}{2}}^{j+\frac{w}{2}} 2\delta_x(u,v)\delta_y(u,v) \qquad (12.1)$$

$$V_y(i, j) = \sum_{u=i-\frac{w}{2}}^{i+\frac{w}{2}} \sum_{v=j-\frac{w}{2}}^{j+\frac{w}{2}} \delta_x^2(u,v)\delta_y^2(u,v) \qquad (12.2)$$

where w is the size of the block. A low-pass filter is used to correct the gradient direction. Equations defined by $\phi_x(i,j)$ and $\phi_y(i,j)$ are used to convert the orientation image into vector fields that are continuous. They are written as follows:

$$\phi_x(i, j) = \cos 2\theta(i, j) \qquad (12.3)$$

$$\phi_y(i, j) = \sin 2\theta(i, j) \qquad (12.4)$$

The following equations perform the low-pass filtering:

$$\phi_x'(i, j) = \sum_{u=\frac{-w_\phi}{2}}^{\frac{w_\phi}{2}} \sum_{v=-\frac{w_\phi}{2}}^{\frac{w_\phi}{2}} W(u,v)\phi_x(i-uw, j-vw) \qquad (12.5)$$

$$\phi_y'(i, j) = \sum_{u=\frac{-w_\phi}{2}}^{\frac{w_\phi}{2}} \sum_{v=-\frac{w_\phi}{2}}^{\frac{w_\phi}{2}} W(u,v)\phi_y(i-uw, j-vw) \qquad (12.6)$$

where W is a two-dimensional low-pass filter with $w_\phi \times w_\phi$ being the size of the filter.

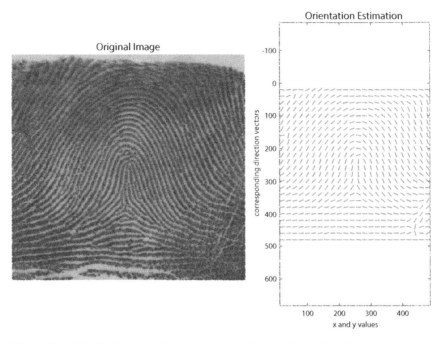

Figure 12.4 Left: Original, raw fingerprint image. Right: Estimated local orientation.

4. Finally, the local orientation at pixel (i,j) is given by

$$O(i,j) = \frac{1}{2} tan^{-1}\left(\frac{\phi_y'(i,j)}{\phi_x'(i,j)}\right) \tag{12.7}$$

The original fingerprint along with the estimated orientation map is shown in Figure 12.4.

12.3.2.2   Singular Region Detection

A commonly used method for singular region detection in a fingerprint image, called the Poincaré index was first proposed by [8]. Let the angle $\theta(i,j)$ denote the direction of the pixel (i,j) in the $N \times N$ fingerprint image. The Poincaré index at pixel (i,j) is computed as follows:

$$\text{Poincaré}'(i,j) = (1/2\pi) \times \sum_{k=0}^{N} \Delta(m) \tag{12.8}$$

Figure 12.5 Left: Tented Arch fingerprint. Right: Whorl fingerprint. The loops are shown in green circles and the deltas in red triangles.

where

$$\Delta(m) = \begin{cases} \delta(m) & if \; |(\delta(m))| < \pi/2 \\ \delta(m) + \pi & if \; |(\delta(m))| \leq -\pi/2 \\ \pi - \delta(m) & if \; |(\delta(m))| \geq \pi/2 \end{cases} \qquad (12.9)$$

$$\delta(m) = \theta(i_{(m+1)modN}, j_{(m+1)modN}) - \theta(i_m, j_m)$$

If Poincaré $(i,j) = 0.5$, the block of the image containing that pixel may contain a core point (or, a loop). If Poincaré $(i,j) = -0.5$, then the corresponding block of the image may contain a delta point. Otherwise, the block does not contain any singular points. However, there are three important points regarding the number of singular points in any given fingerprint image [10]: (i) The arch class has no loops or deltas; (ii) The delta is near the center of the image for tented arch class, near the right for left loops, and near the left for right loops. All the above classes have one loop each; and (iii) The whorl is a complex class, which can contain two loops and two deltas. Figure 12.5 shows the location of the singular points overlaid on the original fingerprint.

12.3.3 Proposed CNN Architecture

Our CNN architecture for fingerprint classification is given in Table 12.2. The original image (size 512×512) is cropped and resized to an image

Table 12.2 The proposed CNN architecture.

Layer type	Size	Stride	Stride
Convolutional	$222 \times 222 \times 32$	1	ReLU
Convolutional	$220 \times 220 \times 32$	1	ReLU
Batch Normalization	$220 \times 220 \times 32$	-	-
Max Pooling	$110 \times 110 \times 32$	2	-
Convolutional	$108 \times 108 \times 64$	1	ReLU
Convolutional	$106 \times 106 \times 128$	1	ReLU
Batch Normalization	$106 \times 106 \times 128$	-	-
Max Pooling	$53 \times 53 \times 128$	2	-
Convolutional	$51 \times 51 \times 128$	1	ReLU
Convolutional	$49 \times 49 \times 128$	1	ReLU
Batch Normalization	$49 \times 49 \times 128$	-	-
Max Pooling	$49 \times 49 \times 128$	2	-
Fully Connected	256	-	ReLU
Dropout	0.5	-	-
Fully Connected	128	-	ReLU
Dropout	0.25	-	-
Fully Connected	5	-	Softmax

of size 224×224. The architecture has a total of 17 layers consisting of 6 convolutional layers, 3 max-pooling, batch normalization, and fully connected layers each and 2 dropout [17] layers. The non-linear activation layer, ReLU, is used in the layers shown in Table 12.2 except for the fully connected layer where the softmax layer is used. While training the network, a few data augmentation methods, such as rescaling, width shift, and height shift, were also used online to enhance the performance of the network on the testing dataset. The following hyperparameters were used for fingerprint classification—the model was run for 150 epochs with a batch size of 32. As for the optimizer, Stochastic Gradient Descent (SGD) was used with a learning rate of 0.001.

12.3.4   Dataset

The dataset used in this study is NIST Special Database 4 (NIST DB-4) [18]. It contains 4,000 fingerprint images in PNG format. They are formatted files which consist of 8-bit grayscale fingerprint images for the 10 fingers on the left and right hands. There are two impressions "F" and "S" for each finger. The size of each fingerprint image is 512-by-512 pixels with 32 rows of white space at the bottom. Each class has an equal number of fingerprints (400), that is, 800 such fingerprint images. After removing corrupted images from the original dataset, a total of 3,816 images were used. These were split into 3,316 training images and 500 testing images randomly. Tables 12.3 and 12.4 show the number of images in each of the fingerprint classes used for training and testing.

12.3.5   Computational Environment

The computations were performed on the following platforms: (i) for feature extraction using conventional methods, MATLAB 2017b was used in a system

Table 12.3 Distribution of the images in the training set.

Fingerprint class	Training images
Whorl	655
Left Loop	677
Right Loop	671
Arch	641
Tented Arch	672

Table 12.4 Distribution of the images in the testing set.

Fingerprint class	Testing images
Whorl	112
Left Loop	74
Right Loop	96
Arch	122
Tented Arch	96

with an Intel i7 processor, 8-GB memory, and a NVIDIA GeForce 830M GPU. (ii) For feature extraction using CNN, Google Colaboratory was used. Keras with Tensorflow backend was used as the deep learning framework.

12.4 Results

Figure 12.6 shows the confusion matrix obtained after classification. The Whorl and Left loop classes have the lowest misclassification error of about 2.7% suggesting that our model learned most of the features of fingerprints from these classes correctly. The Arch class has a misclassification error of 4.9% with a few being classified as Tented arches. The highest misclassification error is observed in the case of Right loop where 15.6% of fingerprints have been wrongly classified as Tented arches. Another important observation from the confusion matrix is that a high number of images are wrongly classified as Tented arch fingerprints. From Table 12.1, we know that this Whorl, Left, and Right loop fingerprints are most commonly observed while Arch and Tented arch fingerprints are quite rare. Therefore, we believe that the lack of variability in the images is reflected in the high misclassification error for this class of fingerprints.

Table 12.5 shows the performance of our CNN architecture. An accuracy of 92.45% was obtained. We also compare our results with the classification

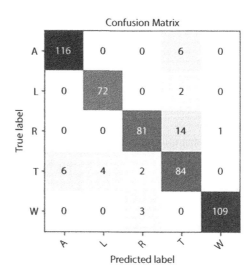

Figure 12.6 Confusion matrix. The diagonal elements show the number of correctly predicted fingerprints of each class.

Table 12.5 Model performance evaluation.

	Proposed CNN architecture
Input Image Size	224×224
Accuracy	92.45%
Training Time	2H 15M

Table 12.6 Comparison of the classification accuracies.

	Accuracy
Proposed CNN architecture	92.45% (NIST-DB4)
Peralta *et al.* [3]	90.73% (NIST-DB4 F) 88.91% (NIST-DB4 S)
Wang *et al.* [14]	93.1% (NIST-DB4)

accuracies reported in the literature. The "F" and "S" suffixes denote that the original dataset was split into two different databases containing two different impressions of the same finger. This is shown in Table 12.6. Wang *et al.* [14] used the tedious conventional method for feature extraction and classification where the features are extracted manually and fed into a NN classifier, whereas our model was directly trained on input fingerprint images and also performs better than that of [3]. It is also worth noting that [14] reported their model's performance on a four-class classification problem by merging the Arch and Tented arch fingerprints into one class. This essentially reduces the class imbalance in the dataset, hence leading to a higher accuracy. Our model, on the other hand, achieves similar performance with all the five classes.

12.4.1   Feature Extraction and Visualization

In order to understand what CNN is learning, we took a simple approach of visualizing the layer activations. Since the model automatically learns the best features while training, we extracted the activations at the output of each convolutional layer to see how the input image has been progressively downsampled by eliminating redundant features. Figure 12.7 (left) shows a subset of the output activations extracted from the 1st to 5th convolutional layers. The outputs of the first convolutional layer (a1

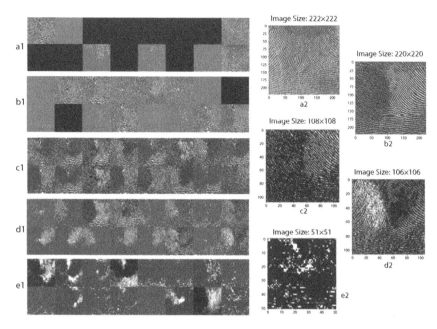

Figure 12.7 The outputs of the 1st to 5th convolutional layers. Figures a1 and a2: Output of 1st convolutional layer and 16th activation enlarged. Figures b1 and b2: Output of 2nd convolutional layer and 16th activation enlarged. Figures c1 and c2: Output of 3rd convolutional layer and 16th activation enlarged. Figures d1 and d2: Output of 4th convolutional layer and 16th activation enlarged. Figures e1 and e2: Output of 5th convolutional layer and 16th activation enlarged.

and a2 in Figure 12.7) contain 32 feature maps out of which 16 activations are randomly chosen and plotted together. The number of feature maps increase as we go deeper into the network; however, the same procedure of randomly picking 16 activations has been used for plotting the outputs of the subsequent convolutional layers (b1, b2; c1, c2; d1, d2; e1, e2 of Figure 12.7). This method was chosen because showing all the feature maps in a single image is impractical. In Figure 12.7 (right), the last activation (16th activation) of each layer output is enlarged to visualize the kind of image that the CNN is learning at each layer.

On observing the extracted activations at the output of the first convolutional layer, it can be seen that some of the activations are completely black, meaning that these are the dead activations that have not helped the network in learning. On the other hand, there are a few activations which bear some resemblance to the original input. When these activations were fed as inputs for estimating the orientation map and locating the singular regions, an interesting phenomenon was observed (see Figure 12.8). The orientation

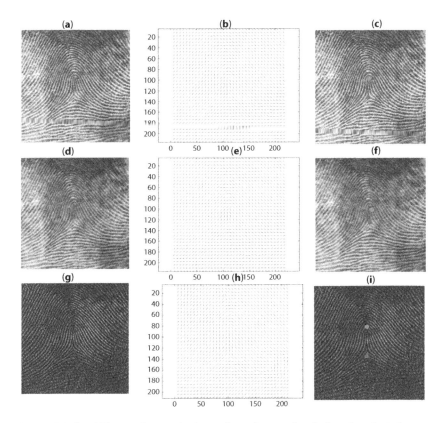

Figure 12.8 (a–c) The raw fingerprint image from the tented arch class, its orientation map, and locations of the singular regions. (d–f) One of the 32 output activations of the first convolutional layer, its orientation map, and the locations of the singular regions. (g–i) An activation from the second convolutional layer, its orientation map, and the locations of the singular regions (best viewed in color).

map of the activation is preserved while at the same time, the location of the singular regions is also intact. When the same process is repeated for the activations from the second convolutional layer output, we could again see some similarity to the features extracted using the conventional methods in Section 12.3.2. However, there are a few important points to note. Compared to the original image, we can see that the output of the second convolutional layer is darker and blurry. In the regions that are blurred, the orientation map cannot be properly estimated, leading to erroneous ridge directions. These lead to the incorrect detection of the singular regions and are removed in the post-processing of the image. However, the centre of the image is still intact which is responsible for detecting the singular regions. Figure 12.8 shows the comparison between the results obtained after using a fingerprint image from the tented arch class of the testing set and the activation outputs of the first and second convolutional layers.

12.5   Conclusion

In this study, features of fingerprints, namely, the local orientation map and the singular regions were successfully extracted. A 17-layer CNN architecture was proposed for fingerprint classification and an accuracy of 92.45% was obtained. The features learned by CNN were interpreted by visualizing the activations of the convolutional layer outputs. A comparison between the features learned by CNN and the features extracted using conventional methods was also performed. From our interpretation of the results, we could understand that the features which are being used for classification using SVMs and k-NNs are being learnt by the network in the initial two layers of the network. The remaining layers are learning more complex representations of the input which are incomprehensible. Instead of manually feeding the encoded feature vectors to the network, the CNNs are learning the class-specific features by themselves which, therefore, is resulting in such high accuracies.

Acknowledgements

The NIST-DB4 fingerprint dataset is currently discontinued and is not available online. However, the dataset will be provided on request. A part of this work was done with the help of the workstation provided by the Energy Science Lab of the Mechanical Engineering Department, Shiv Nadar University.

References

1. Henry, E., *Classification and Uses of Fingerprints*, 2nd ed., George Routledge and Sons, London, 1900.
2. Wilson, C.L., Candela, G.T., Watson, C. I., Journal for Artificial Neural Networks, 1, 2 1994.
3. Peralta, D., Triguero, I., García, S., Saeys, Y., Benítez, J., Herrera, F., On the use of convolutional neural networks for robust classification of multiple fingerprint captures. *Int. J. Intell. Syst.*, 33, 213–230, 2018.

4. Jain, A.K., Prabhakar, S., Hong, L., A multichannel approach to fingerprint classification. *IEEE Trans. Pattern Anal. Mach. Intell.*, 21, 348–359, Apr. 1999.

5. Bazen, A.M. and Gerez, S.H., Systematic methods for the computation of the directional fields and singular points of fingerprints. *IEEE Trans. Pattern Anal. Mach. Intell.*, 24, 905–919, July 2002.

6. Hong, L., Wan, Y., Jain, A., Fingerprint image enhancement: Algorithm and performance evaluation. *IEEE Trans. Pattern Anal. Mach. Intell.*, 20, 777–789, Aug. 1998.

7. Thai, R., *Fingerprint image enhancement and minutiae extraction*, Dissertation report, The University of Western Australia, 2003.

8. Kawagoe, M. and Tojo, A., Fingerprint pattern classification. *Pattern Recognit.*, 17, 295–303, June 1984.

9. Bo, J., Ping, T.H., Lan, X.M., Fingerprint singular point detection algorithm by poincaré index. *WTOS*, 7, 1453–1462, Dec. 2008.

10. Maltoni, D., Maio, D., Jain, A.K., Prabhakar, S., Handbook of Fingerprint Recognition, 2nd ed., Springer Publishing Company, Springer-Verlag, London, 2009.

11. Bay, H., Ess, A., Tuytelaars, T., Van Gool, L., Speeded-up robust features (surf). *Comput. Vis. Image Underst.*, 110, 346–359, June 2008.

12. Srinivas, M. and Mohan, D.K., Medical image indexing and retrieval using multiple features, *Proceedings of the International Conference on Computational Intelligence and Information Technology*, 2013.

13. Srinivas, M., Lin, Y., Liao, H.M., Learning deep and sparse feature representation for fine-grained object recognition, in: *2017 IEEE International Conference on Multimedia and Expo (ICME)*, pp. 1458–1463, 2017.

14. Wang, R., Congying, H., Yanping, W., Tiande, G., Fingerprint classification based on depth neural network. *CoRR*, abs/1409.5188, 2014, https://arxiv.org/pdf/1409.5188.pdf.

15. Simonyan, K., Vedaldi, A., Zisserman, A., Deep inside convolutional networks: Visualising image classification models and saliency maps, in: *Computer Vision – ECCV 2014*, ECCV 2014, (Washington, DC, USA), D. Fleet, T. Pajdla, B. Schiele, T. Tuytelaars (Eds.), pp. 2018–2025, Springer, Cham, 2013.

16. Zeiler, M.D., Taylor, G.W., Fergus, R., Adaptive deconvolutional networks for mid and high level feature learning, in: *Proceedings of the 2011 International Conference on Computer Vision, ICCV '11*, IEEE Computer Society, Washington, DC, USA, pp. 2018–2025, 2011.

17. Srivastava, N., Hinton, G., Krizhevsky, A., Sutskever, I., Salakhutdinov, R., Dropout: A simple way to prevent neural networks from overfitting. *J. Mach. Learn. Res.*, 15, 1929–1958, Jan. 2014.

18. Watson, C.I. and Wilson, C., *Nist special database*, National Institute of Standards and Technology, U.S.A, 4, p. 11, 1992.

13

Facial Expression Recognition Using Fusion of Deep Learning and Multiple Features

M. Srinivas*, Sanjeev Saurav, Akshay Nayak and Murukessan A. P.

Department of Computer Science and Engineering, National Institute of Technology Warangal, Telangana, India

Abstract

Facial emotion recognition plays an important role in machine learning and artificial intelligence applications. Based on the human facial expressions of information, machines can provide personalized services. There are many applications, like virtual reality, personalized recommendations, and customer satisfaction that depend on reliable and an efficient way to recognize the facial expressions. With the help of automated facial emotion recognition, it achieves improvement in the human-machine interface. Emotions are categorized into seven categories and that are anger, disgust, fear, happy, neutral, sad, and surprise. Facial emotion recognition is a very important challenging problem because every individual facial expression varies greatly by slightly change in the head pose, environmental conditions, and so on, and it attracted many researchers for years. In this work, we are proposing deep learning as well as handcraft-based model to detect the facial expressions. In this model, we are using CNN which is a deep learning model, BOVW, and HOG which is handcrafted methods to detect the facial feature. Finally, we use the Support Vector Machine (SVM) classification method to classify the facial expressions. We have evaluated testing results on standard FER 2013 datasets. The proposed method gives promising results compared with other well-known methods.

Keywords: Support vector machine, classification, facial expressions, histogram of gradients, landmark descriptors, convolutional neural networks

---

**Corresponding author*: msv@nitw.ac.in

Mettu Srinivas, G. Sucharitha and Anjanna Matta (eds.) Machine Learning Algorithms and Applications, (229–246) © 2021 Scrivener Publishing LLC

13.1   Introduction

Many components contribute to the transmission of an individual's emotions, and some of them are pose, speech, facial expressions, behaviors, and activities. However, facial expressions are of higher significance from others. In communicating with others, humans can recognize emotions with a considerable level of accuracy. If we can use computer science to find practical solutions for automatic recognition of facial emotions, then we would be able to attain accuracy that is virtually comparable to the human perception.

Facial expression is the most powerful signal using which human beings can express their emotional states and intentions. Emotions can be expressed in three forms such as word of message, vocal part, and facial expression of the speaker. Among these, researchers have found facial expressions of the speaker contribute 55% of the facial emotions. This shows facial expression leaves a major impact on human communication. Many studies have been carried out on automatic facial expression analysis (AFEA) due to its practical uses in social robotics, medical treatment, driver suggestion, and many other human-computer interaction (HCI). Based on cultural studies, seven basic emotions have found. The term basic expression refers to a set of expressions that convey universal emotions they are: neutral, disgust, fear, sadness, happiness, anger, and surprise. Seven basic facial expression sample images are shown in Figure 13.1.

In the course of recent years, numerous FER-related algorithms have been proposed in the article, including perceiving emotions from facial frontal

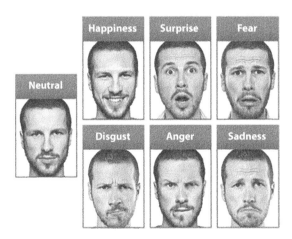

Figure 13.1 Seven basic emotional expressions [22].

and non-frontal pictures. Non-frontal FER is more testing than frontal FER and increasingly relevant in reality. In general, emotion recognition from previous work can be done in three ways, that includes detecting a face in the image, extracting facial features from the image, and classification of expression in the emotion categories. For classification, the most popular classifiers are used is the Support Vector Machine (SVM) [1] and Bayes classifiers, together with some unsupervised learning techniques [2].

However, without any effort or delay, humans easily recognize the facial expression, but machine expression recognition is still a challenging task. Automatic recognition of facial expression is a complex task because faces can vary due to different ages and ethnicity from one individual to another. Even if the recognition of emotion is based on culture-specific factors such as the presence of eyeglasses, facial hair makes this task complex.

Another challenge to this task of emotion recognition is the variation in size and facial orientation in input images. This limits a search for the image's fixed pattern. The facial poses may differ due to the angle of the camera. There could be some frontal or non-frontal faces. Faces can be at different angles, hiding some of the facial characteristics. We can use some good preprocessing technique that applies to input images that have good insensitivity to the scaling, rotation, and translation of the head. Currently, numerous facial expression recognition (FER) methods based on features such as local spatial analysis or geometric information as facial features. Therefore, we can use automatic facial point localization to categorize facial expressions firmly.

The performance of facial point extraction algorithms usually depends on environmental conditions such as lighting in many practical applications, such as robotics. Therefore, if the illumination is not uniform, then the facial point can be detected inaccurately, and therefore, high FER rates are hardly expected. Typically, this factor would make the extraction of features difficult to perform reliably. Preprocessing methods such as Histogram Equalization, DCT normalization, and Rank Normalization can be applied before the extraction of the feature to overcome the variation of illumination in an input image.

In this work, we are using deep learning methods to extract the features from facial emotion data and improves the performance of automatic emotion recognition. The main advantage of deep learning is to remove the pre-processing technique, which uses a physical model, completely or heavily by allowing "end-to-end" learning directly from the input image. That is why deep learning has achieved state-of-the-art results in different fields including face recognition, object detection, scene understanding, and FER.

Given an image dataset, where each entry in datasets are images and their corresponding emotion label, our job is to create a machine learning model that will classify the image into any seven discrete emotion categories that represent universal human emotions.

13.2   Related Work

In recent years, many methods are proposed for automatic emotion recognition such as linear discrimination analysis, principle component analysis, artificial neural networks, Gabor wavelets, and embedded hidden Markov models. Using these methods, accuracy and performance are affected by changes in light, pose, aging, and alignment conditions. These algorithms are mainly based on handcrafted features. However, in practical applications, the handcrafted features have many limitations.

FER Challenge 2013 [3], many deep learning approaches for FER were presented. Interestingly, a deep convolutional neural network is the top-scoring system, while the handcrafted model ranked fourth in the 2013 FER challenge. Currently available methods which are using deep learning methods have proved outstanding performance improvement over the handcrafted features [4].

Mariana Iuliana Georgescu *et al.* proposed a method that combines automatic feature learned and handcraft features [5]. The author uses Convolutional Neural Networks (CNNs) as automatic feature learner and bag-of-visual-words as handcraft feature learning to achieve state-of-art results. To get automatic features the author has performed experiments on numerous CNN architecture, pre-trained model, and training procedures. First, image features are collected from the last dense layer of CNN and also from the bag-of-visual-words. Then, these feature vectors are merged. Then, these merged feature vectors are used to train the multi-classification SVM. Finally, a SVM classifier is used to predict the class labels.

J. Zhang *et al.* have developed a Fully End-to-End Convolutional Network (FEC-CNN) for the detection of facial landmarks [6]. The proposed FEC-CNN has many sub-CNNs, which use finer and finer modeling to refine the shape prediction, each CNN taking the input image directly as input and its previous stage output shape. Finally, the gradient can be propagated back to all the units of each stage from the loss layer, providing promising performance even on wild data for facial landmark detection.

Fuzil Khan *et al.* proposed a method for classifying the facial expression [7]. Initially, facial localization is done, and then, landmark detection and feature extraction are done where landmarks are the fluid features like eyes, lip, and nose. This is performed by the Sobel operator and Hough transformation using Shi Tomasi point detection. Using the Euclidean distance feature vector is formed and trained on a multi-layer perceptron (MLP) for classifying the expression.

S. L. Happy *et al.* described [8] novel approach for expression recognition from selected facial patches. Depending on the facial landmark position, certain facial patches are extracted during emotion elicitation. Using this facial patches, salient patches are obtained, each salient patches differ in the expression classes. The multi-classification method is used for classification. This method is tested on CK+ and JAFFE datasets.

Nazil Praveen *et al.* proposed an uncontrolled framework to detect recognition of spontaneous expression [9]. Initially, the Universal Attribute Model (UAM) which is the form of a large Gaussian model is trained in order to learn how to affect different expressions. The movements of the different facial muscles which are called attributes are combined to form a specific expression of the face. After that, for each expression clip, a super expression vector (SEV) is built by utilizing a maximum UAM posteriori adaptation. This SEV contains the expression attribute's high dimensional representation. Then, the SEV is decomposed to low-dimensional representation to retain only some particular clip. Datasets expression attribute such as BP4D and AFEW, the results show that expression-vector achieves higher accuracy than the state-of-the-art techniques.

Tong Zang *et al.* presented CNNs for facial emotion recognition [10]. The purpose of this study is to classify each facial image into one of the seven categories of facial emotion considered. Using grayscale images from the Kaggle website, the author trained CNN models with different depths. To accelerate the training process, the author developed their models in Torch and used Graphics Processing Unit (GPU) computation. In addition to the networks performing on the basis of raw pixel data, the author used a hybrid feature strategy to train a new CNN model combining raw pixel data and Histogram of Oriented Gradient (HOG) features. In addition to L2 regularization, the author used various techniques to reduce the overfitting of the models, including dropout and batch normalization. To determine the optimal hyper-parameters, the author applied cross-validation and evaluated the performance of the models developed by looking at their training history. The author also presents the visualization of different layers of a network to show what CNN models can learn from the features of a face.

To detect peak expression frame from video, Yuanyuan Ding *et al.* described [11] a Dual Local Binary Pattern (DLBP). This DLBP method can reduce the reduction time successfully and it is of small size. In another way, LBP, Logarithm-Laplace (LL) is used to handle the lighting variations. It is a sturdy facial detection feature. Finally, the theorem of Taylor expansion is first used to extract the feature of facial expression. The author proposed a method which is based on the Taylor feature pattern (TFP) that uses the expansion of LBP and Taylor in order to obtain a precise facial feature from the feature map of Taylor. The result shows that the TFP method is higher précised than some state-of-the-art feature extraction method by performing experimental on JAFFE and Kohn-Kanade datasets.

B. Sun *et al.* proposed a method for continuous FER [12]. In this method, the author has to combine the SIFT feature and multimodal feature, so that they can recognize emotion from the image sequence. To recognize static facial expression from video frames, the authors dense SIFT CNN features. For classifying the emotion, the author train the linear SVM and Partial minimum squares regression. Then, the output is combined with the fusion network from all classifiers.

W. Wang *et al.* proposed a method for expression recognition that relies on evidence theory and local texture [13]. In this method, the facial image is segmented into cells with important identified features, after that, textural features of the cells are separated from the Local Binary Patterns (LBP). Then, a single histogram list is formed by connecting all the local region LBP histograms, and to measure similarity, Chi-square distance is applied for evidence synthesis. Finally, in order to achieve the feature vector combination of all modules, the Dempster-Shafer evidence inference theory (D-S evidence theory) is applied and the class judgment of facial expression is carried out. Nearly every deep learning model uses a softmax activation function to predict and minimize cross-entropy loss for classification tasks. Chen Yu Lee *et al.* made minor changes in [14] by replacing the softmax layer with a linear vector support machine. This new learning minimizes a loss based on margins rather than cross-entropy loss. Although there have been many neural networks and SVM in the past, this simple approach by replacing softmax with SVM gives significant gains in the recognition datasets of popular facial expression.

Amol S. Jumde *et al.* proposed a method that uses a data mining approach for face detection [15]. The proposed method is a two-phase training and detection process. Training image will be converted into an edge and non-edge image during the training phase. A maximum frequent item set algorithm is used to mine edge and non-edge image patterns of both positive and negative features. A face detector is built to remove non-face candidates based on the feature patterns mined. In the detection phase, different scales apply the sliding window approach to the test image. FEI face detection database shows good results.

Most of the previous work is based on the frontal face image. S. Moore *et al.* proposed a method that works on non-frontal images [16]. In this approach, multiple factors on different facial expressions (position, resolution, and global and local characteristics) have been investigated. Local binary pattern and its variations are used for texture descriptors investigation. This feature has an influence on orientation and multi-view FER. The authors used an appearance-based approach that divided the images into sub-blocks and then used vector support machines to learn how to pose dependent facial expressions.

Carlos Orrite *et al.* [17] described a method for emotion detection from a still image. HOG is used to obtain local appearance and face shape. First, the author uses a Bayesian equation for computing class-explicit edge dissemination and log-like maps over the entire adjusted training set. A progressive decision tree is then formed by recurrently bunching and blending the classes at each dimension utilizing a bottom-up technique. We make a list of possibly discriminatory HOG features for each part of the tree utilizing the log-probability maps to support areas we hope to be increasingly biased. Finally, a SVM is used to identify the human emotion from still images taken in a semi-controlled environment. The author uses Kohn-Kanade AU-coded facial expression database.

13.3 Proposed Method

We are proposing a new method that contains AFEA and handcraft based features. In this work, we are using CNN as an AFEA and HOG and Landmark detector as handcraft methods to obtain the features from the image. After that, we fused these features and use a SVM to predict the emotion labels. The block diagram of the proposed model is shown in Figure 13.2.

In our model, we have used the VGG model-based convolution neural network to extract the automatic feature representation for the images of the same sizes. In this work, the FER2013 facial emotion recognition dataset is used, and all the images are of the same size, that is, width = 48 and height = 48.

HOG is a feature detector used to detect features in an image. HOG feature descriptor technique works as follows: first, we divide the image into small regions, each region should be connected. For each small region, we find the edge oriented for the pixel or HoG for the pixel within that region. Next, normalize the result using a block-wise pattern. Finally, we get a descriptor for each region. Now, we will continue this process for the entire image and we will get the individual descriptor vector for each image. The third features are land mark based feature. Once these three

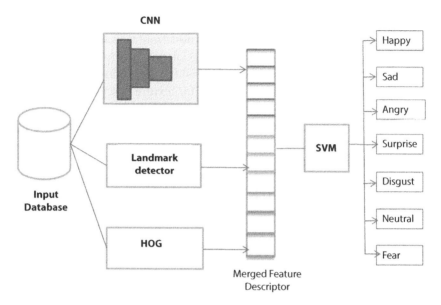

Figure 13.2 Pipeline approach on automatic and handcraft method.

features are extracted, the features are next fused and feed into SVM classifier to predict the emotions.

13.3.1   Convolutional Neural Network

CNN is a very powerful machine learning technique used in the field of deep learning. CNNs are generally used when there is a large collection of data which is divided into large diverse classes and is trained using these diverse images. CNN is self-learning and contains rich feature representations for a large collection of data. These representations tend to outperform classical feature extraction methods which are manually designed with respect to texture, shape, or color. CNNs are composed of multiple layers just like artificial neural networks with the difference that it makes prior assumption that the input will be images, which allows to incorporate certain properties in the model architecture. Deep learning using CNN can be used to extract image features automatically [18]. The CNN model has four layers: convolution layer, Relu layer, pooling layer, and fully connected layer.

13.3.1.1   Convolution Layer

The convolution layer consists of a number of learnable filters that scroll through the entire input image and develop different types of feature maps for activation. Convolution operation has three main advantages: local connectivity, finding out about the relationships between their neighboring pixels; weight sharing on similar feature map, enormously diminishing the quantity of parameters to be learned; and move-invariance is used to locate the object. Usually, the conventional layer is used as an extraction feature in the image. Mathematically convolution operation is represented in Equation (13.1).

$$Conv_{W,B}(I^t)_{i,j,k} = \sum_{x=0}^{p-1}\sum_{y=0}^{q-1}\sum_{u=0}^{c-1} I^t_{i-x,j-y,u}W^t_{k,u,x,y} + B^t_k \qquad (13.1)$$

where I indicate image, W is a kernel weight or filter weight, B is the bias, C is the number of channels, and p and q are size of the filter.

13.3.1.2 Pooling Layer

Pooling layer is used just after the convolutional layer. It is used to reduce the feature maps size and the network's computational cost. Max pooling and average pooling are commonly used for down sampling for translation invariance.

Steps involved in pooling layers are as follows:

- We pick a window size (generally 2 or 3)
- Pick a stride to move on image (generally 2)
- We will slide the window on whole image
- Pick the maximum (max-pool) or minimum (min-pool) from each window.

It divides the image into b × b cell and selects maximum values from each cells. Each channel is used independently. The mathematics for pooling operation is represented in Equation (13.2):

$$pool_b(I^t)_{i,j,k} = \max_{0 \le x < b, 0 \le y < b} I^t_{ib+x,jb+y,k} \qquad (13.2)$$

where $Pool(I)$ is pooling on image I and I is image.

Invariance against image deformation is the main function of pooling operation. The pooled values remain the same when the pattern is changed but the maximum value remains in the same cell. The advantage is that the network remains robust if there are slightly changes in translation or rotation. However, through the pooling operation, spatial information is removed. Although spatial information is important in landmark location and detection. We still benefit from max pooling.

13.3.1.3   ReLU Layer

Rectified Linear Layer is nothing but the activation function. It is used to activate a particular node only when input is above certain threshold. Till the value of input is below zero, the output comes to be zero, but when the input flows over a certain range (threshold), it displays linear relationship with the dependent variable. Relu Layer performs two major tasks: It removes negative values from filtered images and makes them zero. This is generally done to stop the values to sum up to zero. Mathematically, Relu layer is represented in Equation (13.3). Figure 13.3 shows gives an idea of how non-linear function works and represented using graph.

$$s(I^t)_{i,j,k} = g\left(I^t_{i,j,k}\right) \tag{13.3}$$

where g is activation function.

13.3.1.4   Fully Connected Layer

We include a couple of fully connected layers to wrap up the CNN architecture after the convolution with pooling layers. This is the equivalent Artificial Neural Network architecture that is fully associated. Since both convolution and pooling layers' yield are 3D volumes, yet a fully associated layer anticipates a 1D number vector. In this way, the yield of the last pooling layer is straightened to a vector and that is used as a input to the fully connected layer. Straightening simply convert the 3D vector in 1D vector, nothing extravagant occurs here.

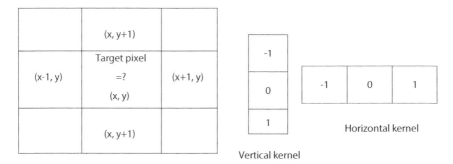

Figure 13.3 Gradient computation depending on kernel.

Now, the output will be in the form of 1×1 image with 2n channels, n is the count of landmarks points. The input data is transmitted through a series of transformations. Equation (13.4) shows how an input data is transmitted through CNN.

$$I^1 = f_0(I^0)$$

$$I^2 = f_1(I^1)$$

(13.4)

....

$$I^t = f_{t-1}(I^{t-1})$$

where f_i is either $Conv_{Wi, Bi}$, $pool_p$, or s, and I^t is input image.

To measure the difference between the output of the network and the ground truth, a loss function is defined. We use the loss function L_2 that sums up the differences in squares. Equation (13.5) represents the loss function.

$$L = \sum_{i=0}^{N-1} \| Y_i - f(X_i) \|_2^2$$

(13.5)

where L is loss in the network, f is calculation in convolution network, and X and Y is pair of data. When we called a network as 10-layer CNN, we mean the network includes 10 W and B pairs.

13.3.2   Histogram of Gradient

HOG is a feature descriptor broadly utilized for describing objects through their shapes in several domains. The appearance and shape of local objects can often be described by the distribution of gradients or edge directions of local intensity. To build object search effectiveness, the image's gamma and colors should be standardized. The object search is depending on the detection technique applied to the small images defined by the sliding indicator window that samples the original input image region by region and its scaled versions. In HOG recognition, the initial step is to isolate the source picture into blocks (for example 16×16 pixels). Little areas, called cells (for example 8×8 pixels), divide each square. Generally, blocks cover one another, with the goal that few blocks may contain a similar cell. The vertical gradients and horizontal gradients are acquired for every pixel in the cell. Utilizing 1D Sobel vertically and horizontally administrators is the simplest approach to do this. Mathematically, Equation (13.6) shows the computation of gradient vector for target pixel location (x, y) and is shown in Figure 13.3.

$$H_x(y, x) = Y(y, x + 1) + Y(y, x + 1) \qquad (13.6)$$

$$H_y(y, x) = Y(y + 1, x) + Y(y - 1, x)$$

where Y(y, x) is pixel intensity at coordinate x and y, $H_x(y, x)$ is horizontal gradient, and $H_y(y, x)$ is vertical gradient.

The magnitude and phase of the gradient are determined by Equation (13.7).

$$H(y,x)=\sqrt{H_x(y,x)^2 + H_y(y,x)^2}$$

$$\theta(y,x)=\arctan\left(\frac{H_y(y,x)}{H_x(y,x)}\right) \qquad (13.7)$$

Next, for each cell, the HOG is created. For the histogram, the angle Q bins are selected (e.g., Q = 9). Usually, unsigned orientation is used, which increases the angles below 0° by 180°. Because different images may have different contrasts, standardization of contrasts can be very useful. Standardization takes place within a block on the histogram vector v. Each detector window is assigned a descriptor. This descriptor is made up of all the cells in the detector window for each block. The descriptor window detector is used for object recognition information. Using this descriptor, training and testing take place. There are many possible methods to use the descriptor to classify objects such as SVMs and neural networks.

13.3.3   Facial Landmark Detection

We are interested in the landmarks (key points) that describe the state of facial attributes such as eyes, eyebrows, nose, mouth, and chin. These points give an extraordinary insight into the face structure analyzed, which can be very useful for a wide range of applications, including face recognition, face animation, emotion recognition, blink detection, and photography. There are numerous technologies that can identify these points: some accomplish superior precision and robustness by analyzing a 3D face model separated from a 2D image, and others depend on the power of

CNNs or RNNs (Recurrent Neural Networks), while others use basic (but fast) features to estimate the point location.

Dlib's Face Landmark Detection algorithm is an implementation of the 2014 Kazemi and Sullivan Ensemble of Regression Trees (ERT) [19]. This technique uses simple and quick features (differences in pixel intensity) to estimate the landmark positions directly. Subsequently, these estimated positions are refined by a cascade of regressors with an iterative process. The regressors produce a new estimate from the previous one, attempting at each iteration to reduce the alignment error of the estimated points. The algorithm blazes quickly.

Basically, from a set of images, annotations, and training options, a shape predictor can be generated. A single annotation is the face region and the points we want to locate labeled. Any face detection algorithm (such as OpenCV, HaarCascade, Dlib HOG Detector, and CNN detectors) can easily obtain the face region, but instead, the points must be manually labeled or detected by already available landmark detectors and models (such as ERT with SP68). Finally, the training options are a set of parameters defining the trained model's characteristics. These parameters can be adjusted properly to obtain more or less the desired behavior of the model generated.

13.3.4   Support Vector Machine

The objective of the SVM algorithm is to find a hyperplane in an N-dimensional space (N the number of features) that distinctly classify the data points. Figure 13.4 shows the SVM classification on two vectors. In Figure 13.4a, there are three hyperplanes, H1, H2, and H3, and among these, we need to select those

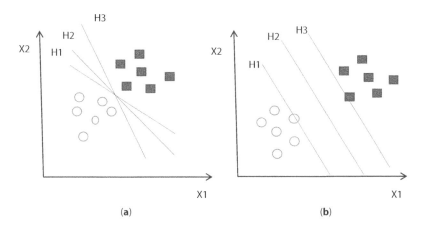

Figure 13.4 SVM classifier for two features.

hyperplanes which are at maximum distance from both the feature point. In Figure 13.4b. H2 is the best hyperplane that we will choose for classification.

There are many possible hyperplanes that could be selected to separate the two classes of data points. Our goal is to find a plane with the maximum margin, i.e., the maximum distance between both classes' data points. Maximizing the margin distance provides some reinforcement in order to be able to classify future data points with greater confidence.

13.3.5   Model Merging and Learning

We merge the deep model and handcraft models (Landmark Detector and HOG) before the learning phase by appending their respective feature descriptors. To get features from the pre-prepared CNN models, the softmax classification layer is evacuated and the activation map of the final remaining fully connected layer is considered. For each image, we will get a feature vector from the last fully connected layer. We can normalize this feature vector using the L_2 norm. Bag-of-visual-words and HOG-based feature descriptor is the kind of handcrafted features. We also normalize this using the L_2 norm. Learning: We use a SVM classifier to learn a model. We train the model using training data, that is, we use a concatenated feature vector. SVM is a discriminative classifier paired classifier that attempts to discover the vector of weight and the term of bias that characterizes the hyperplane that isolates the vectors of the training models.

13.4   Experimental Results

13.4.1   Datasets

In this work, we have used FER 2013 datasets [20]. It contains 28,709 images for training, 3,589 images for public testing, and 3,589 images for validation. Images are of size 48 × 48 pixels. Images belong to seven classes of emotion: sadness, happiness, surprise, disgust, anger, fear, and neutral. We have used Fer2013 datasets because it is challenging datasets. The images are not aligned and some of them are not labeled correctly. Moreover, some samples do not contain faces. Facial expressions we want to use are 0 = Angry, 1 = Happy, 2 = Sad, 3 = Surprise, 4 = Neutral, 5 = Disgust, and 6 = Fear. In this work, we can calculate results with help of accuracy metric. We can define accuracy by below equations:

Accuracy = Number of right expectations/Total number of forecasts

In this work, we use different type features such as CNN, HoG, and landmark-based descriptors to recognize facial emotions efficiently. Firstly, we will use automatic FER CNN for facial emotion recognition and we will use softmax as the last layer of CNN to classify emotion labels. CNN was trained on five emotions and the result is tabulated in Table 13.1.

Table 13.1 shows the performance of the CNN-based classification results. In this work, we are using the VGG model to extract the feature representation and softmax layer to predict facial emotions. Based on results with CNN-based features, surprise emotion recognized more among the other expression. With this method, 68.57% of the average accuracy is achieved.

We will use automatic FER CNN for facial feature extraction. We extract these features from the last dense layer of the CNN. Finally, these extracted features are trained on the SVM for classification. We will use a handcrafted method like 68 landmark detectors which are implemented using the dlib library to detect 68 landmark points from the facial image. Then, these 68 landmark points are used to train SVM, and after that, we will classify our emotion label for test data. Next, we use the handcraft method like the HoG feature descriptor to extract features from the image. After detection HoG feature from the image, then we will train these HoG feature on the SVM for emotion classification. The result of CNN features with SVM classifier and HoG features with SVM classifiers results on seven emotion labels is tabulated in Table 13.2.

Table 13.1 Performance (%) of the CNN classification method on FER 2013 datasets.

Emotion label	Accuracy (%)
0	64
1	79
2	58
3	87
4	62
5	69
6	61
Average Accuracy	**68.57**

Table 13.2 Performance (%) of the different features with SVM classification method on FER 2013 datasets.

Emotion label	CNN + SVM accuracy (%)	Landmarks + SVM accuracy (%)	HoG + SVM accuracy (%)
0	66	51	50
1	79	77	71
2	57	43	44
3	87	74	75
4	61	50	51
5	65	61	64
6	68	59	62
Average	**69**	**59.2**	**59.5**

Table 13.2 shows the different features with SVM classification accuracy results on the emotion dataset. In the case of CNN features with SVM classification method, it gives more accuracy results compared with other features results. The average accuracy of the CNN features with SVM classification method gives 69% highest accuracy and landmarks descriptors and HoG features with the SVM classification average results are 59.2% and 59.5%, respectively.

We use the combination of the CNN as automatic, HoG, and landmark detector as handcraft method. After collecting feature vector, CNN, HoG, and landmark detector corresponding to each image, we will merge these feature and we will have built one merged feature vector. Finally, we will train this merged feature vector on SVM for expression classification. The result is tabulated in Table 13.3.

Table 13.3 shows the combination of merged features with SVM-based classification results on emotion dataset. This three combination of features results give more accuracy compared with the individual features results.

Table 13.3 Fusion of CNN, landmark, and HoG features with SVM classification accuracy results.

Method	Accuracy (%)
Proposed Method (CNN + HoG + Landmark)	72

13.5   Conclusion

In this work, we addressed the task of FER and our aim is to classify images of faces into any of seven discrete emotion categories that represent universal human emotions. We have used automatic as well as handcraft methods to extract features from images. We have used a convolution neural network as automatic feature extraction and histogram of oriented and landmark detector as a handcraft feature detector. After that, we merge all three features and we get a merged feature vector. Then, we train the SVM using the merged feature vector for classification. The purpose method is accurately classified emotions compared with the individual facial features results.

Acknowledgement

The authors would like to thank the anonymous reviewers for their thorough review and valuable comments. This work was supported, in part, by grants Government of India, Ministry of Human Resource Development and NIT Warangal under NITW/CS/CSE-RSM/2018/908/3118 project.

References

1. Srinivas, M., Basil, T., Krishna Mohan, C., Adaptive learning based heartbeat classification. *Bio-med. Mater. Eng.*, 26, 1–2, 49–55, 2015.
2. Srinivas, M. and Krishna Mohan, C., Efficient clustering approach using incremental and hierarchical clustering methods. *The 2010 International Joint Conference on Neural Networks (IJCNN)*, IEEE, 2010.
3. Goodfellow, J., Erhan, D., Carrier, P.L., Courville, A., Mirza, M., Hamner, B., Cukierski, W., Tang, Y., Thaler, D., Lee, D.-H., Zhou, Y., Ramaiah, C., Feng, F., Li, R., Wang, X., Athanasakis, D., Shawe-Taylor, J., Milakov, M., Park, J., Ionescu, R.T., Popescu, M., Grozea, C., Bergstra, J., Xie, J., Romaszko, L., Xu, B., Bengio, Y., Challenges in Representation Learning: A report on three machine learning contests, in: *Proceedings of ICONIP*, vol. 8228, LNCS Springer-Verlag, pp. 117–124, 2013.
4. Srinivas, M., Lin, Y.-Y., Mark Liao, H.-Y., Learning deep and sparse feature representation for fine-grained object recognition. *2017 IEEE International Conference on Multimedia and Expo (ICME)*, IEEE, 2017.
5. Georgescu, Mariana-Iuliana, Radu Tudor Ionescu, and Marius Popescu. Local learning with deep and handcrafted features for facial expression recognition. *IEEE Access*, 7, 64827–64836, 2019.

6. He, Z., Kan, M., Zhang, J., Chen, X., Shan, S., A fully end-to-end cascaded CNN for facial landmark detection. *IEEE International Conference on Automatic Face and Gesture Recognition*, 2017.

7. Khan, F., Facial Expression Recognition using Facial Landmark Detection and Feature Extraction via Neural Networks, arXiv:1812.04510v2, 2018.

8. Happy, S. L., and Aurobinda Routray. Automatic facial expression recognition using features of salient facial patches. *IEEE transactions on Affective Computing*, 6.1, 1–12, 2014.

9. Perveen, N., Roy, D., Krishna Mohan, C., Spontaneous Expression Recognition using Universal Attribute Model. *IEEE Trans. Image Process.*, 27.11, 5575–5584, 2018.

10. Zhang, T. and Zheng, W., A Deep Neural Network Driven Feature Learning Method for Multi-view Facial Expression Recognition. *IEEE Trans. Multimed.*, 18.12, 2525–2536, 2016.

11. Ding, Y. *et al.*, Facial Expression Recognition From Image Sequence Based on LBP and Taylor Expansion. *IEEE Access*, 5, 19409–19419, 2017.

12. Sun, B., Li, L., Zhou, G., He, J., Facial expression recognition in the wild based on multimodal texture features. *J. Electron. Imaging*, 25, 6, 407–407, 2016.

13. Wang, W., Chang, F., Liu, Y., Wu, X., Expression recognition method based on evidence theory and local texture. *Multimed. Tools Appl.*, 76.5, 7365–7379, 2016.

14. Lee, C.-Y., Xie, S., Gallagher, P.W., Zhang, Z., Tu, Z., Deeply Supervised Nets. *International Conference on Artificial Intelligence and Statistics*, 2015.

15. Jumde, A.S., Sonavane, S.P., Behera, R.K., Face detection using data mining approach. *International Conference on Communications and Signal Processing*, 2015.

16. Moore, S. and Bowden, R., Local binary patterns for multi-view facial expression recognition. *Comput. Vision Image Understanding*, 115, 4, 541–558, 2011.

17. Orrite, C., Ganan, A., Rogez, G., Hog-based decision tree for facial expression classification. *Pattern Recognition and Image Analysis*, Springer, pp. 176–183, 2009.

18. Srinivas, M., Roy, D., Krishna Mohan, C., Discriminative feature extraction from X-ray images using deep convolutional neural networks. *2016 IEEE International Conference on Acoustics, Speech and Signal Processing (ICASSP)*, IEEE, 2016.

19. Kazemi, V. and Sullivan, J., One millisecond face alignment with an ensemble of regression trees, in: *Proceedings of the IEEE Conference on Computer Vision and Pattern Recognition*, pp. 1867–1874, 2014.

20. Goodfellow, I.J. *et al.*, Challenges in representation learning: A report on three machine learning contests. *International conference on neural information processing*, Springer, Berlin, Heidelberg, 2013.

22. Fathima, A. and Vaidehi, K., Review on facial expression recognition system using machine learning techniques, in: *Advances in Decision Sciences, Image Processing, Security and Computer Vision*, pp. 608–618, Springer, Cham, 2020.

Part 4

MACHINE LEARNING FOR CLASSIFICATION AND INFORMATION RETRIEVAL SYSTEMS

14

AnimNet: An Animal Classification Network using Deep Learning

Kanak Manjari[1]*, Kriti Singhal[2], Madhushi Verma[1] and Gaurav Singal[1]

[1]Computer Science Engineering Bennett University, Gr. Noida, India
[2]Computer Science Engineering Galgotias University, Gr. Noida, India

Abstract
Image classification is a combination of technologies: Image Processing (IP), Machine Learning (ML), and Computer Vision (CV). The classification of animals has been done in this work that are commonly found in the Indian scenario using two approaches: transfer learning and a custom-built classification network, i.e., AnimNet. For transfer learning, we have used VGG16, VGG19, and Xception network that are existing pre-trained networks and compared the results of the custom-built AnimNet network with these existing networks. The comparison was done on the basis of the accuracy and size of the models as the size of network is as important as the accuracy of network in this era of mobile computing. A lightweight network with good performance is the most optimal choice nowadays. The accuracy was observed to be highest for the Xception network whereas the AnimNet network is lightweight, i.e., 5X smaller than the Xception model with second-highest accuracy.

Keywords: Image classification, animal detection, VGG16, VGG19, computer vision, deep learning

14.1 Introduction

Classification is a methodical categorization of images based on its characteristics in different classes. Some classifiers are binary, leading to a conclusion that is yes/no. Others are multi-class, capable of classifying an object into one of many classifications. Image classification emerged to reduce

---

*Corresponding author: KM5723@bennett.edu.in

Mettu Srinivas, G. Sucharitha and Anjanna Matta (eds.) Machine Learning Algorithms and Applications, (249–266) © 2021 Scrivener Publishing LLC

the lap between computer and human vision by training the computer with data. The conventional methods used for the image classification are segments of the Artificial Intelligence (AI) field, called Machine Learning (ML). ML includes two modules: feature module and classification module. Feature module is responsible for extracting viable features such as textures and edges. Classification module classifies based on the extricated characteristics. Classification is a very common case of ML; classification algorithms are used to solve problems such as filtering email spam, categorization of documents, recognition of voice, recognition of images, and recognition of handwriting. The main drawback of ML is the need of large amount of training data which should be unbiased and of good quality. This is rectified by Deep Learning (DL).

DL is a sub-segment of ML, able to learn via its own computing method. DL uses complex, multi-algorithm framework represented as an artificial neural network (ANN). The ANN's architecture is replicated using the human brain's biological neural network. This makes DL more able than the standard models of ML. In DL, we consider the neural networks which recognize the image on the basis of its characteristics [1]. This is achieved by the construction of a complete characteristic extraction model which can solve the difficulties faced by conventional methods. In DL, to perform classification duties, a computer model learns directly from images, text, or sound. DL models, often exceeding human-level efficiency, may achieve state-of-the-art accuracy. Models are trained by the use of a large set of labeled data and architectures of neural networks that involve multiple layers.

14.1.1 Feature Extraction

The extraction of features is a reduction of dimensions where an initial set of unprocessed data is reduced to more convenient groups for processing. A feature of such big data sets is the great number of variables that require heavy computing resources for processing. Extraction of features is the term coined for methods that select and merge variables into characteristics, whilst decreasing the quantity of data to be processed and still accurately and completely describing the original unprocessed data.

14.1.2 Artificial Neural Network

In DL, a model masters at first hand from pictures, text images and audio to carry out classification task [2]. DL models can achieve pioneering precision, often exceeding output at the human level. DL models are trained

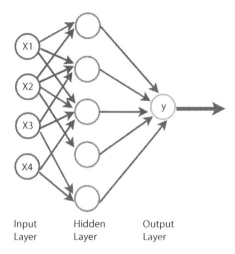

Figure 14.1 Artificial neural network.

using huge amount of labeled data and architectures of neural networks, which contain a lot of layers. ANN [3] is a value system of information processing, inspired by our own nervous system, such as information about the brain process as shown in Figure 14.1. ANNs are built like the human brain, with neuron nodes interconnected like a web.

An ANN has hundreds or thousands of artificial neurons that are interconnected by nodes, called processing units. Input and output units are made up of these processing units. Based on an internal weighting scheme, the input units obtain different types and structures of information and the neural network attempts to learn about the information provided to generate one output report. ANNs often use a series of learning rules called backpropagation to perfect their performance outcomes, just as humans need rules and instructions to come up with a result or performance. The ANN is taught what to look for and what its performance should be during the training and supervisory process, using yes/no query types of binary numbers. We train the network's data by providing an input image and conveying its output to the network.

14.1.3   Transfer Learning

Transfer learning [4] is a ML expression in which a model designed for a specific problem statement is reused for a second problem statement as the base model. In DL, it is a popular approach where pre-trained models are used because of their vast computational and time resources needed to construct neural network models on these problems and the enormous skill leaps they provide on related issues [5]. Transfer learning is an optimization technique, time saving shortcut or performance optimizer. The types of pre-trained model mainly used for effective image classification are vgg-16, vgg-19, and Xception.

Here, a network to classify different types of animals commonly found in the Indian scenario has been presented. The aim is to build a network having good accuracy and make it light-weight so that it becomes suitable for the real-time usage. A customized network, i.e., AnimNet has been developed using the transfer learning approach that is both light-weighted as well as provides a good accuracy. Section 14.2 describes the related work done recently. The remaining part of the chapter is organized as follows: The proposed methodology is illustrated in Section 14.3 which includes details of dataset preparation and model development. The results obtained from the proposed solution are described in Section 14.4 followed by conclusion in Section 14.5.

14.2   Related Work

A variety of work has been done to perform animal classification and detection. A few of them has been discussed here in brief. Authors in [6] have tried to solve the CAPTCHA challenge that is based on the issue of distinguishing dog and cat images. They have used Dense-SIFT features, combining dense SIFT and color features, and features learned from convolution neural network (CNN). They have achieved a good accuracy of 94% using support vector machine (SVM) classifier.

Authors in [7] have proposed a novel method of fully connected dual deep convolution neural network (DCNN), which extracts and analyzes the image features on a large scale. This method has gained the capability of analyzing a large amount of dataset as well as extracting more features than before including batch normalization layer and exponential linear unit (ELU) layer. The proposed DCNN outruns its counterparts as it has fewer computing costs and was able to achieve an accuracy of 92%. In [8], authors have tried to study household animals' demeanor and body language using DL technique. Their aim was to find out whether the animals are sick or not and provide necessary help in time if required. They have applied transfer learning on vgg16, and the accuracy increased from 80% to over 95%.

Authors in [9] have opted for a robust learning method for animal classification using images captured in an extremely cluttered natural environment and annotated with noisy marks. To divide the training samples based on different characteristics, they used k-means clustering, which was then used to train various networks. Two publicly accessible camera-trap image datasets were evaluated for the performance of the proposed method: Snapshot Serengeti [10] and the Panama-Netherlands datasets. The results suggested that the approach selected by the authors outperformed the literature's state of the art methods and enhanced the precision of the classification of animal species from camera-trap images which contain noise.

In paper [11], a classification system for classifying images of real animals has been developed by the authors. Using the toy photos of animals to account for factors other than just the physical appearance of animals, the model was educated. The segmentation was performed using the k-means clustering technique after pre-processing the image. Following segmentation, the extraction of hog features from the segmented image was performed. The extracted features were used in the final step to classify the image into a suitable class using the supervised multi-SVM classifier. In paper [12], the authors have shed light on different methods available for feature extraction and features these methods extract to perform an efficient identification and classification. They presented the results obtained from a dataset containing 111,467 photos in the training of a CNN to identify 20 African wildlife species with an overall accuracy of 87.5%. In order to generate a visual similarity dendrogram of known organisms, hierarchical clustering of feature vectors associated with each image has also been used.

In classifying camera trap data, how to process datasets with only a few classified images that are generally difficult to model and applying a trained model to a live online citizen science project, authors in [13] found the accuracy of DL. In order to distinguish between images of various animal species, human or vehicle images, and empty images, CNNs were used. Accuracies ranged between 91.2% and 98.0% for identifying empty images through programs, while accuracies ranged between 88.7% and 92.7% for identifying individual organisms.

Authors in [14] have attempted to resolve the challenge faced during CNN-based fine-grain recognition. Generally, the need for large sets of training data and the learned approaches to feature presentations are high-dimensional, leading to less efficiency. The authors suggested an approach where online dictionary learning is incorporated into CNN to resolve these issues. A significant amount of weakly labeled information on the Internet can be learned from the dictionary by an incremental process.

During fine-grained image classification, the authors discussed the problems of elevated inter-class similarity and broad intra-class variations in paper [15]. They also suggested a system of fine-grained image classification that performs identification of bird species. An online dictionary learning algorithm has been proposed where the concept of sparsity is incorporated into the use of bilinear convolutional neural network (BCNN) classification. This method performs classification based on sparsity, where a lower number of dictionary atoms can reflect training data.

Although there are existing networks, but they are not lightweight that can be deployed on edge devices. AnimNet network, that is accurate and lightweight than the existing networks has been developed and is the key contribution of this work. AnimNet network is five times lighter than Xception model and can accurately classify different types of animals commonly found in the Indian scenario.

14.3 Proposed Methodology

The proposed approach consists of data collection measures, preparation, and performance assessment of models. Each procedure is therefore outlined briefly as follows.

14.3.1 Dataset Preparation

The dataset has been self-created which has six categories of animals commonly found in India. The six categories of animals include cat, cow, dog, horse, goat, and monkey. The images were captured in very common circumstances. The samples for each class are taken from different scenarios and has high-resolution as well as low-resolution images. These images were captured from raspberry pi and Mi Note 8 Pro mobile phone to achieve images with a combination of high and low resolutions. The dataset is not only focused on the images of the animals in their natural habitat but also contains pictures of animals in common surroundings. For example, the image of horses is from the barn, roads, and side of roads to have more natural and common surrounding areas. The dataset has been divided into two sets, i.e., training images and testing images containing 2,519 and 629 images, respectively.

14.3.2 Training the Model

We have used two approaches in building a classification model for animals in Indian scenario: 1) using transfer learning and 2) creating a custom model (AnimNet).

1) *Using Transfer Learning:* We have trained our dataset using available pre-trained models, i.e., VGG19, VGG16, and Xception. In this section, we will look into the structure of each of these models and perform training on the custom-built dataset. Using transfer learning, we first train a base network on a base dataset, and then transfer the learned features to a second target network to be trained on a target dataset. If the features are general, this mechanism would appear to perform, meaning that they are appropriate for both tasks, rather than unique to the base task. Here, we use pre-trained weights and retrain the network using the custom dataset which increases the accuracy. The analysis of the obtained results is provided in the later section.

VGG16 [16] is a model developed by K. Simonyan and A. Zisserman. ImageNet [17] is a dataset of over 14 million images in 1,000 classes, with a test accuracy of 92.7 %. The input to the cov1 layer is an image of fixed size 224 × 224. The image is executed through a stack of convolutional layers and the filter was used with less receptive fields: 3 × 3 which is the smallest size that captures the up/down, center, left/right. The padding layers are one pixel long. There are five layers of max pooling layer following the convolution layer. Max-pooling is achieved using a 2 × 2-pixel window with a stride of 2. The design of the fully connected layer is similar to other networks. Non-linearity of the rectification (ReLU) is fitted on all the hidden layers. None of the networks provide Local Response Standardization (LRN), except for one, such standardization does not boost the ILSVRC dataset efficiency, but results in increased memory usage and computation time.

In Figure 14.2, the architecture of VGG16 and VGG19 has been presented. The difference between both the architecture is that VGG16 has 16 layers of 3 × 3 convolution and VGG19 has 19 layers of 3 × 3 convolution. It means that VGG16 contains 16 layers that has some weights, whereas VGG19 contains 19 layers that has some weights. VGG16 is a large network which has a total of about 138 million parameters. In terms of the number of parameters to be trained, it is really large. VGG19 network, which is bigger than VGG16, but because VGG16 does almost as well as the VGG19, a lot of people will use VGG16. But, in order to achieve more accuracy, VGG19 is preferred in some cases.

VGG19 [18] is a convolution neural network with 19 layers. ImageNet database has a pre-trained version of the network on a million images. The pre-trained network has learned accurate attribute representations

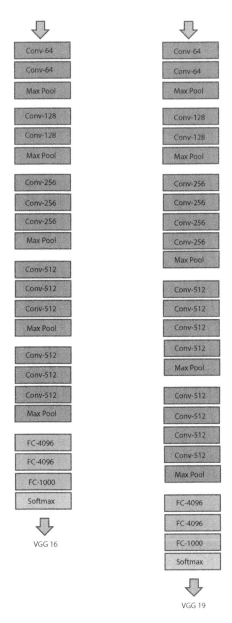

Figure 14.2 Layers of VGG16 and VGG19 network.

for a large image dataset. Its frame size is 224 × 224. A fixed-size RGB image of size 224 × 224 has been inputted into this network. This suggests the matrix would have been (224,224,3). The mean RGB value was subtracted from each pixel. Kernels of 3 × 3 size with a step size of

1 pixel were used which made covering the whole notion of image possible. Spatial information of the image was retained with the help of spatial padding. A 2 × 2-pixel window with stride 2 was used to perform max pooling. Rectified linear unit (ReLU) was used after this to add non-linearity. It is better than models using tanh or sigmoid functions as non-linearity increases the computational time. Three fully connected layers were implemented: the first two layers have 4,096 channels each, the third layer performs ILSVRC 1,000-way classification and thus has 1 channel per 1,000 channel class. Softmax is applied in the last layer for classification.

Xception [19] is a convolutional, 71-layer, deep neural network. It is a CNN architecture that relies completely on depth-wise separable convolution layers. A pre-trained version of the trained network can be loaded from the ImageNet database which has over a million images. As a result, the network has learned rich representations of features for a wide array of images. The network size is 299 × 299 input images. It is a convolutional architecture of the neural network, formed entirely on depth-wise, separable layers of convolution. Later, the following hypothesis was proposed that in the feature maps of CNN the mapping of cross-channels correlations and spatial correlations can be completely decoupled. As this hypothesis is a firmer version of the Inception architecture hypothesis, this architecture was coined the term "Xception" which stands for "Extreme Inception". The architecture consists of 36 convolutional layers which form the network's base for extracting features. These 36 layers are arranged into fourteen modules, all except for the first and last modules, which have residual linear ties around them.

2) *Creating a Custom Model (AnimNet):* The main aim to develop a custom model is to have a good performance model that is lightweight to make it suitable for mobile devices. AnimNet required no pre-trained weights for training. This model has been trained from scratch by adjusting the weights, adding customized layers and tried to make the proposed model as light as possible with enough neurons for efficient feature extraction along with a good accuracy. The convolution is followed by max pooling and then dropout of 0.5 has been added. The input shape is (128 × 128 × 3), kernel is of (3 × 3), and l2 regularizer of 0.01 has been used. After this, flattening is done followed by adding dense layers and dropout. Rmsprop has been used as optimizer, ReLU as activation function, and categorical cross-entropy

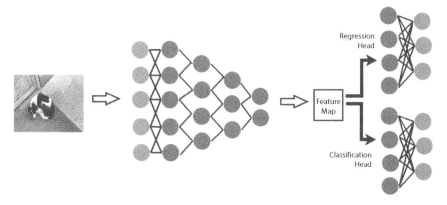

Figure 14.3 The architecture of convolution neural network.

has been used for the training. The typical classification and localization network architecture has been shown in Figure 14.3 with an additional regression head on the top right with CNN classification network.

14.4   Results

The result achieved by applying transfer learning and by AnimNet has been presented in this section. The training, validation, and testing performance of the models has been shown in graphs and tables. The training loss, training accuracy, validation loss, validation accuracy, and size of the network are the performance evaluation parameters which we have used in this chapter to discuss the performance of networks. The loss and accuracy achieved during training and validation process for each of the networks has been compared to analyze their performance. Along with the loss and accuracy, size of each networks has been compared to understand their compatibility with mobile devices. These evaluation parameters are discussed briefly below:

- Training Loss: The loss encountered at each epoch during the training process which tends to be decreasing for a good model is called as training loss.
- Training Accuracy: The accuracy achieved at each epoch during the training process which tends to be increasing for a good model is called as training accuracy.

- Validation Loss: The loss encountered during the validation process which is done after the training process and before the testing process is called as validation loss.
- Validation Accuracy: The accuracy achieved during the validation process which is done after the training process and before the testing process is called as validation accuracy.
- Size: The overall size of the network after the training and validation process is complete. A network with lower size is the preferred choice.

14.4.1   Using Pre-Trained Networks

As can be seen in Table 14.1, the model with highest accuracy (training - 89% and validation - 92%) and minimum loss (training - 0.354 and validation - 0.0862) among all is Xception model. There is no problem of over-fitting or under-fitting has been observed; hence, it is the best choice to go for when size of the model is not an issue. It has lowest validation loss as well as training loss. The highest loss was encountered when we have trained using VGG19 network for training.

The loss encountered during training and validation has been shown by a plot in Figure 14.4a and the accuracy achieved during training and validation has been shown by a plot in Figure 14.4b. It can be clearly observed that the validation loss is lower than the training loss and the validation accuracy is higher than the training accuracy.

14.4.2   Using AnimNet

A self-created dataset, customized layers, and adjusted neurons have been used for custom network development. The training process took a longer time than the time taken by training using pre-trained model. AnimNet was trained using conv2D and dense layers, with less neurons as compared to

Table 14.1 Results obtained using pre-trained networks.

Pre-trained network	Training loss	Training accuracy	Validation loss	Validation accuracy	Size (mb)
VGG16	0.6125	0.7345	0.5326	0.8231	89
VGG19	1.0318	0.6748	0.9873	0.8154	93
Xception	0.354	0.8849	0.0862	0.9201	87

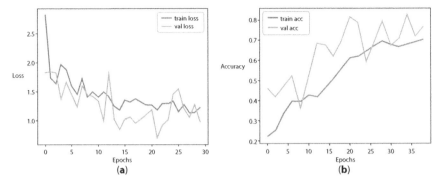

Figure 14.4 Plots of Xception network. (a) Training loss of Xception network (b) accuracy of Xception network.

Table 14.2 Results obtained using AnimNet network.

Training loss	Training accuracy	Validation loss	Validation accuracy	Size (mb)
1.2617	0.7948	0.6797	0.8467	16

pre-trained model to make it lightweight. Although the accuracy achieved using Xception model is higher than AnimNet network, but this network is light-weight of 16mb which is five times lighter than Xception model as shown in Table 14.2. One of the major reason of this is the dataset which we have used had limited number of images (≤3,200).

The loss and accuracy of the AnimNet network during training and validation has been shown in form of a graph in Figures 14.5a and b. It has been observed that the validation loss reached below 1, whereas the training loss is more than that. Also, the validation accuracy is higher than the training accuracy which is clearly visible in the graph.

14.4.3   Test Analysis

In this section, the qualitative performance analysis of Xception (pre-trained) and AnimNet (custom-built) network has been shown on the test data. The difference in testing accuracy obtained by using pre-trained network, i.e., Xception and AnimNet network, has been shown. The classification result is shown class-wise, i.e., for six classes. The time taken for

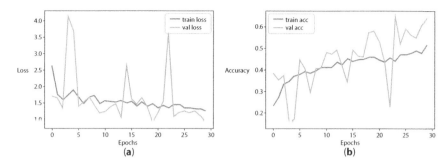

Figure 14.5 Plots of AnimNet network. (a) Training loss of AnimNet network (b) accuracy of AnimNet networks.

classification of each image by both the networks are almost same, i.e., 9–11 ms/step. By looking over the validation accuracy obtained by these two models, it can be assumed that the Xception model would provide a better accuracy while predicting images from our test dataset. Although Xception network achieved the highest accuracy, the accuracy of AnimNet is also acceptable. However, if the need is to have a lightweight as well as accurate model, then the proposed network (AnimNet) may be preferred.

The test results of the model on the test images along with the accuracy obtained for each class has also been shown. The test results obtained on test images for Xception and AnimNet (custom-built) network has been shown in Figures 14.6, 14.7, 14.8, 14.9, 14.10, and 14.11, respectively. These results are after training all the models for the self-created dataset. It has been observed from the test results that the accuracy was higher when Xception model was used as it is pre-trained on large dataset. Although

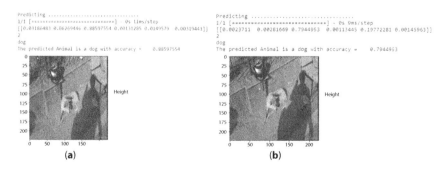

Figure 14.6 Accuracy of class "dog" (size of image = 200*200 pixels). (a) Using Xception network (b) using AnimNet network.

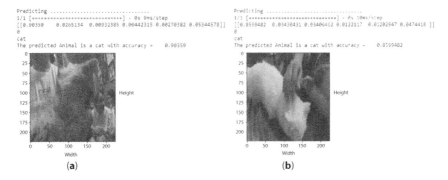

Figure 14.7 Accuracy of class "cat" (size of image = 200*200 pixels). (a) Using Xception network (b) using AnimNet network.

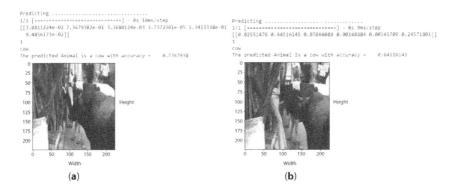

Figure 14.8 Accuracy of class "cow" (size of image = 200*200 pixels). (a) Using Xception network (b) using AnimNet network.

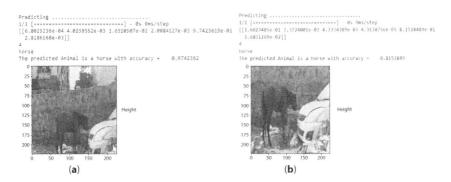

Figure 14.9 Accuracy of class "horse" (size of image = 200*200 pixels). (a) Using Xception network (b) using AnimNet network.

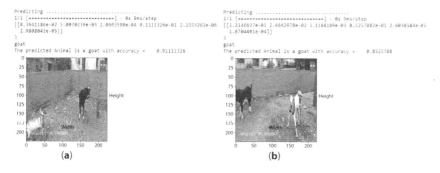

Figure 14.10 Accuracy of class "goat" (size of image = 200*200 pixels). (a) Using Xception network (b) using AnimNet network.

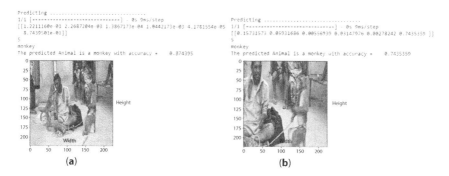

Figure 14.11 Accuracy of class "monkey" (size of image = 200*200 pixels). (a) Using Xception network (b) using AnimNet network.

AnimNet network achieved less accuracy than Xception, it can also be used where size of the model is a constraint. The Xception model is quite heavy, i.e., 87 mb which makes it five times heavier than AnimNet which is of 16 mb size. As per the requirement and need, one can choose either Xception or AnimNet network.

14.5 Conclusion

A quantitative as well as qualitative performance analysis of the pre-trained networks and AnimNet has been provided in this chapter for clear understanding. As can be observed from result analysis, the accuracy given by the AnimNet network is very well though the images have many things other than animals like human and vehicles. A demonstration of how a technology called deep neural networks is capable of extracting the valuable features that can classify a plethora of real-life objects including internal human body tumors as well. It was observed that Xception model gave us a better testing accuracy than the AnimNet for different classes of animals. A point can also be concluded that this AnimNet network was good at predicting test images from dataset, which is acceptable and good to go as our classification was focused on animals commonly found in Indian scenario. AnimNet can be used for classification where it is aimed to be used for edge devices that are resource-constrained. A pre-trained model would always give us better accuracy as they are trained on a huge dataset, when it comes to feature extraction, nevertheless were able to achieve a good accuracy with AnimNet network in limited time period. Also, the size of the AnimNet network is five times lighter than Xception model. So, the selection of network is clearly up to the choice of end user. As a future work, AnimNet network can be improvised to have higher accuracy than all the pre-trained networks but not at the cost of size.

References

1. Manjari, K., Verma, M., Singal, G., A Survey on Assistive Technology for Visually Impaired. *Internet Things*, Elsevier, 11, 100188, 2020.
2. Manjari, K., Verma, M., Singal, G., A Travel Aid for Visually Impaired: R-Cane, in: *International Conference on Smart City and Informatization*, 2019, November, Springer, Singapore, pp. 404–417.
3. Jain, A.K., Mao, J., Mohiuddin, K.M., Artificial neural networks: A tutorial. *Computer*, 29, 3, 31–44, 1996.
4. Torrey, L. and Shavlik, J., Transfer learning, in: *Handbook of research on machine learning applications and trends: algorithms, methods, and techniques*, pp. 242–264, IGI Global, New York, 2010.
5. Manjari, K., Verma, M., Singal, G., CREATION: Computational ConstRained Travel Aid for Object Detection in Outdoor eNvironment, in: *2019 15th IEEE International Conference on Signal-Image Technology & Internet-Based Systems (SITIS)*, 2019, November, pp. 247–254, 2020.
6. Suryawanshi, M.S., Jogdande, M.V., Mane, M.A., Animal classification using Deep learning. *Int. J. Eng. Appl. Sci. Technol.*, 6, 305–307, 2020.
7. Khan, R.H., Kang, K.W., Lim, S.J., Youn, S.D., Kwon, O.J., Lee, S.H., Kwon, K.R., Animal Face Classification using Dual Deep Convolutional Neural Network. *J. Korea Multimed. Soc.*, 23, 4, Korea multimedia society, 525–538, 2020.
8. Lin, L. and Link, Y., *Household Animals Classification Using Deep Learning*, CS230: Deep Learning, Winter 2020, Stanford University, CA, 2020.

9. Ahmed, A., Yousif, H., Kays, R., He, Z., Animal species classification using deep neural networks with noise labels. *Ecol. Inf.*, 57, 101063, 2020.

10. Swanson, A., Kosmala, M., Lintott, C., Simpson, R., Smith, A., Packer, C., Snapshot Serengeti, high-frequency annotated camera trap images of 40 mammalian species in an African savanna. *Sci. Data*, 2, 1, 1–14, 2015.

11. Nanditha, D. and Manohar, N., Classification of Animals Using Toy Images, in: *2020 4th International Conference on Intelligent Computing and Control Systems (ICICCS)*, IEEE, pp. 680–684, 2020, May.

12. Miao, Z., Gaynor, K.M., Wang, J., Liu, Z., Muellerklein, O., Norouzzadeh, M.S., Getz, W.M., Insights and approaches using deep learning to classify wildlife. *Sci. Rep.*, 9, 1, 1–9, 2019.

13. Willi, M., Pitman, R.T., Cardoso, A.W., Locke, C., Swanson, A., Boyer, A., Fortson, L., Identifying animal species in camera trap images using deep learning and citizen science. *Methods Ecol. Evol.*, Wiley, 10, 1, 80–91, 2019.

14. Srinivas, M., Lin, Y.Y., Liao, H.Y.M., Learning deep and sparse feature representation for fine-grained object recognition, in: *2017 IEEE International Conference on Multimedia and Expo (ICME)*, IEEE, pp. 1458–1463, 2017, July.

15. Srinivas, M., Lin, Y.Y., Liao, H.Y.M., Deep dictionary learning for fine-grained image classification, in: *2017 IEEE International Conference on Image Processing (ICIP)*, IEEE, pp. 835–839, 2017, September.

16. Alippi, C., Disabato, S., Roveri, M., Moving convolutional neural networks to embedded systems: the alexnet and VGG-16 case, in: *2018 17th ACM/IEEE International Conference on Information Processing in Sensor Networks (IPSN)*, pp. 212–223, 2018, April.

17. Deng, J., Dong, W., Socher, R., Li, L.J., Li, K., Fei-Fei, L., Imagenet: A large-scale hierarchical image database, in: *2009 IEEE conference on computer vision and pattern recognition*, pp. 248–255, 2009, June.

18. Carvalho, T., De Rezende, E.R., Alves, M.T., Balieiro, F.K., Sovat, R.B., Exposing computer generated images by eye's region classification via transfer learning of VGG19 CNN, in: *2017 16th IEEE International Conference on Machine Learning and Applications (ICMLA)*, 2017, December, pp. 866–870.

19. Chollet, F., Xception: Deep learning with depthwise separable convolutions, in: *Proceedings of the IEEE*, 2017.

15

A Hybrid Approach for Feature Extraction From Reviews to Perform Sentiment Analysis

Alok Kumar* and Renu Jain†

Department of Computer Science and Engineering, University Institute of Engineering and Technology, CSJM University, Kanpur, India

Abstract

In this chapter, a hybrid approach to extract the important attributes called features of a product or a service or a professional from the textual reviews/feedbacks has been proposed. The approach makes use of topic modeling concepts and the linguistic knowledge embedded in the text using Natural Language Processing tools. A system has been implemented and tested taking the feedbacks of two different domains: feedback of teachers and feedback of laptops. The system tries to extract all those features (single word and multiple words) for which users have expressed their opinion in the reviews. The syntactic category and the frequency contribute in deciding the importance of a feature and a numerical value between zero and one called weight is generated for each identified feature representing its significance. Results obtained from the proposed system are comparable if extraction from the text is done manually.

Keywords: Feature identification, aspect extraction, sentiment analysis, natural language processing, item overall sentiment score, text mining, PLSA

**Corresponding author*: akumar.uiet@gmail.com
†*Corresponding author*: jainrenu@gmail.com

Mettu Srinivas, G. Sucharitha and Anjanna Matta (eds.) Machine Learning Algorithms and Applications, (267–288) © 2021 Scrivener Publishing LLC

15.1   Introduction

Sentiment analysis is a process to understand and quantify the feelings or emotions of users from the text called reviews expressed in a natural language. It tries to quantify the effectiveness and usefulness of a product/service/professional on the basis of experiences shared by different users conveyed through written communication. Sentiment analysis can either simply classify something good or bad but a fine grained sentiment analysis is performed by feature-based analysis. Feature-based analysis takes as input a list of features and then for each feature, sentiments according to some pre-defined scale are evaluated. To get the feedback of users, traditionally, a questionnaire-based method Kumar *et al.* [6] is used where a form containing a set of questions related to the item is given to users for their evaluation. Every question in the questionnaire represents an important aspect or property of the item and it can be referred as one of the feature of the item. On the basis of users' responses, an overall analysis of the item and of required question-based analysis is done. But, through questionnaire, users give their opinion only about those attributes/features which are mentioned in the form and feel deprived of expressing their views on other aspects if there are any. The selection of appropriate features of any item plays a very important role in sentiment analysis of that item.

Though there is no standard method to decide the list of features for inclusion in the questionnaire but most of the time, some authorities decide features on the basis of their knowledge and experience. If we think how each one of us would write feedback about a person or about a product, we tend to write only about those features which are important to us while other persons may comment on entirely different set of features depending upon their requirements. Hence, the accurate way of identifying the features would be to extract the features from feedbacks itself. In addition to this, the importance of each feature may vary according to domain/environment. For example: "knowledge" and "dress sense" are two features for teachers but their weights would be different according to their importance while calculating the effective sentiment score of a teacher. Hence, to correctly evaluate the overall usefulness/performance of any product or any individual, the list of relevant features needs to be identified and categorized as strong and weak features.

In this chapter, we have proposed a statistical unsupervised-based method to identify relevant features from feedbacks. A weight estimated statistically and representing the importance of a feature is associated with each feature. The implementation has been done for two sets of data: one for feedbacks of laptops and another one for feedbacks of teachers. Feedbacks of laptops were collected from a public repository "SemEval-2014" [18] and feedbacks of teachers were collected from three different sources: Online platform for American teachers' feedback [17], Online platform for Indian teachers' feed-back [10], and feedbacks collected from engineering students of our institute [2]. The chapter has been broadly divided into five sections including Introduction, Related Work, The Proposed System, Results, and Conclusions and References.

15.2   Related Work

The feature extraction methods can be divided into three categories, i.e., rule-based methods, supervised machine learning and unsupervised machine learning–based methods. In rule-based methods, a set of rules are defined by the researchers to identity relevant features from the textual feedbacks. Rules are formed by taking into account syntactic and semantic relations among the tokens in the sentences. In supervised machine learning methods, systems are trained to classify whether a word is a feature or not and for training the system a labeled data set (training set) is required. In unsupervised methods words are grouped on the basis of syntactic and semantic similarities. Each group is known as cluster and cluster head represents a feature.

Poria *et al.* [14] proposed a rule-based approach to extract features of product from the reviews of the product. Authors suggested twelve rules to identify explicit features in review. Rules were based on the syntactic relations among the tokens of the sentences and clustered-based approach is used by the authors to identify implicit features. Pavlopoulos *et al.* [12] developed three new datasets for three different domains which are publically available for the researchers. Three most popular techniques (baseline methods) are implemented by the authors to process new developed datasets. Authors have combined continuous space vector representation word and phrases to enhance performances of system.

Qiu *et al.* [16] proposed a double propagation system to extract aspect words and opinion words on the basis of syntactic relationships between aspect and sentiment terms. By using known sentiment words (seed words) and syntactic patterns between aspect and sentiment terms new aspect terms are identified. On the basis of identified aspects and syntactic patterns between aspect and sentiment terms, new sentiment words are identified and this process is continued till aspect or sentiments words are identified or we can say that set of aspect terms and opinion terms are expanded simultaneously.

Liu *et al.* [7] have modified double propagation algorithm that is given by Qiu *et al.* [16] through including semantic similarity and aspect and aspect association-based knowledge. It performs better than baseline algorithm and is also able to capture multi-word aspect terms with high accuracy. Siqueira *et al.* [19] proposed a method to extract features from the reviews of services. This method is used in the design of a prototype system "What Matter". Valid features are identified using linguistic knowledge. It works in four steps, i.e., frequent noun identification, relevant noun identification, feature indicator mapping, and unrelated noun removal.

Hamdan *et al.* [4] proposed a Conditional Random Field (CRF)–based system to extract multi-word aspect terms in reviews. Authors have used IOB (Inside, Beginning, and the Outside) notation in review sentences. Each single word is extracted with set of features and on the basis of extracted features, it is decided whether a word is valid aspect or not. System is implemented by using CRF suite. Wang *et al.* [20] proposed a model-based on Restricted Boltzmann Machines to extract aspect terms and sentiment words in unsupervised setting. Model is designed with three types of hidden layers in neural network. Hidden layers represent aspect, sentiment, and background, respectively.

Poria *et al.* [13] proposed a method to tag each word in review as aspect term or non-aspect term. Authors have used seven-layer deep convolutional neural network for it. Linguistic patterns are also combined with neural network. Chen *et al.* [1] pro-posed a clustering-based method for feature extraction and feature categorization simultaneously. Features are grouped on the basis of their domain similarities and merging constraints. Domain similarities are captured with public lexicon WordNet. Hamdan [3] used CRF to learn system for feature extraction. Main features used by author were terms itself, part of speech tag to each term, word shape (capital letter, small letter, digit, punctuation, and other symbol), word type (uppercase, digit, symbol, and combination), prefixes (all prefixes having length between one to four), suffixes (all suffixes having length between one to four), and stop word (word is a stop word or not). Pranali and Borikar [15] suggested an artificial neural network system to classify movie reviews. Authors trained and tested the system using training and test data sets which were collected from public IMDB movie review. In this system, fuzzy logic was used to handle the sentiment negations like no, not, and never. Integration of fuzzy logic and artificial neural network was helpful in improving system accuracy.

Huey and Renganathan [5] proposed a system to find the sentiment polarity of comments on electronics items written in Chinese language. System is implemented using Maximum Entropy–based approach.

Authors have also analyzed feature selection and pre-processing of the Chinese comments using Maximum Entropy concept.

Muqtar *et al.* [9] proposed an unsupervised machine learning–based method to divide tweets in positive and negative clusters. In this method, clusters are created with the help of K-means algorithm. Authors have used hierarchical clustering to visualize the results generated by the system. Results given by the authors show that the performance of suggested method is comparable to SVM.

15.3 The Proposed System

A hybrid approach for the identification of features of an item has been proposed. The approach integrates the concept of topic modeling and linguistic knowledge extracted from the text to find the important features. The proposed system identifies features of a product/service/professional dynamically from the textual feedbacks and the importance of each feature is decided on the basis of statistical knowledge present in the text. The architecture of the proposed system is shown in Figure 15.1. Main modules

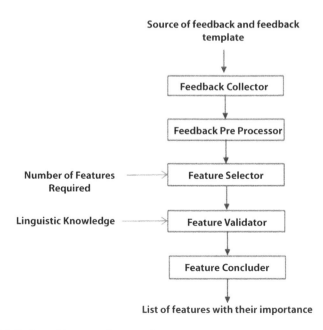

Figure 15.1 Basic architecture of proposed system.

of the system are Feedback Collector, Feedback Pre-Processor, Feature Selector, Feature Validator, and Feature Concluder.

Feedback Collector is responsible to collect textual feedbacks from specified sources. Feedback Pre-Processor performs the basic processing tasks on collected feedbacks. Feedback Collector and Feedback Pre-Processor are implemented using libraries of Natural Language Toolkit (NLTK) [11]. Feature Selector module is used to generate K probabilistic distribution of words, where each probabilistic distribution represents a topic/feature. Implementation of this module is based on topic modeling-based approach known as Probabilistic Latent Semantic Analysis (PLSA). Valid features of a product or a service or an individual are identified with the help of Feature Validator module and various linguistic tests are applied on probable words generated by Feature Selector module. Importance or weight of each feature is statistically estimated by Feature Concluder module. Implementation details and basic functions of modules are given in next sub sections.

15.3.1   Feedback Collector

This module collects all the feedbacks of an item from the local or remote source. Module can collect textual feedbacks from different kind of documents, i.e., html, xml, pdf, and doc. Input to this module is source address of feedbacks, document type, and feedback template in which feedbacks have been stored at the source address. To implement this module, we have used standard libraries of Python and NLTK.

15.3.2   Feedback Pre-Processor

Feedbacks collected by the Feedback Collector are in raw form. It may contain unwanted characters, symbols, comments, tags, etc. One major function of this module is to remove unwanted characters, symbols, comment, and tags from the collected textual feedbacks. Other important functions of this module are text normalization, removal of stop words and spelling corrections of misspelled words in the feedbacks.

15.3.3   Feature Selector

Input to this module is pre-processed feedbacks and an integer number K (number of possible topics). In this module, it is assumed that all sentences are generated from K different topics. Each topic/feature is represented by a probabilistic distribution of vocabulary words. K topics (probabilistic distribution words) are predicted by using the topic modeling-based technique called PLSA. PLSA is an unsupervised approach and the basic intuition of PLSA is that a topic or a feature of a sentence can be captured by the probability distribution of words. For one feature, some words are more probable with respect to other feature. In a sentence, students may highlight more than one feature, for example, "Presentation and knowledge is awesome but he is not punctual". In this sentence, three features are mentioned, i.e., "Presentation", "Knowledge", and "Punctual".

PLSA extracts related features in the form of words distribution along with coverage of each topic in all sentences. Input to the model is a corpus (i.e., collection of feedbacks) and a number decided by the users, i.e., K. Let $C = \{s_1, s_2, \ldots s_n\}$ is the collection of input sentences, $\{\Theta_1, \Theta_2, \ldots \Theta_k\}$ are K different topics where Θ_i represents the probabilistic distribution of all words for topic i, i.e., $P(w| \Theta_i)$ and $\{\pi_{i1}, \pi_{i2}, \ldots \pi_{ij}, \ldots \pi_{ik}\}$ where π_{ij} is the coverage of ith sentence by j^{th} topic.

Vocabulary V is automatically identified from the corpus. A word of any sentence can be generated from K possible topics $(\Theta_1, \Theta_2, \ldots \Theta_k)$ with the assumption that there are **m** words in vocabulary V. Probability of observing a word "w" from distributions is denoted as P(w) and it is estimated by considering the probability of word in different topics and coverage of that topic as given in Equation (15.1).

$$P(w) = \sum_{j=1}^{k} \pi_{sj} * P(w|\Theta_j) \qquad (15.1)$$

where π_{sj} is converge of sentence s by topic j while $P(w| \Theta_j)$ word probability distribution of word w in topic j. Logarithmic probabilities have been used instead of direct probabilities to perform computations to desired number of decimal because normal probability values are of the order of 10^{-5}. Logarithmic probability of a sentence's (Log(P(s))) is defined as follows:

$$LogP(s)) = \sum_{w \in V} C(w,s) * log\left[\sum_{j=1}^{k} \pi_{sj} * P(w|\Theta_j)\right] \qquad (15.2)$$

where $C(w,s)$ is the frequency count of word "w" in sentence "s" and π_{sj}, $P(w| \Theta_j)$ are as defined in equation (1). Similarly, logarithmic probability of whole corpus is sum of all individual feedbacks, i.e., P(C) given in Equation (15.3).

$$\text{LogP(C))} = \sum_{s \in C} \sum_{w \in V} C(w,s) * \log \left[\sum_{j=1}^{k} \pi_{sj} * P(w|\Theta_j) \right]$$

$$(15.3)$$

Expectation-Maximization algorithm (Algorithm 15.1) is used to estimate topic model parameters (Λ), i.e., word distribution in each topic $\{\Theta_1, \Theta_2, \ldots, \Theta_k\}$ and the coverage captured by each topic for each sentence $\{\pi_{i1}, \pi_{i2} \ldots \pi_{ij} \ldots \ldots \pi_{ik}\}$ such that it maximizes the probability of whole corpus, i.e., $\Lambda^* = \text{argmax}_\Lambda P(C| \Lambda)$. Basically, it is a constraint optimization problem where two constraints in model are as follows:

(i) Sum of word probabilities in all topics to be 1, $\sum_{i=1}^{N} P(w_i | \Theta_j) = 1$ for every topic j $\in$ [1,K].

(ii) Sum of coverage probabilities of all topics to be 1 in each sentence, i.e., $\sum_{j=1}^{k} \pi_{sj} = 1$ for every sentence s $\in$ C.

In this problem, K latent variables for K topics are included. An Expectation-Maximization algorithm consists of E steps and M steps where in E steps, latent variable are introduced and the probability of generating each word from the latent topic is estimated. E step starts with initial random values of parameters after that E step iteratively uses the values computed by M step.

15.3.4   Feature Validator

A fixed number of words of higher probabilities from each topic (probabilistic words distribution generated by PLSA) are selected and inserted into a tentative list of features. An algorithm that makes use of linguistic properties of features, contextual knowledge to filter the unwanted words is applied to tentative list to select the most significant features. The algorithm uses different filters as shown in Figure 15.2. Each filter is used to remove irrelevant aspects from probable aspects list.

15.3.4.1   Removal of Terms From Tentative List of Features on the Basis of Syntactic Knowledge

It is known that, normally, syntactic categories of features are noun, adjective, or adverb. Therefore, as a first step, common sentiment words which

Algorithm 15.1 Expectation-Maximization to estimate topic model parameters.

Inputs:	Term by sentence matrix for all the sentences after removing background (stop) words and the number of topics K.
Output:	K distribution of vocabulary words (Topics),

Step 1:	Initialize all parameters $\{\Theta_1, \Theta_2...\Theta_k\}$ and $\{\pi_{i1}, \pi_{i2}... \pi_{ij}... \pi_{ik}\}$ randomly with numbers between zero and one.
Step 2:	Normalize the parameters so that sum of word probabilities in all topics is 1 and the sum of coverage probabilities of all topics is also 1.

Step 3: Estimate probability of generating each word from the latent topics, i.e., $P(Z_{s,w} = j) = \dfrac{\pi_{sj} * P(w|\theta_j)}{\displaystyle\sum_{j=1}^{k} \pi_{sj} * P(w|\theta_{j'})}$ using latest values of π_{sj} and $P(w|\theta_j)$.

Step 4: Using inferred Z values to spilt the counts and then collecting the right count to re-estimate the parameters $\pi_{s,j}$ and $P(w|\theta_j)$ as

$$\pi_{s,j} = \frac{\displaystyle\sum_{w\varepsilon V} C(d,w) * P(w|\theta_j)}{\displaystyle\sum_{j'\varepsilon K} \sum_{w\varepsilon V} c(d,w) * P(w|\theta_{j'})} \text{ and}$$

$$P(w|\theta j) = \frac{\displaystyle\sum_{d\varepsilon C} C(d,w) * P(w|\theta_j)}{\displaystyle\sum_{w'\varepsilon V} \sum_{d\varepsilon C} c(d,w) * P(w|\theta_{j'})}.$$

Step 5: Iterate step 3 and step 4 till convergence maximum likelihood of corpus, i.e., P(C) and modify $\{\Theta_1, \Theta_2...\Theta_k\}$ and $\{\pi_{i1}, \pi_{i2}... \pi_{ij}... \pi_{ik}\}$ using latent variables.

Step 6: Last modified values $\{\Theta_1, \Theta_2...\Theta_k\}$ and $\{\pi_{i1}, \pi_{i2}... \pi_{ij}... \pi_{ik}\}$ are the final optimum parameters of the model, where $\Theta_j = P(w|\Theta_j)$ is words distribution for topic "j" and π_{ij} is the coverage of ith document by j^{th} topic.

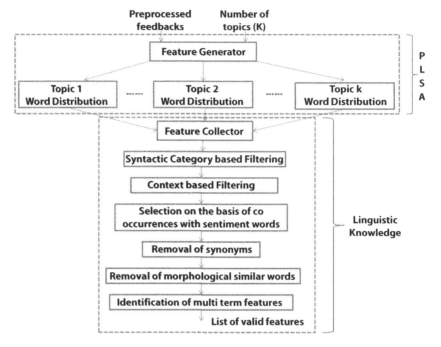

Figure 15.2 Filtering based on linguistic knowledge.

are adjective or adverb like "good", "awesome", "bad", and "worst" are removed and then all those words whose syntactic categories are not noun, adjective, or adverb are removed from the tentative list of features.

15.3.4.2 Removal of Least Significant Terms on the Basis of Contextual Knowledge

It is observed that many valid features are paradigmatic (similar context) words. Relation between words is called paradigmatic if one word can be used in place of other word without violating syntactic structure or acceptability of the sentence. Degree of paradigmatic reflects agreement between lexical neighborhoods. Generally, parts of speech of paradigmatic words are same. To extract most of the significant feature terms, we add two well-known features of each valid syntactic category, i.e., noun, adjective, and adverb, respectively, in seed feature list as seed features and compute context similarities between words in tentative and seed feature list. Contextual similarities between terms are cosine similarities between contextual vectors of both terms. Term frequency and inverse document (TF-IDF) weighting scheme is used in vector representation of contexts.

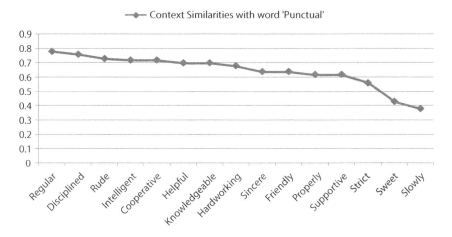

Figure 15.3 Contextually similar terms of word "Punctual".

Terms in seed feature list and terms of tentative list having higher context similarities with terms in seed feature list are added in the final feature list. Again, context similarities between terms in final feature list and terms in tentative feature list are computed and highly contextually similar words of tentative list are added in final feature list. This process is continued till new terms keep adding to the final list. Paradigmatically similar terms of word "Punctual" in teachers' feedbacks (on x axis) with their contextual similarities (on y axis) are shown in Figure 15.3.

From Figure 15.3, it is identified that "Regular" and "Disciplined" are more relevant compared to "Sweet" and "slowly".

15.3.4.3 Removal of Less Significant Terms on the Basis of Association With Sentiment Words

It is known that feature and sentiment words frequently co-occur in feedbacks or we can say that features of an item and sentiment bearing terms are syntagmatic words. In this step, we remove those terms from final feature list whose syntactic category is noun and are weakly associated with sentiment words. To measure the association, we computed Point wise Mutual Information (PMI) between the terms in final feature list and words in sentiment list. Sentiment list contains general sentiment words like "good", "bad", "worst", and "excellent". Few strongly and weakly sentiment associated words in teachers' feedback and in "laptop" feedback are shown in Tables 15.1 and 15.2.

Table 15.1 Most strongly and weakly sentiment associated words in teachers' feedbacks.

Terms strongly associated with sentiment words (Kept in final feature list)		Terms weakly associated with sentiment words (Removed from feature list)	
Words	Degree of association	Words	Degree of association
Teaching	0.96	Book	0.487805
Knowledge	0.918221	Board	0.328694
Presentation	0.859541	Bit	0.128694
Skills	0.837565	Minutes	0.028694
Regular	0.812575	Class	0.114347

Table 15.2 Most strongly and weakly sentiment associated words in laptops' feedbacks.

Terms strongly associated with sentiment words (Kept in final feature list)		Terms weakly associated with sentiment words (Removed from final feature list)	
Words	Degree of association	Words	Degree of association
Price	0.898234	Store	0.037645
Touchpad	0.897215	Power	0.026792
Size	0.783419	Night	0.024876
Screen	0.718394	Area	0.018721
Keyboard	0.688890	Network	0.012543

15.3.4.4   Removal of Terms Having Similar Sense

In this step, redundant features are removed by using sense similarities between words in final feature list. Sense similarities between words are computed using "Wordnet" lexicon. In the analysis of teachers' feedback, we have found that words "skill", "way", "method", and "style" have same sense. Therefore, we are retaining only one word out of four similar words.

15.3.4.5   Removal of Terms Having Same Root

We also observed that sometimes different syntactic forms of a same root word (like knowledge and knowledgeable) are present in final feature list. To remove such terms, first we find root form of all the terms present in final feature list and retain only one term having syntactic category noun. We have used NLTK stammer to find root word of all words present in the final feature list.

15.3.4.6   Identification of Multi-Term Features

In this step, we try to join two or more terms to form a new feature. Words are joined on the basis of their co-occurrences. Highly co-occurring words are considered as a single valid feature. Point wise mutual information gain is used to estimate co-occurrences between the terms present in final feature list. "Paper Pattern", "Teaching Way", and "Communication Skill" are valid features in teachers' feedback while "Battery Life", "Screen Size", and "Hard Drive" are valid features in laptops' feedback.

15.3.4.7   Identification of Less Frequent Feature

In this step, less frequent and missing features of an item are identified on the basis of syntactic and semantic relations between terms in final feature list and sentiment words. All other words of feedbacks having similar relations are treated as significant features and are added in final feature list. Algorithm used in implementation of Feature Validator (Algorithm 15.2) is given below.

Algorithm 15.2 Feature Validator.

Input:	Tentative list of features, list of general sentiment bearing words, WordNet lexicon, Users' feedbacks.
Output:	Most significant of features.
Step 1:	Remove all words from the tentative list of features whose syntactic category are not Noun, Adjective, and Adverb.
Step 2:	Remove general sentiment bearing words from the tentative list.

(Continued)

Algorithm 15.2 Feature Validator. (*Continued*)

Step 3:	Add seed features in seed list.
Step 4:	Compute contextual similarities between each terms present in seed and tentative feature list.
Step 5:	All terms of seed feature list and highly contextual similar words of tentative feature list are added in final feature list and removed from tentative feature list.
Step 6:	Compute contextual similarities between each terms present in final and tentative feature list.
Step 7:	Highly contextual similar words of tentative feature list are added in final feature list and removed from tentative feature list.
Step 8:	Repeat step 6 and step 7 until new words are added to final feature list.
Step 9:	Remove all words having syntactic category noun from final feature whose occurring with general sentiment word is less than threshold.
Step 10:	Compute sense similarities between each term present in final feature list and only single entry is maintained for all terms having similar sense.
Step 11:	Remove all words adjective and adverb whose stem word is present in final feature list and its syntactic category is noun.
Step 12:	Remove all neighboring and co-occurring terms from final feature list and co-occurring multi-term is added in final feature list.
Step 13:	Add all terms from the vocabulary to final feature list whose syntactic structure are similar to the terms present in final feature list.
Step 14:	All words in final feature list are the significant features of the item.

15.3.5   Feature Concluder

This module is responsible to estimate the importance of each feature. In estimation of importance of features, we assume that users try to mention all important features in their feedback during writing textual feedback of any item while less important features are ignored or we can say that degree of inclusion of a feature in feedbacks represents its importance. Most significant features of teachers' with their importance are shown in Figure 15.5. Weight of feature plays significant role during the computation of overall sentiment score of product/service/professional. Overall sentiment score of an item should be estimated by taking the weighted average of sentiment score of all the significant features. Role of features' weights in estimation of overall sentiment score of an item is demonstrated below. Let there be two items having five features, where weights and sentiment scores are given in Table 15.3. Feature weights are considered in the range of 0 to 1 while sentiment scores are in the range of 1 to 10. It seems in Table 15.3 that item 2 is better than item 1 because sentiment scores of

Table 15.3 Estimation of overall sentiment score of an item.

Feature	Weight	Feature sentiment score of item 1	Feature sentiment score of item 2	Effective sentiment score item 1	Effective sentiment score item 2
F1	0.9	8	3	Average sentiment score without considering weights = $(8 + 8 + 8 + 3 + 2)/5 = 5.8$ Weighted average sentiment score with considering weights = $(8 \times 0.9 + 8 \times 0.8 + 8 \times 0.6 + 3 \times 0.3 + 2 \times 0.2)/5 = 3.94$	Average sentiment score without considering weights = $(3 + 8 + 9 + 5 + 7)/5 = 6.4$ Weighted average sentiment score with considering weights = $(3 \times 0.9 + 8 \times 0.8 + 9 \times 0.6 + 5 \times 0.3 + 7 \times 0.2)/5 = 3.48$
F2	0.8	8	8		
F3	0.6	8	9		
F4	0.3	3	5		
F5	0.2	2	7		

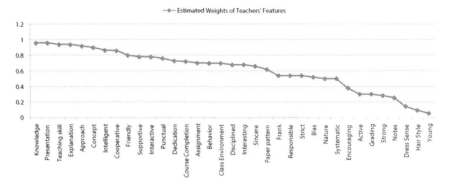

Figure 15.4 Teachers' features with its importance.

all features of item 2 are better than item 1 except feature F1 and average sentiment score of item 2 is also better than item 1 but if weights of features are taken into account, then it can be seen that the effective sentiment score of item 1 is better than item 2.

It can be easily seen from Figure 15.4 that dominating or most important features like "Knowledge", "Presentation", and "Intelligent" having higher weights in comparison to the features "Young", "Hair Style", "Notes", etc.

15.4   Result Analysis

We have processed feedback in two different domains. In the first domain, we have processed textual feedbacks of product, i.e., laptops, and in the second domain, we have processed feedbacks of professionals, i.e., teachers. Summary of results accomplished by different important modules/ phases/steps are given in Table 15.4.

To measure the effectiveness of proposed system, we have compared features identified by our system with pre tagged features. In laptops' feedback dataset, each sentence is labeled with appropriate aspect term and its sentiments while in teachers' feedback, we have manually assigned related aspect term with each sentence. In our experiment, we have found that our system is performing better than baseline method [8]. To estimate system performance, we have divided feedbacks of teachers and laptops into training and test sets in the ratio of 3:1. System is trained by using statistical and linguistic knowledge extracted from the training set. Average accuracy, precision, and recall of our proposed system for teachers and laptops are shown in Figure 15.5.

Table 15.4 Summary of results accomplished by different important modules/steps.

Module/phase/step	Processing remark	No. of words are treated as valid features in teachers feedbacks	No. of words are treated as valid features in laptops feedbacks
Data Collection	Feedback collection from specified remote location.	No of Sentences: 7,342 Total words: 66,767 Unique words: 6,047	No of Sentences: 3,048 Total words: 29,623 Unique words: 3,005
Feature Selector (Topic modeling)	Number of topics has taken, i.e., K (20).	Words from each topic = 15 Total no of words = 15 × 20 = 300	Words from each topic = 15 Total no of words = 15 × 20 = 300
Removal of invalid words on the basis of syntactic categories of words	Only nouns, adjectives, and adverbs are kept in tentative list.	Remaining words in tentative feature list = 210.	Remaining words in tentative feature list = 210.
Removal of sentiment bearing words	General sentiment bearing words (adjective and adverb) are removed from the tentative list.	Remaining words in tentative feature list = 177.	Remaining words in tentative feature list = 167.

(*Continued*)

Table 15.4 Summary of results accomplished by different important modules/ steps. (*Continued*)

Module/phase/ step	Processing remark	No. of words are treated as valid features in teachers feedbacks	No. of words are treated as valid features in laptops feedbacks
Context Similarity– based removal	Only those words of tentative list are considered valid features which are contextually similar.	Remaining words in tentative feature list = 102.	Remaining words in tentative feature list = 93.
Occurrence- based removal	Features having part of speech noun are frequently co-occur with sentiment word, PMI is used to measure concurrences	Remaining words in tentative feature list = 55.	Remaining words in tentative feature list = 48.
Removal of features which have similar sense	To remove redundant feature, sense of each features is compared with other features using WordNet lexicon.	Remaining words in tentative feature list = 44.	Remaining words in tentative feature list = 39.

(*Continued*)

Table 15.4 Summary of results accomplished by different important modules/steps. (*Continued*)

Module/phase/step	Processing remark	No. of words are treated as valid features in teachers feedbacks	No. of words are treated as valid features in laptops feedbacks
Removal features which are derived form of other features	Those features are remove that have more than one syntactic categories but its stem (root) is same.	Remaining words in tentative feature list = 41.	Remaining words in tentative feature list = 37.
Multi-word feature formation	Highly co-occurring terms are considered as a multiword features.	Remaining words in tentative feature list = 35.	Remaining words in tentative feature list = 33.

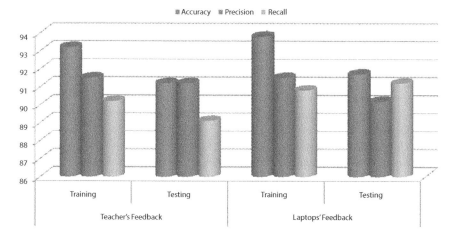

Figure 15.5 System performance in teachers' and laptops' feedbacks.

15.5   Conclusion

With the proposed approach, we are able to identify relevant features of a product/service/professional with their weights representing significances of features. Proposed system works in two phases: First, a tentative list of features is identified using topic modeling-based technique PLSA and further linguistic knowledge is used to extract significant features. This system will be helpful in performing a fine gained sentiment analysis on textual feedbacks. We have tested proposed system with the feedbacks of laptops and teachers. In future, we will test the proposed system on feedbacks of other domains like feedbacks of movies, restaurants, books, employees, etc., to identify the significant features in each domain. Our future plan is develop a topic model-based system to identify sentiment orientation of the mentioned features. It can be integrated with our proposed feature extraction system to build a new feature-based sentiment analyzer. We are also planning to incorporate domain specific linguistic knowledge to enhance performance of our system.

References

1. Chen, L., Martineau, J., Cheng, D., Sheth, A., Clustering for Simultaneous Extraction of Aspects and Features from Reviews. *Proceedings of NAACL-HLT*, San Diego, California, pp. 789–799, 2016.
2. *Collected Textual Feedback: Textual feedbacks collected from 120 engineering students for 20 teachers of University Institute of Engineering and Technology*, CSJM University, Kanpur, 2018.
3. Hamdan, H., SentiSys at SemEval-2016 Task 5: Opinion Target Extraction and Sentiment Polarity Detection. *Proceedings of SemEval-2016*, San Diego, California, pp. 350–355, 2016.
4. Hamdan, H., Bellot, P., Bechet, F., Lsislif: CRF and Logistic Regression for Opinion Target Extraction and Sentiment Polarity Analysis. *Proceedings of the 9th International Workshop on Semantic Evaluation (SemEval 2015)*, Denver, Colorado, pp. 753–758, 2015.
5. Huey and Renganathan, H., Chinese Sentiment Analysis Using Maximum Entropy, in: *Proceedings of the Workshop on Sentiment Analysis where AI meets Psychology (SAAIP), IJCNLP 2011*, Chiang Mai, Thailand, November 13, 2011, pp. 89–93, 2011.
6. Kumar, A. and Jain, R., Sentiment Analysis and Feedback Evaluation. *IEEE 3rd International Conference on MOOCs, Innovation and Technology in Education (MITE)*, India, 2015.

7. Liu, Q., Liu, B., Zhang, Y., Kim, D.S., Gao, Z., Improving Opinion Aspect Extraction Using Semantic Similarity and Aspect Associations. *Proceedings of the Thirtieth AAAI Conference on Artificial Intelligence (AAAI-16)*, 2016.

8. Minqing, H. and Bing, L., Mining and summarizing customer reviews, in: *Proceedings of ACM SIGKDD International Conference on Knowledge Discovery and Data Mining (KDD-2004)*, 2004.

9. Muqtar U., Ameen, A., Raziuddin, S., Opinion Mining on Twitter Data using Unsupervised Learning Technique. *Int. J. Comput. Appl.* (0975 – 8887), 148, 12, 12–19, 2016.

10. Myfaveteacher : Online Indian platform for teachers' feedback.

11. NLTK: http://www.nltk.org.

12. Pavlopoulos, J. and Androutsopoulos, I., Aspect Term Extraction for Sentiment Analysis: New Datasets, New Evaluation Measures and an Improved Unsupervised Method. *Proceedings of the 5th Workshop on Language Analysis for Social Media (LASM)*, Gothenburg, Sweden, pp. 44–52, 2014.

13. Poria, S., Cambria, E., Gelbukh, A., Aspect extraction for opinion mining with a deep convolutional neural network. *Knowledge-Based Syst.*, 108, 42–49, 2016.

14. Poria, S., Cambria, E., Ku, L.W., Gui, C., Gelbukh, A., A Rule-Based Approach to Aspect Extraction from Product Reviews. *Proceedings of the Second Workshop on Natural Language Processing for Social Media (SocialNLP)*, Dublin, Ireland, pp. 28–37, 2014.

15. Pranali, P. and Borikar, D.A., An Approach to Sentiment Analysis using Artificial Neural Network with Comparative Analysis of Different Techniques. *IOSR J. Comput. Eng. (IOSR-JCE)*, 18, 2, 64–69, 2016.

16. Qiu, G., Liu, B., Bu, J., Chen, C., Opinion Word Expansion and Target Extraction through Double Propagation, *Assoc. Comput. Linguist.*, 37, 1–21, 2011.

17. Ratemyprofessor: Online American platform for teachers' feedback.

18. SemEval2014: http://alt.qcri.org/semeval2014/task4/index.php?id=data-and-|tools.

19. Siqueira, H. and Barros, F., A Feature Extraction Process for Sentiment Analysis of Opinions on Services. *Proceeding of International Workshop on Web and Text Intelligence*, 2010.

20. Wang, L., Liu, K., Cao, Z., Zhao, J., Melo, G.D., Sentiment-Aspect Extraction based on Restricted Boltzmann Machines. *Proceedings of the 53rd Annual Meeting of the Association for Computational Linguistics and the 7th International Joint Conference on Natural Language Processing*, Beijing, China, pp. 616–625, 2015.

16

Spark-Enhanced Deep Neural Network Framework for Medical Phrase Embedding

Amol P. Bhopale* and Ashish Tiwari

Department of Computer Science and Engineering, Visvesvaraya National Institute of Technology, Nagpur, India

Abstract

The fundamental problem in information retrieval (IR) technique is the limited set of query words and, when used, cannot be helpful in retrieving documents having similar context words. Although word embedding has greatly benefited the field of NLP by considering similar meaning words, it is not capable of dealing with contextually similar phrases. This paper presents a deep neural embedding–based solution which not only considers the similar context words but also takes care of semantic phrases. To ensure the scalability, a spark-based map-reduce framework is employed to extract phrases using NLP techniques and prepare a new annotated dataset using these phrases. This paper uses Word2Vec Continuous Bag-of-Word (CBOW) model to learn embeddings over the annotated dataset and extracts contextually similar phrases. Considering the advancements in medical field and requirements of effective IR techniques for clinical decision support using medical artefacts, the proposed methodology is evaluated on a dataset provided by TREC-2014 CDS track. It consists of 733,125 PubMed articles which have been used in many IR experiments. In the result, meaningful phrases and their contextually similar forms are observed. These phrases can further be used for query expansion task.

Keywords: Phrase embedding, information retrieval, medical concept, deep neural network, spark

*Corresponding author: amolpbhopale@gmail.com

Mettu Srinivas, G. Sucharitha and Anjanna Matta (eds.) Machine Learning Algorithms and Applications, (289–304) © 2021 Scrivener Publishing LLC

16.1 Introduction

In numerous NLP applications such as sentiment analysis, web search, and language translation, phrases are considered to be one of the important language units. It is assumed that the words occurred in the similar context usually have similar meaning [1]. Advancements in deep neural network technique have benefited word vector representation into its contextually similar form with more information in hand. Compare to the symbolic linguistic representations, these rich informative embedding helped in various NLP tasks [2]. With the huge success of low-dimensional word embedding, it has been widely used for other domains, such as network [3] and user [4] embedding. Initially, embeddings are derived only for words, but in recent years, it is extended to phrases as well. In information retrieval (IR) tasks, phrase embedding helps by enriching the meaning of a word with its contextually similar forms. It has many applications in scientific and medical domains where technical concepts are mainly represented as multi-word terms.

The motivation is to perform medical phrase embedding in the vast growing digital content about patients, diseases, and medical reports on the Internet. Many times, practitioners find difficulties in retrieving decision supportive documents with fewer query words or using only acronyms. Phrase embedding can be used to infer the attributes of the context they enclosed with and they also can capture non-compositional semantics. This paper presents a study to build the phrase embedding model trained on a large dataset. It is used for contextually similar phrase extraction based on similarity scores to leverage the query expansion task which may improve the quality of the retrieved documents.

To achieve scalability a spark map-reduce framework is employed which leverages CPU power using its multi-threading architecture to process massive amount of data. Map function is used to split the dataset and generate phrases. This process is generalized to include phrases by identifying their boundaries at each special character and stop word. This technique is also known as chunking. Reduce function collects the frequent phrases and explicitly annotated corpus with the derived phrases. For learning phrase embedding, the adopted approach treats phrases as one unit and learns to embed them in the same way as the word embedding technique proposed in paper [5]. The key contributions of this paper are as follows:

- An unsupervised phrase generation technique is proposed to extract meaningful phrases and annotate them in the dataset.

- A spark-based map-reduce framework is used to work efficiently with large datasets for phrase extraction and corpus annotation.
- A word2vec CBOW–based phrase embedding model is proposed to learn embeddings for phrases as well as words in the same vector space.
- An effectiveness of the proposed model is evaluated on the TREC-CDS 2014 dataset.

The rest of the paper is organized as follows. In Section 16.2, related work is discussed followed by proposed phrase extraction and embedding technique which is discussed in Section 16.3. In Section 16.4, experimental setup is described. In Section 16.5, results are presented and outcomes are discussed followed by conclusion in Section 16.6, and then finally, the references are listed.

16.2   Related Work

Document representation has a long history. In paper [6], authors have presented a latent semantic analysis (LSA) technique to represent documents in low-dimensional term space; singular value decomposition is applied to decompose large term vs document matrix into set of orthogonal factors. In latent Dirichlet allocation (LDA), term dependencies are represented by considering them derived from latent variables [7]. Major challenge faced by these techniques is that they consider document level word co-occurrences to compute term associations.

More recently, word embedding has been used as one of the solutions to represent word in low-dimensional vector space which may lead to better term-dependency models. Several count-based and prediction-based methods are devised to learn embedding [8]. In [5], authors have applied neural language model to learn word embedding by maximizing the probability of co-occurrence of a word and its context.

Inspired from the word embedding, distributional approach is proposed for phrase embedding in [9], where phrases are treated as a single unit. However, phrases are critical for capturing the lexical meaning for many tasks. In [10], authors have presented a feature-rich compositional transformation (FCT) model for phrase representation which takes the weighted sum of word vectors based on lexical feature template list for each phrase type. Zhao *et al.* [11] have proposed a compositional model to construct phrase or sentence meaning. They applied vector-tensor-vector multiplication model to learn phrase representations. In [12], authors have presented the application of phrase embedding in extracting and ranking keywords from long scientific papers. In [13], authors have proposed a hybrid method to learn phrase embedding representation which is based on the linear combination of the distributional component and the compositional component with an individualized phrase compositionality constraint.

16.3 Proposed Approach

Phrase embedding is a three-stage process as shown in Figure 16.1; in first stage, frequent phrases are discovered from the corpus. In second stage, corpus is annotated with the captured phrases followed by word2vec model training in the third stage using a newly annotated dataset.

16.3.1 Phrase Extraction

The very first step in generating phrase embedding is to extract phrases which are made up of a group of words. In [14] has proposed "chunking" as one of the most linguistically heavy approach of detecting phrases. As shown in Figure 16.2, the first step is to split-up entire corpus into segments based on the occurrences of special characters such as a period, semicolon, and comma. Stop words are used to set the boundary for each candidate phrase. This process produces a large number of candidate phrases which are filtered out based on the frequency count.

This study has employed a built-in multi-threaded spark-based lightweight approach to ensure scalability and efficiency. Thus, a PySpark package is used to avail the spark environment in python. As shown in Figure 16.3, multiple map threads read text documents and apply basic NLP techniques such as converting texts into lower case and consider stop words as boundary to generate candidate phrases. Reduce function collects all phrases which satisfy minimum frequency count.

Figure 16.1 The three-phase proposed approach.

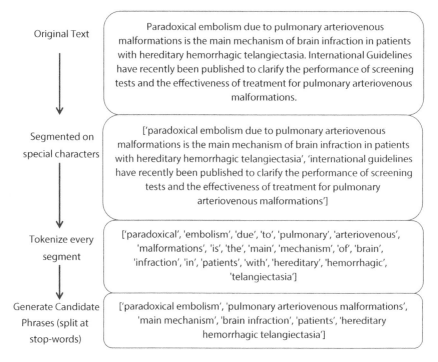

Figure 16.2 Phrase extraction sequence.

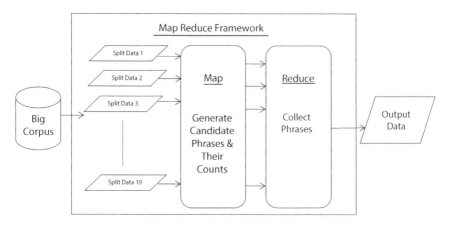

Figure 16.3 Map-reduce framework.

16.3.2 Corpus Annotation

It is the process of highlighting phrases in corpora. There are two ways to annotate corpora: first is pre-annotating entire corpora with phrases and building a new annotated corpora; the other way is to add one more layer in neural network to annotate documents prior to learning the embedding. This paper has followed the first way to make it simple and built a new annotated corpus. In the corpus, at every occurrence of phrase, a white space between sub-words is replaced by underscore "_" character as shown in Figure 16.4.

16.3.3 Phrase Embedding

Explicitly tagged phrase corpus is used to learn phrase embedding and train the neural network model. A Word2Vec CBOW–based training model is adopted for vectorizing and modelling pre-annotate phrase corpus. CBOW model was first proposed in [5] for representing words efficiently in their vector space. It is an iterative model and successor of neural network language model proposed in [15]. CBOW model predicts the probability of missing word from a given window of context words. It also helps in extracting semantically rich set of bi-grams.

CBOW model contains three identifiable layers, i.e., input layer, hidden layer, and output layer as shown in Figure 16.5. It is a three-phase process; in first phase, feed forward techniques are being used to train the model. In the input and output layer, the number of nodes depends upon the vocabulary size, whereas in the hidden layer, the number of nodes represents the vector dimensions. To train the neural network one-hot vector of context words is fed to input layer which uses feed forward technique and calculates the values of neurons at hidden layer. Unlike the traditional artificial neural network, weights of neurons at hidden layer are calculated just by considering the summation of products of input parameter to the weight of each neuron at input layer. In this process, activation function is

Paradoxical_embolism due to pulmonary_arteriovenous_malformations is the main_mechanism of brain_infraction in patients with hereditary_hemorrhagic_telangiectasia. International Guidelines have recently been published to clarify the performance of screening_tests and the effectiveness of treatment for pulmonary_arteriovenous_malformations.

Figure 16.4 Sample annotated document.

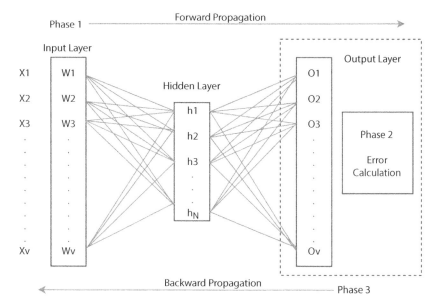

Figure 16.5 Single context CBOW model.

not considered in weight calculation. At output layer, probability value of different neurons is calculated using the weighted vector matrix between hidden layer and output layer. In output layer, the probabilities obtained for each context vector are summed up to predict the target word vector as shown in Equation (16.1).

$$y_j = \frac{1}{V} \sum_{t=1}^{V} \log p \left(w_t \Bigg| \sum_{-c \leq j \leq c, j \neq 0} w_{t+j} \right) \qquad (16.1)$$

where c is the size of context window, w_t is the target word, and V is vocabulary size. Probability at output is expressed in terms of softmax function as shown in Equation (16.2).

$$p(w_t|w_c) = \frac{\exp\left(u_{w_t}^T u_{w_c}\right)}{\displaystyle\sum_{w=1}^{V} \exp\left(u_w^T u_{w_c}\right)} \qquad (16.2)$$

Here, u_w is a target embedding vector for w_t and v_w is a context embedding vector. The vector u_w is the final embedding vector which is kept as a result, whereas v_w is considered as a side product.

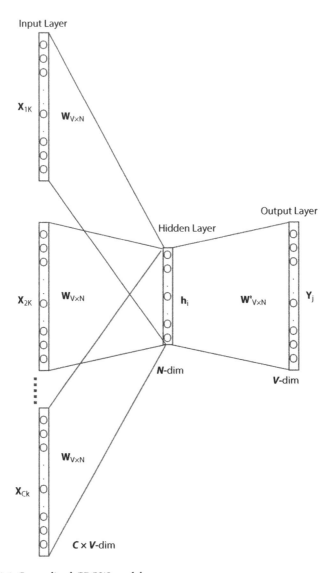

Figure 16.6 Generalized CBOW model.

In the second phase, error is calculated at output layer between the actual target word vector values and the summed-up values. If an error is detected, then traditional back propagation is being performed in the third phase to adjust the weights at hidden layers. The objective of training model is to maximize the conditional probability of observing the actual output word w_t, given the input context words w_c. Thus, the loss function is defined as $max(p(w_t|w_c))$. This loss function can also be considered as a special case of cross entropy measurement between two probabilistic distributions. Back-propagation weights at neurons are updated with the help of gradient descent optimization algorithm. In CBOW model, weight matrix adjusted between the inputs to hidden layer and hidden to output layer are essentially word vectors which are being learned. The process is performed iteratively until all neurons achieve optimal weights. These learned vectors between different layers are also known as embedding. Once the model is trained, it can then be used for predicting words based on context sequence. Figure 16.6 gives the generalized CBOW model with C contexts.

16.4   Experimental Setup

This section briefly discusses about the processes followed for data collection and data pre-processing. In the later part, the parameter tuning required to perform experiments is presented.

16.4.1   Dataset Preparation

For evaluating the proposed work a widely known dataset for IR, i.e., TREC-Clinical Decision Support dataset, which has 733,138 PubMed articles is used. The articles are in the NXML format; thus, it is parsed to extract title and abstract in text file format. Each article is pre-processed by applying NLP techniques such as lowering the case, removing special characters and prepared a single text document of entire Trec corpus which has one document per line.

16.4.2   Parameter Setting

A spark framework that parallelizes the phrase extraction process is used to ensure scalability. Using 10 map-reduce function threads the given corpus is partitioned and different NLP operations are performed to generate phrases and annotate dataset. Stop words are used to mark the boundary for phrases, each mapper function divides sentences into phrases based on their boundary, and the reduce function collects phrases that have a frequency count greater than 50. This study has used the python gensim library to implement word2vec CBOW model. It obtains vocabulary by representing each word or phrase vectors in 150 dimensions and then set context window size as 10 and trained the embedding model for 10 epochs. Table 16.1 summarizes the parameter details and their values.

Table 16.1 Parameter details and their values.

Parameter	Description	Value
Threads used in Spark	It is the number of map-reduce function threads.	10
Phrase Frequency Count	Minimum threshold value to be considered for phrase extraction.	50
Vector Length	The length of vector for representation of word or phrase.	150
Context Window Size	Number of words to be considered on both side of the target word/phrase.	10 (5 on each side)
Epoch Count	It is the number of allowed iterations to be performed for training the model.	10

16.5 Results

Objective of this study is to learn embedding for phrases as the word embedding does. This section describes the results obtained, i.e., phrases extracted using chunking technique and spark architecture from the TREC dataset. In the latter section, the sample phrase and word embeddings generated by the proposed phrase embedding model is shown.

16.5.1 Phrase Extraction

Table 16.2 shows the sample phrases extracted from the corpus. As shown in the table, the proposed technique has extracted bi-grams, tri-grams, and, in some cases, higher order n-grams. It is evident from the table that many meaningful candidate phrases are extracted.

16.5.2 Phrase Embedding

Phrase embedding is very much similar to word embedding. Tables 16.3 and 16.4 show the sample results generated by the proposed embedding model for both phrases and words, respectively. The proposed phrase embedding model works for both phrases as well as words. It is evident from Table 16.4 that similar phrases are extracted along with words for any targeted word. In the result, it is observed that highly correlated and

Table 16.2 Sample candidate phrases extracted from corpus.

Gene associated	Patient treated	Prospectively included
Review attempts	Measles virus	Stochastic model
Kidney diseases	Therapeutic agent	Cold acclimation
Neural basis	Iron homeostasis	Ocean acidification
Radiation exposure	Risk assessment	Detailed review
Spinal surgery	Investigate effects	Personality traits
Proteolytic cleavage	Specific differences	Gren syndrome
Major goals	Deep venous thrombosis	Cardiac arrest
Optimal level	Different processes	Synapse formation
Highest affinity	Large parts	Clinical consequences
Showed improvement	Large range	Differentially regulated genes
Functional networks	Tumor regression	Obsessive compulsive disorder
Rheumatoid arthritis	Warranted conclusion	Retrospectively reviewed patients
Clinically suspected	Chemical carcinogens	Inter xadmolecular inter xadactions

Table 16.3 Sample phrases and their embedding with similarity score.

Contextually similar to "chest pain"		Contextually similar to "human_genome"	
Word/phrase	Similarity score	Word/phrase	Similarity score
Palpitations	0.700	Genome	0.742
Syncope	0.699	Mouse genome	0.710
Dyspnea	0.693	Human genes	0.706
Epigastric pain	0.681	Entire genome	0.657

(Continued)

Table 16.3 Sample phrases and their embedding with similarity score. (*Continued*)

Haemoptysis	0.670	Genomes	0.656
Abdominal pain	0.662	Yeast genome	0.643
Dyspnoea	0.658	Human genomes	0.642
Palpitation	0.647	Coding regions	0.621
Pleuritic	0.646	Mouse genomes	0.609
Exertional	0.645	Plant genomes	0.608
Contextually similar to "measles_virus"		**Contextually similar to "kidney_diseases"**	
Word/phrase	**Similarity score**	**Word/phrase**	**Similarity score**
Poliovirus	0.661	Renal_diseases	0.700
Virus	0.627	Kidney_disease	0.624
Paramyxovirus	0.600	Renal_disease	0.613
Edmonston	0.590	Nephropathies	0.609
Vaccinia_virus	0.590	Nephropathy	0.547
Influenza_virus	0.587	Kidney_failure	0.533
Viral	0.581	Renal	0.528
Measles_viruses	0.568	Glomerulopathy	0.523
Reovirus	0.566	Kidney	0.516
Ectromelia	0.563	Hyperfiltration	0.509
Contextually similar to "spinal_surgery"		**Contextually similar to "cardiac_arrest"**	
Word/phrase	**Similarity score**	**Word/phrase**	**Similarity score**
Spine_surgery	0.791	Ohca	0.727
Spinal_fusion	0.725	Resuscitation	0.718
Discectomy	0.674	cpr	0.689

(*Continued*)

Table 16.3 Sample phrases and their embedding with similarity score. (*Continued*)

Laminoplasty	0.661	Asystole	0.680
Surgery	0.642	rosc	0.673
Microdiscectomy	0.625	Cardiac_arrests	0.672
Decompression	0.609	Pulseless	0.650
Durotomy	0.609	Comatose	0.629
Thyroid_surgery	0.605	Asystolic	0.624
Arthrodesis	0.598	Hypothermia	0.616

Table 16.4 Sample words and their embedding with similarity score.

Contextually similar to "tachycardic"		Contextually similar to "ribosomal"	
Word/phrase	Similarity score	Word/phrase	Similarity score
Tachypneic	0.719	rrna	0.743
Pulse rate	0.678	Large subunit	0.659
Tachypnea	0.646	Small subunit	0.651
Afebrile	0.642	ssu	0.626
Diaphoretic	0.640	Ribosome	0.614
Vitals	0.606	lsu	0.598
Tachypnoea	0.605	rrna genes	0.571
Drowsy	0.582	rdna	0.571
Hypotensive	0.571	rrnas	0.570
Diaphoresis	0.562	Processome	0.560
Contextually similar to "echocardiogram"		Contextually similar to "dermatologist"	
Word/phrase	Similarity score	Word/phrase	Similarity score
Angiogram	0.655	Dermatologists	0.785

(*Continued*)

Table 16.4 Sample words and their embedding with similarity score. (*Contitnued*)

Echocardiograms	0.654	Dermatology	0.687
Cardiomegaly	0.655	Dermatological	0.600
Transesophageal	0.639	Rheumatologist	0.574
Transthoracic	0.619	Acral	0.573
Murmur	0.612	Dermoscopy	0.571
ekg	0.603	Allergist	0.568
tte	0.600	Dermatoses	0.560
Hypokinesis	0.579	Skin_lesions	0.559
Physical_exam	0.573	Artefacta	0.550
Contextually similar to "distress"		**Contextually similar "diabetes"**	
Word/phrase	**Similarity score**	**Word/phrase**	**Similarity score**
Anxiety	0.708	dm	0.796
Psychological	0.664	Type diabetes	0.767
Depression	0.643	Hypertension	0.714
Psychosocial	0.642	Obesity	0.706
Feelings	0.629	cvd	0.704
Emotional	0.599	Dysglycemia	0.699
Hopelessness	0.593	Hyperglycemia	0.688
Physical stress	0.593	Prediabetes	0.688
Social problems	0.590	Diabetic	0.685
Somatization	0.586	Dyslipidemia	0.677

meaningful medical concepts and their similarity score are derived for each target phrase and word.

16.6   Conclusion

This paper has proposed an idea of phrase embedding on a pre-annotated corpus. The spark-based map-reduce framework is employed to achieve scalability on large volume dataset and chunking technique is applied to extract frequent word phrases from it. A word2vec CBOW model–based phrase embedding technique is used to learn phrase and word representation in the same vector space and capture meaningful concepts. These concepts have many applications in the field of IR and recommender systems. It can be widely used for query expansion. In the future, it is proposed to investigate the effect of medical query expansion using the phrase embedding technique in the field of IR for clinical decision support.

References

1. Harris, Z.S., Distributional structure. *Word*, 10, 2–3, 146–162, 1954.
2. Collobert, R., Weston, J., Bottou, L., Karlen, M., Kavukcuoglu, K., Kuksa, P., Natural language processing (almost) from scratch. *J. Mach. Learn. Res.*, 12, 2493–2537, 2011, Aug.
3. Grover, A. and Leskovec, J., node2vec: Scalable feature learning for networks. *Proceedings of the 22nd ACM SIGKDD international conference on Knowledge discovery and data mining*, 2016.
4. Yu, Y., Wan, X., Zhou, X., User embedding for scholarly microblog recommendation. *Proceedings of the 54th Annual Meeting of the Association for Computational Linguistics (Volume 2: Short Papers)*, 2016.
5. Mikolov, T., Chen, K., Corrado, G., Dean, J., Efficient estimation of word representations in vector space, *1st International Conference on Learning Representations (ICLR) Scottsdale*, Arizona, USA, Workshop Track Proceedings, http://arxiv.org/abs/1301.3781, 2013
6. Deerwester, S., Dumais, S.T., Furnas, G.W., Landauer, T.K. and Harshman, R., Indexing by latent semantic analysis. *JASIST*, 41, 6, 391–407, 1990.
7. Blei, D.M., Ng, A.Y., Jordan, M., II, Latent dirichlet allocation. *J. Mach. Learn. Res.*, 3, 993–1022, 2003, Jan.
8. Baroni, M., Dinu, G., Kruszewski, G., Don't count, predict! A systematic comparison of context-counting vs. context-predicting semantic vectors, in: *Proceedings of the 52nd Annual Meeting of the Association for Computational Linguistics (Volume 1: Long Papers)*, pp. 238–247, 2014.

9. Yin, W. and Schtze, H., An exploration of embeddings for generalized phrases, in: *Proceedings of the ACL Student Research Workshop*, pp. 41–47, 2014.

10. Yu, M. and Dredze, M., Learning composition models for phrase embeddings. *Trans. Assoc. Comput. Linguist.*, 3, 227–242, 2015.

11. Zhao, Y., Liu, Z., Sun, M., Phrase Type Sensitive Tensor Indexing Model for Semantic Composition, in: *Twenty-Ninth AAAI Conference on Artificial Intelligence*, 2015.

12. Mahata, D., Shah, R.R., Kuriakose, J., Zimmermann, R., Talburt, J.R., Theme-weighted Ranking of Keywords from Text Documents using Phrase Embeddings, in: *2018 IEEE Conference on Multimedia Information Processing and Retrieval (MIPR)*, IEEE, pp. 184–189, 2018.

13. Li, M., Lu, Q., Xiong, D., Long, Y., Phrase embedding learning based on external and internal context with compositionality constraint. *Knowledge-Based Syst.*, 152, 107–116, 2018.

14. Abney, S.P., Parsing by chunks. Principle-based parsing, in: *Principle-based parsing*, pp. 257–278, Springer Dordrecht, 1991.

15. Bengio, Y., Ducharme, R., Vincent, P., Jauvin, C., A neural probabilistic language model. *J. Mach. Learn. Res.*, 3, 1137–1155, Feb 2003.

17

Image Anonymization Using Deep Convolutional Generative Adversarial Network

Ashish Undirwade* and Sujit Das†

Dept. of Computer Science and Engineering, NIT Warangal, Warangal, India

Abstract

Advancement in deep learning requires significantly huge amount of data for training purpose, where protection of individual data plays a key role in data privacy and publication. Recent developments in deep learning demonstrate a huge challenge for traditionally used approch for image anonymization, such as model inversion attack, where adversary repeatedly query the model, in order to reconstruct the original image from the anonymized image. In order to apply more protection on image anonymization, an approach is presented here to convert the input (raw) image into a new synthetic image by applying optimized noise to the latent space representation (LSR) of the original image. The synthetic image is anonymized by adding well-designed noise calculated over the gradient during the learning process, where the resultant image is both realistic and immune to model inversion attack. More presicely, we extend the approach proposed by T. Kim and J. Yang (2019) by using Deep Convolutional Generative Adversarial Network (DCGAN) in order to make the approach more efficient. Our aim is to improve the efficiency of the model by changing the loss function to achieve optimal privacy in less time and computation. Finally, the proposed approach is demonstrated using a benchmark dataset. The experimental study presents that the proposed method can efficiently convert the input image into another synthetic image which is of high quality as well as immune to model inversion attack.

Keywords: Adversarial learning, generative adversarial network, data privacy, deep learning, model inversion attack, machine learning

---

Corresponding author: ashishundirwade37@gmail.com
†*Corresponding author*: sujit.das@nitw.ac.in

Mettu Srinivas, G. Sucharitha and Anjanna Matta (eds.) Machine Learning Algorithms and Applications, (305–330) © 2021 Scrivener Publishing LLC

17.1   Introduction

Image anonymization technique has been developed to make it more difficult to identify a particular image from provided altered image. In image anonymization, one is provided with the original image, and our task is to convert that original image into some another anonymized image by changing the pixel or adding random noise, etc., in such a way that an image recognition model or a human eye, would not be able to label/recognize the original image. Image anonymization plays an important role in today's world, as many tasks in today's world require realistic data and these realistic data may contain confidential information of an individual and the particular individual does not want to disclose the information because making this dataset public will affect the privacy of the individual. Even if the dataset is made private, but if the model is not constructed properly, there are some attacks possible over these private datasets to capture the original image by continuously querying the model.

Social media is also one of the domains, where confidential data may be captured in an image, which alarms the privacy issue. Usually, social media get millions of images from all his users, and these images may contain some confidential information of a person, which he/she does not want to disclose. This raises to a privacy issue and may lead to legal actions. Image anonymization is one of the tasks which can be carried out to prevent such privacy issue and legal actions. Machine learning also requires big amount of data to prepare their model; more precisely, this large amount of data is required to train the weights of the model so that, for some random data also, their model should work. Therefore, big amount of data is necessary to train these types of machine learning model. This large amount of data can be made public or just be used to train the model only making this dataset private. Public dataset is available to the entire user in the world who has access to the link to download the same and should not contain any sensitive information corresponding to a user. But private dataset is considered to be having confidential data; therefore, privacy of these dataset is also an important task while training the model. Recent researches on the field of adversarial machine learning reveal that training data can also be fetched form the trained model creating privacy issue for the training data. One of such attack is model inversion attack in which the adversary tries to query the trained machine learning model over a random image and changes the random image according to the confidence value attain.

Another major importance of image anonymization is because of the new European law, GDPR. In which, an organization/institute, cannot use any personal information of a respective person, without its concern/approval. As machine learning requires large amount of such data, where fetching such approval would be a tedious task. To avoid violating this rule, researchers/developers have used image anonymization model, which will change the original image into one another anonymized image, providing no relationship between original and anonymized image. Consequently, those large datasets can be used effectively to train our model and these generated anonymized datasets are real and immune to model inversion attack.

There are different types of image anonymization techniques, which are mainly classified into two categories: transfer domain and pixel level. In transfer domain, the image is anonymized by using scalability provision of used codec. The error or random noise is introduced in the coding process, which makes the generated image different from original image. This process can be reversed by providing the keys. Here, higher privacy means less probability to detect the feature. In pixel level image anonymization, the pixel value of an image is changed. Here, pixel intensities and chrominance are changed or altered to hide the identity of the confidential object/person. Some examples of pixel level image anonymization techniques are blurring, pixelization, k-same, and k-same select. K-same is an anonymization technique in which similarity between focus area/image is calculated using distance metrics over the saved dataset and a new image is created by averaging the image components of k images, which have less distance metric with the given image. Therefore, when check by the facial recognition system, the anonymized image leads to k images (having same distance metric). In blurring, convolution 2D network is used to generate the anonymized image. In Pixelization, the image is split down into m*m squares that are non-overlapping and the pixels within an image are replaced by the average value within each square, resulting in a new anonymized image. However, the traditional image anonymization technique mentioned above are not attack prone in today's world, where machine learning model can be trained to fetch the original image with high confidence value. Therefore, we aim to study one image anonymization model, which anonymize the image at latent space (not at pixel level), by adding random optimized noise making the anonymized image realistic and immune to such machine learning attacks. Some relevant studies on image anonymization are narrated below.

Datasets are formed by collecting speeches, images, and videos from a numbers of individuals and are used for model training, which are now bound to privacy risks. Chaudhuri *et al.* [1] stated that by just simply releasing the pre-trained model or statistics of the machine learning model may not be sufficient to remove the risk of privacy over the training data. To achieve the privacy preserving goal, they have used objective permutation given in [2]. Synthetic data generation [3–5] has been in the main focus for privacy-preserving data publication in recent years, where sensitive data is fully or partially replaced with synthetic data before it is allowed to be published. Beaulieu-Jones *et al.* [3] have used ACGAN and have applied objective perturbation over it, to generate sharable data. However, T. Kim and J. Yang [6] have stated that Generative Adversarial Network (GAN) [7, 8] with objective permutation, with training on image dataset [9–12], lead to mode collapse, on their prior attempts. Objective permutation is complex, costly, and time consuming, when used to generate synthetic data using GAN, in differential private way. Instead of performing these costly operations, T. Kim and J. Yang [6] have proposed one methodology to add optimized noise to the latent space representation (LSR) of the image to generate anonymized image, which are also differential private. In our study, we have improved the performance of this methodology by optimizing the loss function to provide us the same privacy gain or same level of anonymized image in less time and computation. Recent research by Fredrikson *et al.* [13] introduced a medical related case study by defining model inversion attack, where the adversarial had access to the machine learning–based model and was able to learn sensitive genomic function about some individual. The authors in [14] stated that using model inversion attack an adversary can recover (up to certain degree) the original individual face of a particular person using the blurred face image, which are removed by adding optimized noise generated via a neural network, which takes input as a random noise and optimized this noise in such a way that, when added to the original image, one is able to produce anonymized image, which are immune to these privacy attacks.

A flowchart for image anonymization using GAN is given in Figure 17.1, where the latent space of an image is captured using encoder network, then a well-designed noise is added to these latent spaces. Using decoder network, a new anonymized image is constructed. The quality of the constructed image is supervised using discriminator which allows the generator network to train/construct new anonymized images which are more realistic in nature. Figure 17.1 asserts the process used to convert a raw input image into another synthetic image. In this process, firstly, the LSR of an image is extracted, over which, optimized noise is added to make noised latent space representation. Then, the GAN is trained, in min-max game, so that the model gives highly anonymized, but realistic images.

Objective of this study is to present an image anonymization technique using GAN, which will transform an image by adding optimized noise

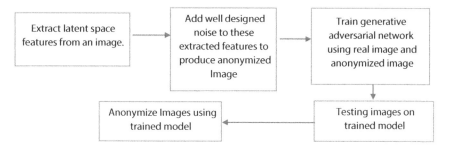

Figure 17.1 Flowchart for image anonymization.

to the latent space depiction of that image, to produce another synthetic image. The synthetic image is anonymized by adding well-designed noise calculated over the gradient during the learning process. In this study, mainly our aim is to increase the efficiency of the model by changing the loss function to achieve optimal privacy, in less time and computation. Our contributions in this study are given below in bulleted points.

- Image anonymization techniques proposed by T. Kim and J. Yang [6] used WGAP-GP loss function, which is a highly efficient but requires more time and computation cost than the tradition GAN Loss function.
- The loss function of the image anonymization model proposed by T. Kim and J. Yang [6] has been changed in this study to enable our model to generate highly anonymized image and to converge faster.
- The loss function has been changed from WGAN-GP to Deep Convolutional Generative Adversarial Network (DCGAN) as in WGAP-GP we have to calculate the gradient penalty which enforces the Lipschitz constraint which in turn increases the overall cost to train the discriminator.
- Instead of WGAN-GP discriminator's loss function, this study has used DCGAN loss function because of following reasons:
    - Our model will add optimized noise to the original image to generate synthetic image. Therefore, this model will have overlapping probability distribution. Hence, usage of DCGAN will reduce the overall computational cost of the whole model.
    - Our proposed model has used DCGAN Loss function which only requires the discriminator and generator

to be train once per epoch, whereas in WGAP-GP, one needs to train the discriminator "n" number of times for one generator training per epoch.

Rest of this study is planned as follows. Section 17.2 summarizes the necessary ideas linked to this paper. The proposed model is presented in Section 17.3 followed by the experimental study in Section 17.4. Key observations are found in Section 17.5.

17.2   Background Information

Here, some important concepts related to this chapter are briefly introduced such as black vs. white box attack, model inversion attack, differential privacy, GAN, Wasserstein distance, WGAN, WGAN-GP, KL and JS divergence, and, lastly, DCGAN.

17.2.1   Black Box and White Box Attacks

The major difference between "black box" and "white box" attacks is found on the basis of knowledge of the adversary, whether the adversary knows the internal working of the model or not. In white box attack, the adversary tries to get sensitive information from the model, where the adversary has complete access to the internal working of the model (underlying code and properties, but not the training data). As an example, some organization/companies provide entire pre-trained machine learning model to some third party to be used in their domain of work. This machine learning model is required to be trained using their own private data for better efficiency. In white box attack, adversary have access to the code and properties of the machine learning model (but not to the third-party private training data), which is used to infer sensitive information from the model. In black box attack, the adversary does not have information regarding the internal working of the model (code and properties of machine learning model is not known to the adversary). Here, the adversary can only query the model and tries to establish relationship between input and output, to infer sensitive information. As an example, many organizations/companies provide access to the machine learning model using API's, with the help of which a customer/user can query the machine learning model online and can have the output as response. Here, the adversary will continuously query the machine learning model with some well-crafted random sample to infer sensitive information from the model. As a summary, white box attack can be performed by a producer, customer or anyone else who can access to the internal of the model (code and properties), whereas black box attack can be performed by anyone who can query the model to generate the output.

17.2.2   Model Inversion Attack

Model inversion attack is a type of attack in which the adversary can access to the trained machine learning model with few private datasets, and the adversary can query the model to generate the output. Here, the adversary tries to get certain sensitive information from private dataset, by finding the relationship between the input and output of the model. One good example of model inversion attack is associated with facial recognition system, where attacker previously have some personal data (such as name) belonging to some specific individuals included in the training data, using this information, attacker try can infer further personal information (image of that individual) about those same individuals by observing the relationship between the inputs and outputs of the machine learning model. Another such example of model inversion attack is related with blurring/anonymization model, where an image is given to the machine learning model and the model outputs an anonymized image. Here, the adversary can reconstruct the original image by continuously querying the model with some crafted images to construct the inverse of the anonymization model, which can produce the original image. The main concept in model inversion attack is that the adversary tries to infer sensitive information by observing the relationship between input and output. Fredrikson *et al.* [14] have shown that adversary can access sensitive/confidential information from the training data using machine learning API's by model inversion attack. They have also provided an algorithm to infer sensitive information from face recognition system using some personal information/some non-sensitive information available regarding that user like name. This concludes that model inversion attacks are possible in machine learning API's. Mainly, model inversion attack is classified into two categories namely reconstruction attack and de-blurring attack. In reconstruction type of attack, the adversary tries to get the sensitive information or original image by continuously querying the machine learning model with some crafted raw input which adversary optimize after every output from the model based on the confidence value for that crafted input value. Based on the confidence value, the adversary will change the crafted input to achieve maximum confidence value. In this way, the adversary captures the sensitive information or original image up-to certain degrees. Attack on facial recognition system is an example of reconstruction attack. Whereas, in de-blurring type of attack, adversary have access to the model and by observing the relationship between the input and output, adversary tries to construct an inverse model for given machine learning model. This inverse model will undo the changes made by our model based on the parameters observed by fetching the relationship between the input and output.

17.2.3   Differential Privacy

Many data breach is observed in 21st century, which trigger's the importance of privacy in dataset. Although researchers and developers require large amount of data to train their machine learning model, these datasets may contain confidential information regarding some individual. Improper disclosure of this data may lead to catastrophic consequences and legal actions. To avoid such situations, we have a privacy models such as differential privacy which guarantees that sensitive information will be protected in a given dataset, if differential privacy constraints are satisfied. Dwork *et al.* [2, 15, 16] first proposed differential privacy, and it is a strong measure of privacy for aggregate databases. Differential privacy has been used extensively to specify the privacy guarantee on aggregate database algorithms. It is being used to specify the risk on individual's privacy, when the data of that individual is stored in the databases, on which such algorithms are applied. Differential privacy basically measures the privacy of an individual record, when participated in a database. It was initially defined for two databases which differ only by one single record.

17.2.3.1   Definition

"A randomized mechanism $M{:}D{\rightarrow}R$ with domain D and range R satisfies (ϵ,δ)-differential privacy if for any two adjacent inputs d, d$'$ $\in$ D and for any subset of outputs S $\subseteq$ R, it holds that

$$\Pr [M(d) \in S] \le e^{\epsilon} \Pr [M(d') \in S] + \delta \text{''} \qquad (17.1)$$

The real valued function f: D->R is basically approximated with the help of Gaussian and Laplace noise mechanism (shown in Tables 17.1 and 17.2), which is basically, done by adding noise calculated from f's sensitivity s_f. This s_f can be calculated by fetching the maximum value from the absolute difference between d and d', where d and d' are two adjacent inputs. Therefore, one can define s_f as s_f = Max |f(d) – f(d')|.

This paper has used Gaussian noise mechanism in the noise amplification module. We can change the intensity (strength) of the noise by changing the value of ϵ and δ. One can also magnify (amplify) the noise from

Table 17.1 Laplace noise mechanism.

Laplace Noise Mechanism:
M(d) = f(d) + lap (0, b)
where
Lap (0,b): Laplace Distribution
b: scale
If $b = \dfrac{sf}{\epsilon}$ (satisfies e-differential Privacy)

Table 17.2 Gaussian noise mechanism.

Gaussian Noise Mechanism:
M(d) = f(d)+N (0,∞)
where
N (0,σ^2): Normal Distribution with 0 mean.
σ : Standard Deviation.
If $\sigma = \sqrt{2\log\left(\dfrac{1.25}{\delta}\right)} * \dfrac{sf}{\epsilon}$ (satisfies (ϵ, δ) – Differential Privacy)

lap (0,1) or N (0,1) to lap (0,b) or N(0, σ^2), by just multiplying by b or σ, respectively.

17.2.4   Generative Adversarial Network

GAN [17–23] is an architecture consisting of two neural networks fighting against one another to achieve new instances of data that are realistic in nature. GANs are widely used to generate new images, videos, and speech from the provided training data. To be able to understand GAN, one should be familiar with generative and descriptive algorithms. Descriptive algorithm is like a classifier which will predict the label for the given input data. When the input features are given, descriptive algorithm should be able to specify the label or category to which this input data instance belongs to. For example, your task is to differentiate a spam from the rest of the emails; your input data instance would be the content of an email. You will check for certain relationship or certain rules in the input data to classify that the provided email is spam or not. Therefore, we can say that it behaves like a two-way classifier. In the same way, the descriptive network in GAN will be trained on real as well as fake images and the task of the discriminator is to label the real image as 1 (real) and fake image as fake (0). Unlike discriminator, the generator networks try to predict the features of an image that are realistic or can be passed through a discriminator network as a real image feature. The generator network tries to generate such features that are like the real data distribution. The generator network tries to predict what should be features of a real data distribution. For example, you have the same email spam task; our generator will try to generate emails which are most likely to be a spam. So, it can be stated that our generator tries to answer, if a given email is a spam, how likely are their features. Based on this, our generator will generate emails which are most likely to be spammed as they contain features of a spam. GANs are basically consist of two neural networks which are generator or protector network and discriminator or critic network. Generator or protector network will generate random samples and our task is to generate such samples which are most likely to be classified as a real data. The task of the generator is to optimize the weights of the generator network in such a way that, when an random sample is given to the generator network, it should be able to produce new instance of data, which have similar features as that of real data or when passed through the discriminator, the discriminator should classify that data instance as real data instance. Discriminator or critic network will classify the data instance as real or fake. Depending upon the training it receives from the real dataset to confidently classify real data instance as real images (1). We first train our discriminator network to classify real images as real and fake images as fake having generator module at not trainable for those instance of real and fake data, i.e., we will not optimize the weights associated with generator network but will optimize the weights associated with discriminator network. Then, generator network is trained to produce images which are from random noise and tries to optimize the generator network to construct such synthetic images which will pass though discriminator as a real image. While training the generator network, we will have our discriminator network as not trainable. In the proposed method, the fake image is generated by adding noise to the real image, making it an anonymized image. Below given are the steps GAN takes to generate new data samples:

i.   Generate random numbers and construct image from that random sample.

ii. Train your discriminator network, with real data sample as well as with fake images generated above.

iii. The discriminator network will return probabilities, stating whether the given image is real (1) or fake (0).

iv. A feedback loop is associated with the discriminator with the known ground truth of the images.

v. Generator is in a feedback loop associated with discriminator.

Block diagram of GAN is shown in Figure 17.2.

Nowadays, GANs are used to generate realistic images which can be used as a training dataset for machine learning models. The main concept behind GAN is that one can train our generator and discriminator in an adversarial mode. GAN is a min-max game between two players (generator and discriminator), which tries to minimize the divergence or distance between the real distribution P_r and model distribution P_θ. Wasserstein GAN and WGAN-GP has objective function as Earth Mover (EM) and achieve state of the art performance. GANs are widely used for style transfer domain, where some predefined style/feature of an image is transferred to another image, making the new synthetic image having same feature/style. Implementation part will contain the deep-convolution encoder-decoder network which will be used as a generator to find relationship between the two different image domain and discriminator to evaluate the quality of the mapped images. Here, we are also keen to find one such mapping from one

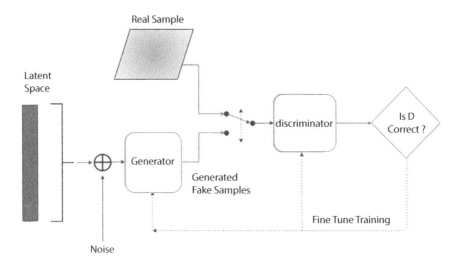

Figure 17.2 GAN.

image domain to another, making our new anonymized image realistic. This study will also be using deep-convolution encoder-decoder network with added noise amplifier module which will add optimized noise to the generated latent space from the encoder network. The noise amplifier will add random optimized noise, making it hard for an adversary to rebuild the original image from the anonymized image. This study will also be having an adversarial network with encoder-decoder network, which will try to reconstruct the original image from the anonymized image provided and our generator is trained in such a way that one should not be able to rebuild the original image from the generated anonymized image, hence protecting the model from deblurring attack.

17.2.5   Earth-Mover (EM) Distance/Wasserstein Metric

Wasserstein distance is the minimum distance required to make/convert the random data distribution q into real data distribution p. In simple terms, it is the minimum cost required to turn one pile of data distribution into another (if we assume, each data distribution is of unit amount pilled over M). Mathematically, it can be formulated as (for one single move): distance dirt has moved * mean distance it has moved. As stated above, Wasserstein distance is the minimum distance from all transportation plans. Wasserstein distance (Figure 17.3) is defined as

$$W(\mathbb{P}_r, \mathbb{P}_g) = \inf_{\gamma \in \Pi(\mathbb{P}_r, \mathbb{P}_g)} \mathbb{E}_{(x,y)\sim\gamma}\left[\|x - y\|\right], \qquad (17.2)$$

where $\mathbb{P}_r$ is the real data distribution, $\mathbb{P}_g$ is the generated data distribution, and infimum refers to greatest lower bound from all the transportation plan.

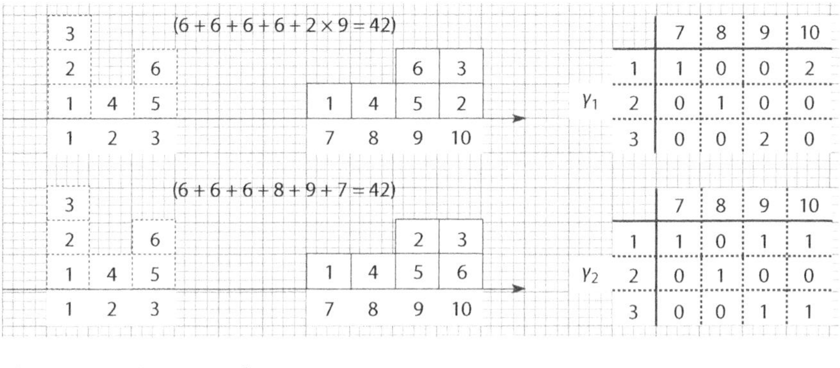

Figure 17.3 Wasserstein distance.

For example, suppose one needs to move the blocks (Figure 17.3) from position 1, 2, 3 to 7, 8, 9, 10 with defined shape at destination position, which has been shown above. There are many ways to performing this task to move the box from one location to another so that we have the defined shape at the last output/destination. Each of these ways of performing the task are called as transportation plan and each plan contains a transportation cost calculated using (source position (i) – destination position (j)) * number of blocks moved (value at i, j). In such a way, one can calculate the transportation cost of each transportation plan and the minimum among them can be classifies as Wasserstein distance.

17.2.6   Wasserstein GAN

The traditional GAN has a vanishing gradient problem or it can be said that the discriminator will not learn anything as the KL diversion as well as JS divergence will be constant, when two probability distribution does not have any overlap in between them. To solve this problem, Wasserstein distance has been used in this paper to calculate the distance between two distributions. These types of GANs are called WGAN [24], and the new loss functions for them are given below:

$$g_w \leftarrow \nabla_w \left[\frac{1}{m} \sum_{i=1}^{m} f_w(x^{(i)}) - \frac{1}{m} \sum_{i=1}^{m} f_w(g_\theta(z^{(i)})) \right] \quad (17.3)$$

where f has to be a 1-Lipschitz function, therefore, must follow below given equation.

$$|f(x_1) - f(x_2)| \leq |x_1 - x_2|. \quad (17.4)$$

To enforce this constraint, clipping is applied to have the output from "f" to be in between certain range of "c" and "$-c$", where, c is a hyper-parameter.

17.2.7   Improved Wasserstein GAN (WGAN-GP)

Clipping is used in WGAN to enforce a 1-Lipschitz constraint. But, because of this, the model may produce bad results and may not converge. As the performance of the model also depends upon the hyper parameter "c", if the value of "c" is huge, then large amount of time will be taken by the model to get its weights reach their limit, and if the value of "c" is small, then vanishing gradient can happen (when number of layers are large or batch normalization is not used). From this, one can state that the performance of the model also depends upon the hyper parameter "c". To avoid this, we can use gradient penalty instead of clipping to enforce the 1-Lipschitz constraint.

$$L = \mathop{E}_{\tilde{x} \sim P_g} [D(\tilde{x})] - \mathop{E}_{x \sim P_r} [D(x)] + \lambda \mathop{E}_{\hat{x} \sim P_{\hat{x}}} \left[\left(\left\| \Delta_{\hat{x}} D(\hat{x}) \right\|_2 - 1 \right)^2 \right] \quad (17.5)$$

17.2.8   KL Divergence and JS Divergence

KL divergence is one of the ways to calculate the statistical difference between two statistical objects, such as probability distribution. KL divergence is basically used to compute the distance between two probability distributions while training the GAN. If two distributions are of perfect match, then KL divergence of them will be 0. KL divergence ranges from 0 to infinity. The lower the KL divergence, the less will be the distance between the two statistical distribution. KL divergence is defined as

$$D_{KL}(P \| Q) = \sum_{x=1}^{N} P(x) \log \frac{P(x)}{Q(x)} \quad (17.6)$$

where $D_{KL}(P \| Q)$ is the notation for KL divergence, and P and Q are two difference distributions. The main intuition behind KL divergence is that one will have large divergence, when probability of P is large but probability of Q is small. In the same way, we will have large diversion, when we have large probability of Q, but small probability of P. In this way, we have a metric score to generalize the distance between two distributions. KL diversion is not symmetric in nature, i.e., KL(P || Q) != KL(Q || P). JS Divergence uses KL divergence to normalize the score, to have it symmetric in nature. That is, with JS divergence, the divergence from p to q will be same as that of from q to p, i.e., JS(P || Q) == JS(Q || P). The JS divergence can be calculated using below given formula

$$D_{JS}(p \| q) = \frac{1}{2} D_{KL} \left(p \| \frac{p+q}{2} \right) + \frac{1}{2} D_{KL} \left(p \| \frac{p+q}{2} \right) \quad (17.7)$$

One of the major advantages of JS divergence is that it produces smoothened and normalized version of KL divergence, with scores between zero and one, when log with base 2 is used. KL- divergence and JS divergence will have gradient vanishing problem, when two data distribution are not overlapping.

17.2.9   DCGAN

DCGAN [25] is considered as an extension of GAN with few changes over the model, with main change corresponds to the usage of convolutional and convolutional-transpose layers in the discriminator and generator network, respectively. In DCGAN, discriminator consists of convolution layers, batch normalization layers, and leaky ReLU activation. The input to this discriminator is an image, whereas the output comprises of scalar probability stating whether this image is from real data distribution or not. The generator consists of convolutional-transpose layers, batch norm layers, and ReLU activation, which will take input as a random latent vector, and using strided conv-transpose layers it converts the random latent vector into an image. DCGAN has a min-max game between the generator and discriminator. The generator is given, which produces random samples and we have real samples also, both of these samples are given to the discriminator with real samples as value 1 and fake samples as value 0. Whereas our generator is train with fake images and value as 1. Therefore, our discriminator tries to correctly mark the fake image and generator tries to generate images which can have label value as 1. Below given is the loss function used in DCGAN:

$$\min_G \max_D V(D,G) = E_{x \sim P_{data}(x)}[\log D(x)] + E_{z \sim p_z(z)}[\log(1 - D(G(z)))]$$

$$(17.8)$$

17.3   Image Anonymization to Prevent Model Inversion Attack

Image anonymization is a type of image sanitization, where the original image has been modified in such a way that new anonymized image does not point to the original image, when matched with each other. Image anonymization plays a key role in preserving the privacy of the training data, where many images are made public for testing the efficiency of the algorithm. With recent developments in deep learning, an adversary can attempt to rebuild the original image from the anonymized image. Here, an image anonymization methodology is presented, which will convert the original image into another synthetic image which is both realistic and immune to machine learning attack. The model is described in Figure 17.4, which comprises of three parts: protector M, attacker N, and critic O,

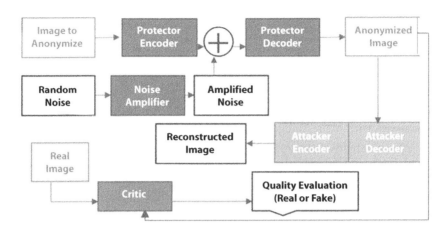

Figure 17.4 Image anonymization to prevent model inversion attack.

where M gets the original image I, anonymize it into another image I', N attempts to rebuild the original image I from the new anonymized image I', and O checks the quality of I'.

The noise amplifier is added into the generator module in such a way that it will generate anonymized image as well as it will prevent the model inversion attack over the trained machine learning model. The noise amplifier is trained in such a way that it will generate optimized noise which will help us to attain differential privacy. The traditional image anonymization technique using GAN and noise amplifier was introduced in [6], but they have used WGAP-GP as a loss function. WGAP-GP produces effective anonymized images but is time consuming and requires more computation power than tradition GAN. The reason for this large overall training time and higher computation is basically due to involvement of gradient penalty, which has to be calculated to define the discriminator loss. This calculation of gradient penalty makes the model more time consuming and requires more computation power. Gradient penalty is calculated to withhold the Lipschitz constraint. Another reason for higher computation time is due to that fact that the discriminator in the WGAP-GP must train discriminator loss "n" number of times for one generator loss per epoch. This makes WGAP-GP discriminator more time consuming and because of this the overall time to train the model increases. Instead of using WGAN-GP, DCGAN loss function is used to train our model. The DCGAN loss function is given below.

$$\min_G \max_D V(D,G) = E_{x \sim Pdata(x)}[\log D(x)] + E_{z \sim p_z(z)}[\log(1 - D(G(z)))]$$

$$(17.9)$$

The DCGAN loss function requires only one additional parameter to satisfy which is basically to fetch sigmoid output from the discriminator. From the loss function of DCGAN, it can be stated that one do not require any gradient penalty to be calculated for this loss function, making our loss function less time consuming and requires less computational power. Also, DCGAN does not require the discriminator to be trained "n" number of times for single generator training, per epoch. It only requires that the generator and discriminator to be trained once per epoch.

17.3.1   Algorithm

Initialize: protector (Generator) parameters: θ_0, critic (Discriminator) parameters: w_{c0}, and attacker parameters, w_{a0}, at initial stage of the training, i.e., before the training starts.

Require: attacker iterations: $n_{attacker}$ and critic iterations : n_{critic}, per protector iteration.

Default values: Adam hyperparameters: α, $\beta1$, and β, Batch size: m, gradient penalty coefficient: λ,

---

while (θ has not converged):
    for (t = 1, ... n_{critic}):
        for (i = 1, ..., m):
            Sample real data sets y ~ Pr and y' ~ Pr and a random number ε ~ U[0, 1].
            $\tilde{y} \leftarrow P_\theta(y)$
            $\hat{y} \leftarrow \varepsilon y' + (1 - \varepsilon)\tilde{y}$
            $L_c^{(i)} \leftarrow \log(C_{wc}(\tilde{y})) + \log(1 - C_{wc}(y'))$
        wc $\leftarrow$ Adam $(\nabla(1/m) \sum_{i=1}^{m} L_c^{(i)}$, wc, α, $\beta1$, $\beta2$)
    for (t = 1, ..., n_{attack}):
        for (i = 1, . . . , m):
            Sample real data set y ~ Pr.
            $\tilde{y} \leftarrow P_\theta(y)$
            $L_a^{(i)} \leftarrow \|y - A_{wa}(\tilde{y})\|_2$
        wa $\leftarrow$ AdamOptimizer($\nabla(1/m) \sum_{i=1}^{m} L_a^{(i)}$, wc, α, $\beta1$, $\beta2$)
    for (i = 1, ..., m):
        Sample real data set y ~ Pr.
        $\tilde{y} \leftarrow P_\theta(y)$
        $L_p^{(i)} \leftarrow -C_{wc}(\tilde{y})$
    $\theta \leftarrow$ AdamOptimizer($\nabla(1/m)) \sum_{i=1}^{m} L_p^{(i)}$, wc, α, $\beta1$, $\beta2$)

The proposed model consists of three networks:

1. Protector: It consists of encoder-decoder network, where encoder is used to convert the image into its vector representation (z). It has also one noise amplifier which will add noise to this vector presentation of the image, and lastly decoder which will convert the modified vector representation into one new image, which will be an anonymized image of the original image.
2. Attacker: Attacker is an encoder-decoder network, which attempts to recreate the original image from the anonymized image provided by the protector.
3. Critic: The DCGAN critic directs the protector network to produce realistic images by evaluating its quality.

LSR is a vector representation of an image, which depicts the crucial features, such as hair style, hair color, facial expression, and skin color of an image, which can be extracted using convolutional autoencoders.

17.3.2 Training

To evaluate the performance of an attacker network, we have defined a new term called as privacy gain, where privacy gain can be calculated as L2 loss between original image and reconstructed image. The main objective of the adversary network is to minimize this privacy gain (L_{priv}). Privacy gain can be expressed as $L_{Priv} = \| x\text{-}x'\|^2$, where x is the original image and x' is the anonymized image. Discriminator tries to categories the original image as real (label = 1), and anonymized image as fake (label = 0). DCGAN loss function is used since we are adding additional noise toward the original image. So, we would be having overlapping data distribution for these two images. DCGAN Loss function is expressed as

$$\nabla_{\Theta d} \frac{1}{m} \sum_{i=1}^{m} [\log D(x^{(i)}) + \log(1 - D(G(z^{(i)})))] \qquad (17.10)$$

where x(i) is the ith original image, D(x(i)) is the probability value of this image to be categorized as a real image, z(i) is the noise added LSR of original image, G(z(i)) is the anonymized image, and $(1 - D(G(z(i))))$ is the probability value of this anonymized image to be categorized not as a real image. The generator in our experiment has trained twice for one discriminator training per epoch. The generator network would like to construct images which can pass through the discriminator as a real image. Generator network tries to maximize the log(D(G(z(i)))). Generator loss (LP) can be defined as

$$LP = -E_z(\log(D(G(Z^{(i)}))))\qquad(17.11)$$

The attacker's task is to minimize L_{Priv}, i.e., $L_A = L_{priv}$, and the attacker network will try to minimize this distance. When training of our model is started, firstly, all the weights associated with protector, critic and attacker network are fine-tuned by performing adversarial training. Then we will try to converge the protector's parameters, when this happens protector is optimized to generate synthetic image, which are realistic and immune to model inversion attack.

17.3.3 Noise Amplifier

Noise amplifier is basically a module, positioned in-between, encoder and decoder network of the generator. The encoder network of generator outputs the LSR of an image to which this optimized noise has been added and the output is given to decoder to reconstruct a new anonymized image. Noise amplifier is a neural network which tries to find an optimal value σ^*, which can be thought of as a scale factor. This scale factor is then multiplied with the noise sample generated from the probability distribution to produce overall noise, which is then added to the LSR produced by encoder of generator network to produce anonymized image. Mathematically, the above given noise amplifier is stated as $z_d' = z_d + \sigma^* n$, where, z_d be the LSR of an image produced by the encoder of generator network of d-dimension, σ^* is the optimal scaling facto, n is the random noise generated from probability distribution, z_d' is the LSR of the anonymized image, which when provided to the decoder network produces anonymized image. The random noise can be generated using Laplace or Gaussian distribution. We can fetch the value of Lap(0,b) by multiplying Lap(0,1) by b, and N(0, σ) by multiplying it by σ. Both of these distributions can be used in noise amplifier to generate random noise as follows:

$$\sigma(S_e, \epsilon) = \frac{Se}{\epsilon}\qquad(17.12)$$

$$\sigma(S_e; \epsilon, \delta) = \sqrt{2\log\left(\frac{1.25}{\delta}\right)} * \frac{Se}{\epsilon}\qquad(17.13)$$

To find the exact value of sensitivity, firstly, our autoencoder is pretrained with all the images in the dataset using L2 loss minimization. This step is important, since the exact value of sensitivity is not found, while we are training with unknown values of encoder weights. Therefore, it is necessary to pretrain our autoencoder with all the images. Now, one can have the exact value of sensitivity as

$$S_e = \text{Max } E_p(x_i) - \text{Min } E_p(x_j) \qquad (17.14)$$

where x_i and x_j both belongs to sample images S_t. With the sensitivity value added to the anonymized vector, one will have z_i' value as

$$z_i' = z_i + \sigma(s_e) n_0 \qquad (17.15)$$

where, z_i is the original LSR of the ith image, s_e is the appropriate sensitivity, noise amplifier function σ, and n_0 is the initial noise. The value of ϵ is 1 and δ is 1e-8.

17.3.4 Dataset

This paper used the MNIST dataset which is downloaded from "tensorflow.examples.tutorials.mnist" library using input_data() function and is divided into three sections, such as 55,000 datapoints of training data (mnist.train), 10,000 datapoints of test data (mnist.test), and 5,000 datapoints of validation data (mnist.validation).

17.3.5 Model Architecture

The encoder part of generator P and attacker A consists of five convolution layer 5*5 and stride is of size 2, which is followed by batch normalization and activation function: Leaky ReLU. The encoder part of generator P has one additional additive noise layer and noise amplifier. This noise amplifier is placed in-between encoder and decoder of generator P to add noise to the latent feature vector of the image, so that, after decoding the vector, we will obtain the anonymized image. The final output of the encoder is converted into a 128-dimensional vector z, to which, the noise generated by the noise amplifier is added, which will change the feature vector of the original image. The Decoder part of generator P and Attacker A are consisting of five de-convolution layers with 5*5 and a stride of size 2, which is followed by batch normalization and activation function: ReLU. To get the final image of the decoder in the range of [0, 1], sigmoid is used instead of ReLU, in the last activation function of the decoder in the attacker. The discriminator network will take the image generated by the generator network x' of size N*N*k and determines whether it is fake or real. Discriminator C contains four or five convolutional layers with 5*5 and stride of size 2, which is followed by batch normalization and leaky ReLU. Five convolution layers will be used for an image of size 64*64*3, i.e., for color images and four convolution layers for rest of image sizes. From discriminator network, the output is sent through sigmoid layer.

17.3.6   Working

Encoder present at generator's side will take the image of size N*N*K and will convert it into vector representation of that image (z). On this vector representation, we will add noise generated using noise amplifier and this modified vector representation will be given to generator's decoder to convert the vector representation into modified image, which would be our anonymized image. Attacker is a network of encoder-decoder, which will take input as this anonymized image and will try to generate the original image form this. The image generate by generator network will be given to the discriminator to evaluate, i.e., to check whether the image generated by the generator is real or not. Discriminator evaluates the performance of the generator network, so that generator will generate more realist image, which would be hard for attacker to generate the original image out of it.

17.3.7   Privacy Gain

This study used an adversary network to check the privacy preserving performance of our model. This network is consisting of denoising autoencoder, which will aim to recreate the original image, from the noised image provided to it. The efficiency of the model over these attacks has been classified as privacy gain, which is basically a L2 loss between the original image and the reconstructed image. One will have better anonymized images, when the model is having higher privacy gain. In simpler terms, higher the privacy gain, better the anonymized images. T. Kim [6] has proven that, using denoising autoencoders, one can perform reconstruction attack on blurred out images. Making pixel-level anonymization such as blurring is vulnerable for machine learning attacks. Therefore, we have used optimized random noise generated from our trained neural network, to anonymize our original image at LSR. In our experiments, our model is trained over MNIST dataset using WGAN-GP and DCGAN loss function. Both the loss function gives the nearly the same privacy gain, but DCGAN takes less time and computation, as compared to WGAN-GP.

17.4   Results and Analysis

Here, DCGAN loss function has been used to train our model and tested image from the same dataset, producing highly anonymized images. We have also compared the privacy gain for our model with traditional image anonymization model to prevent model inversion attack and came to know that our model requires less time and computation to generate anonymized image to achieve same privacy gain as compared with anonymized images generated by traditional image anonymization model which prevents model inversion attack. Figure 17.5 depicts the result of image anonymization technique stated above, showing top image as an original image, middle one as an anonymized image, and the last one is the image constructed by the attacker.

This study has also compared the privacy gain of our proposed model with traditional image anonymization model which prevents model inversion attack, and from the graph given in Figure 17.6, it can be stated that we can achieve same privacy gain, in less time and less computation compared with the traditional image anonymization model which prevents model inversion attack. WGAN-GP requires an additional gradient penalty calculation per epoch which is not required in our proposed method and also WGAN-GP requires discriminator to train "n" number of times per epoch, which is also not required in our proposed method.

The main reason for this improvement in speed is due to that fact that DCGAN uses KL divergence, and WGAN-GP uses EM distance to differentiate/compare two distributions. EM distance or WGAP-GP is preferred on those problem statements in which one has vanishing gradient problem on starting phase due to that fact that two data distributions are not overlapping, but, in our case, as depicted below (Figure 17.7), we always will be having overlapping data distribution as we are adding up noise to

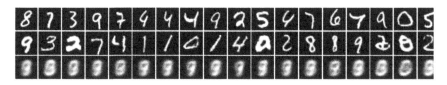

Figure 17.5 Result over MNIST dataset.

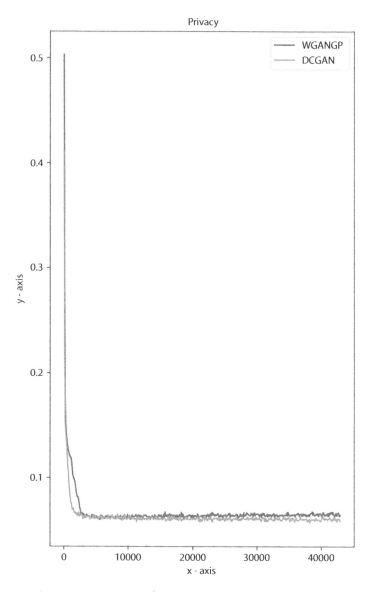

Figure 17.6 Comparing privacy gain for WGAN-GP and DCGAN.

the original image, and this noise is also first optimized. Therefore, from Figure 17.7, we can state that DCGAN will provide same privacy gain in much less time and will also require less computation than WGAN-GP.

Figure 17.7 comprises of anonymized image (left most), original image (middle one), and data distribution graph of anonymized image (red) vs.

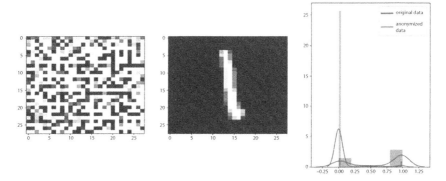

Figure 17.7 MNIST data distribution: left-hand figure shows anonymized data, middle one shows original data, and right figure shows overlapping between these two images.

original image (blue). These images are taken from the first few images given to our proposed model at initial stage of training. Therefore, it is concluded that vanishing gradient problem will not arrive in our proposed model due to non-overlapping data distribution. So, instead of WGAN-GP, we can use DCGAN loss function to train our model.

17.5   Conclusion

Image anonymization is an important aspect to hide the privacy of a user in an image captured with/without user concern and allow those images to be used for project development purpose, mainly to train machine learning model. This also allows an organization to work on those images without concerning European Union data privacy act (GDPR). Therefore, it is important to anonymize these images to protect the privacy of user as well as to provide compliance with GDPR. In this study, we have presented one training model, which will anonymize the image by adding noise to its latent feature vector, constructing new anonymized images, which are realist and immune to model inversion attack. More precisely, we have contributed to present an image anonymization methodology to prevent model inversion attack, which requires less time and computation power than the traditional image anonymization to prevent model inversion attack. In future, to enhance the efficiency of the network or to increase the privacy gain, one can use RNN type structure to add noise at every convolutional layer which should be optimized with a dense layer. Future scope of this project can also be directed toward face and background anonymization.

In the same way, one can use it for gait, speech, video, text anonymization, and exploring different domains.

References

1. Chaudhuri, K., Monteleoni, C., Sarwate, A.D., Differentially private empirical risk minimization. *J. Mach. Learn. Res.*, 12, 1069–1109, 2011.
2. Dwork, C., Differential privacy, in: *Automata languages and programming*, pp. 1–12, Springer, Berlin, Germany, 2006.
3. Beaulieu-Jones, B.K., Wu, Z.S., Williams, C., Greene, C.S., Privacy-preserving generative deep neural networks support clinical data sharing. *BioRxiv*, 2017.
4. Li, H., Xiong, L., Zhang, L., Jiang, X., DPSynthesizer: Differentially private data synthesizer for privacy preserving data sharing. *Proc. VLDB Endowment*, vol. 7, pp. 1677–1680, 2014.
5. Zhang, J., Cormode, G., Procopiuc, C.M., Srivastava, D., Xiao, X., PrivBayes: Private data release via Bayesian networks. *ACM Trans. Database Syst.*, 42, 4, 25:1–25:41, 2017.
6. Kim, T. and Yang, J., Latent-space-level image anonymization with adversarial protector networks. *IEEE Access*, 7, 84992–84999, 2019.
7. Arjovsky, M., Chintala, S., Bottou, L., Wasserstein generative adversarial networks. *Proc. 34th Int. Conf. Mach. Learn*, vol. 70, pp. 214–223, 2017.
8. Berthelot, D., Schumm, T., Metz, L., BEGAN: Boundary equilibrium generative adversarial networks. *CoRR*, 2017. arXiv preprint arXiv:1703.10717.
9. Yu, F., Zhang, Y., Song, S., Seff, A., Xiao, J., LSUN: Construction of a large-scale image dataset using deep learning with humans in the loop. *CoRR*, 2015. arXiv:1506.03365.
10. Krizhevsky, A., Nair, V., Hinton, G., *Cifar-10*, 2020. http://www. cs.toronto. edu/kriz/cifar.html
11. LeCun, Y. and Cortes, C., *MNIST handwritten digit database*, 2010. http:// yann.lecun.com/exdb/mnist/
12. Liu, Z., Luo, P., Wang, X., Tang, X., Deep learning face attributes in the wild. *Proc. Int. Conf. Comput. Vis. (ICCV)*, 3730–3738, 2015.
13. Fredrikson, M., Lantz, E., Jha, S., Lin, S., Page, D., Ristenpart, T., Privacy in pharmacogenetics: An end-to-end case study of personalized warfarin dosing, in: *23rd Security Symposium ({USENIX} Security 14)*, pp. 17–32, 2014.
14. Fredrikson, M., Jha, S., Ristenpart, T., Model inversion attacks that exploit confidence information and basic countermeasures, in: *Proceedings of the 22nd ACM SIGSAC Conference on Computer and Communication*, 2015.
15. Dwork, C., McSherry, C.F., Nissim, K., Smith, A., Calibrating noise to sensitivity in private data analysis, in: *Theory Cryptography*, pp. 265–284, Springer, Berlin, Germany, 2006.

16. Dwork, C., Differential privacy: A survey of results, in: *Theory and Applications of Models of Computation*, pp. 1–19, Springer, Berlin, Germany, 2008.

17. Goodfellow, I., Pouget-Abadie, J., Mirza, M., Xu, B., Warde-Farley, D., Ozair, S., Courville, A., Bengio, Y., Generative Adversarial Networks. *Proceedings of the International Conference on Neural Information Processing Systems*, pp. 2672–2680, 2014.

18. Salimans, T., Goodfellow, I., Zaremba, W., Cheung, V., Radford, A., Chen, X., Improved Techniques for Training GANs. arXiv:1606.03498 [cs.LG], 2016.

19. Isola, P., Zhu, J.-Y., Zhou, T., Efros, A., Image-to-image translation with conditional adversarial nets. *Computer vision and pattern recognition*, 2017.

20. Ho, J. and Ermon, S., Generative adversarial imitation learning. *Adv. Neural Inf. Process. Syst.*, 4565–4573, 2016.

21. Zhao, J.J., Mathieu, M., LeCun, Y., Energy-based generative adversarial network. *CoRR*, 2016. arXiv:1609.03126.

22. Radford, A., Metz, L., Chintala, S., Unsupervised representation learning with deep convolutional generative adversarial networks. *CoRR*, 2015. arXiv:1511.06434.

23. Odena, A., Olah, C., Shlens, J., Conditional image synthesis with auxiliary classifier GANs, *arXiv:1610.09585*, 2016.

24. Arjovsky, M., Chintala, S., Bottou, L., *Wasserstein GAN*, Courant Institute of Mathematical Sciences 2Facebook AI Research, 2017.

25. Mehralian, M. and Karasfi, B., RDCGAN Unsupervised representation learning with regularized deep convolutional generative adversarial networks. *9th Conference on artificial intelligence and robotics and 2nd Asia-Pacific international symposium*, Kish Island, Iran, pp. 31–38, 2018.

Index

Printed and bound by CPI Group (UK) Ltd, Croydon, CR0 4YY

27/10/2024

14580126-0004